MEMOIRS OF A PROSECUTING MAN

– DOUGLAS RICHARD BINSTEAD –

An environmentally friendly book printed and bound in England by
www.printondemand-worldwide.com

Mixed Sources
Product group from well-managed forests, and other controlled sources
www.fsc.org Cert no. TT-COC-002641
© 1996 Forest Stewardship Council

PEFC Certified
This product is from sustainably managed forests and controlled sources
www.pefc.org
PEFC/16-33-415

This book is made entirely of chain-of-custody materials

FastPrint Publishing

http://www.fast-print.net/bookshop

MEMOIRS OF A PROSECUTING MAN

A catalogue record for this book is available from the British Library

ISBN 978-178456-147-5

First Published 2015 by
Fast-Print Publishing of Peterborough, England.

INTRODUCTION

Despite the title, this book is not a biography of the author and it is not intended to be a biography of the author. Whilst the period of time covered by the book coincides with the period of the author's career in the criminal law and follows the chronology of that career, the narrative does not touch upon the writer's earlier or later life or dwell upon any personal domestic matters in between, save where that is considered necessary to assist the progression of that narrative.

The book is intended to paint a picture of the criminal justice system during the four decades from 1971 and, in particular, of the courts and of the often larger-than-life characters who frequented some of those courts in this period, be they defendants, advocates, police officers, or those charged with sitting in judgment or involved in that process. This picture is drawn from a litany of anecdotes and events from the author's own experiences over a long career, first as a magistrates' legal adviser and then, more so, as a prosecutor in the criminal courts in several different parts of the country.

The period in question is an important one because there are a number of seminal events which lead to probably the most profound changes in the criminal justice system in generations, if not in its entire history. There are also evolutionary changes which, together with the statutory ones, see the criminal justice system move from the way it has largely operated since the nineteenth century into the very different contemporary model. The way we did things and the people who did them are quite unrecognisable now, but hopefully this book will capture them and that 'moment in time', and also the evolution and change that has occurred since.

As its creation is one of the most significant developments in this period, the Crown Prosecution Service will feature large in this work. The book, however, is not intended to be an apologia for that organisation and its reputation will not emerge much enhanced by anything written in this book by this author. The author, however, does reserve most of his criticism for the higher management of that body and not for the rank-and-file.

As a largely anecdotal account, the book is intended to be humorous and it is to be hoped the reader will find it so! Although much of the content may appear to be written in light-hearted vein, however, the intention is also to strip off some of the veneer of respectability of the criminal justice system and its incumbents and knock the latter off their lofty pedestals!

There is also an 'instructive' element to be found – some hopefully practical advice to the young or would-be prosecuting advocate, drawn from the experience, if not the wisdom, of the author! This features throughout the book, but is largely to be found in Chapter Five – this hopefully does not detract from the reader's enjoyment of the work as a whole, but he may feel free to skip this section if he so wishes!!

CHAPTER ONE

Early Days

1st October 1971. Warm and sultry. Not a typical autumnal day, more like the weather we had enjoyed two or three months before. I remember it well, even after more than 40 years, as it was the day I started out on my long career in the law in a market town in the East Midlands, known then only for a church with a crooked spire, although years later also for having an MP called Anthony Wedgwood Benn.

I had presented myself that morning at the office of the Clerk to the Chesterfield Justices in a nondescript three-storey building in a busy street off the main thoroughfare. To be more precise, it was the office of the Clerk to the County Justices - at that time there were two Justices' Clerks in the town, the other being the Clerk to the Borough Justices. The latter's jurisdiction, as the name suggests, was confined to the town itself, whereas the County Clerk dealt with matters arising in the rural areas of North East Derbyshire, and indeed, as I was soon to discover, in part of the Peak District as well.

The Borough Clerk had an office in a brand-new courthouse in the town and inevitably, in my ignorance, I had gone there first, certain that was my correct destination. I was faintly disappointed when a pleasant and very buxom blonde lady, only a few years older than myself, greeted me at the reception desk, told me of my error and redirected me to the right place. I was indeed to be articled to the Clerk to the County Justices.

The detour meant that I was late on my first morning, and my embarrassment continued when I eventually arrived at the office of the County Clerk only to physically bump into the man himself as he emerged, somewhat flustered, from the building, clutching a bunch of papers, pausing only to announce that he was on his way to Bakewell Court, and that I should "go and find Royd". Then he was gone.

Left to my own devices, and not without some trepidation, I entered the building and, finding no-one about, I climbed the stairs to look for "Royd". I found him on the top floor in an untidy office, cigarette in mouth, hunched over a typewriter. His cheerful and easygoing manner, however, was soon to put me at my ease and most of what I was to learn over the next twelve months, I learnt from him. Like me he was an articled clerk, but was also a senior court clerk in his own right, and had entered articles only latterly in a bid to qualify as a solicitor and progress his career. It is unfortunate that, despite his obvious competence, he was to achieve neither aim.

Nothing had prepared me for what confronted me on that first day and in the weeks that followed. I had never been in a courtroom; I had never worked in an office. My first experience of both was to prove a revelation.

⋆ ⋆ ⋆

On that first morning Royd confirmed what I already knew - that the principal role of the Clerk to the Justices, and indeed his "court clerks", was to provide legal advice to the lay magistrates in court. What I also learnt, however, was that the Clerk and his staff were responsible for the administration of the magistrates' courts and the recording and, to some extent, the implementation and enforcing of the courts' decisions. Amongst other things this meant issuing summonses, arranging court sittings, preparing court lists, preparing court orders, serving papers, and collecting and enforcing fines and maintenance payments.

One of my first jobs was to prepare a matrimonial order that had been made by the magistrates in exercising their family court jurisdiction (they also had a liquor and betting-and-gaming jurisdiction as well as the more obvious jurisdiction in criminal matters). Whilst I expected the order to be typed, to my horror I was told that I had to do the typing as well and was presented with a Remington noiseless typewriter for this purpose. I had never used a typewriter in my life and had never envisaged that I would ever use one. Within twelve months, however, I became reasonably proficient as a 'two-fingered' typist, a skill that indeed stood me in good stead in later life!!

That afternoon I also had my first experience of being in court. I accompanied Royd on the ten-mile trip to Renishaw Magistrates' Court in the north-east of the county. The police had charged a man with an assault on his wife and did not wish to release him on bail. This meant he had to appear before a magistrate, who would determine whether he should be released on bail or remanded in custody pending his next court appearance (at that time a defendant could be remanded in custody before conviction for a maximum of only eight clear days).

The courthouse was on the edge of Renishaw village, next to the *Sitwell Arms*, and surrounded by fields. Courts would not be found in such locations now. The many rural courts that existed then have long since been swept away, their business transferred to large courts in urban centres, and their buildings demolished or converted into dwellings, offices or gastro-pubs.

The bigger of the two courtrooms had the appearance of a Baptist chapel, with rows of "pews" for the public and the advocates and other officers of the court, press, police, etc. There was a raised dais for the magistrates and a table below that for the court clerk and his assistant. To the rear of the courtroom and behind a closed door was the magistrates' "retiring room" whence they would depart to discuss, consider and make their decisions. Here it was that I met my first magistrate - a local shopkeeper called Billy French. He was affable, still dressed in his working apparel and had a strong Derbyshire accent. Not the patrician haughty plutocrat that I had expected or had envisaged as the typical member of the lay magistracy! (But at that stage I had not been exposed to the experience of Bakewell Court!)

Shortly after this, in the courtroom, I had my first encounter with a 'prisoner' when two uniformed police officers brought in from the adjoining police station a dishevelled, middle-aged man. He was brought to the front of the court - as I recall there was no dock for persons in custody, such an obvious lack of security that would not be tolerated in today's courtrooms! The prisoner - one Harry Gordon Hill - had a palpable limp, appeared to be a little battered, and was very subdued. He had no solicitor to represent him in court - a not-uncommon feature in those days but much rarer now.

A uniformed police inspector made the application for the defendant to be remanded in custody. Looking back, he referred to no grounds for opposing bail other than "the seriousness of the offence". The defendant had little by way of previous convictions and the "offence" was not that serious in the overall scheme of things. Nowadays such persons would almost certainly be granted bail, subject to appropriate conditions. This was, however, long before the Bail Act 1976 and the more stringent regime that was ushered in when bail was to be opposed by the prosecution, and magistrates were much more ready then to accede to police requests for persons to be refused bail, even on comparatively flimsy grounds. And so it was here! The hapless Mr Hill made a semi-coherent and half-hearted application for bail and was duly remanded in custody by Mr French, who didn't even move from his seat or apparently contemplate "retiring" to consider the merits of the case. Mr Hill was handcuffed and bundled away into the police station. (A few weeks later, having been remanded in custody for several weeks, he pleaded 'guilty' and received a non-custodial sentence!)

This was not the end of my first day in the job, as we travelled back to the office in Chesterfield and found that my principal had returned from Bakewell. "Mitch" Nevins, the Clerk to the Chesterfield County Justices, I had indeed met once before when I was interviewed a couple of months previously by a panel consisting of three of the Clerks from the county. Mitch had stood out as the only one with an obvious sense of humour and he confirmed this as he and his deputy, a bluff Yorkshireman called Geoff Clarke, regaled Royd and me with shocking and humorous anecdotes from Bakewell Court that day. More of that to come.

In the days that followed I learnt more about my colleagues, the nature of the job, the courts in which we worked, and the many and various characters that frequented those courts. These early experiences have stayed with me and have shaped my working life.

* * *

Mitch Nevins was my principal and my boss. He was a man of about fifty years of age, tall, owlish and bespectacled, fond of a drink, and, as I have hinted already, possessed of a ready sense of humour. I was to accompany him to court many times over the next three years and was able to appreciate firsthand the commanding and disarming way he dealt with defendants, magistrates and solicitors. Particularly with truculent or combative defendants, he could defuse situations with a quip or by talking to them in a language they could understand. He was universally respected and treated with almost godlike reverence by the magistrates he served. He commanded the same respect and admiration from his staff. From what I was to learn later about the character and personality of other Clerks to the Justices around the county, I realised that I had indeed been fortunate to have become articled to the Clerk to the Chesterfield County Justices!

I have many memories of Mitch and his humour, but one stands out and really underlines his personality. He and I were looking through court registers in the downstairs office - where defendants attended to pay fines or maintenance payments, or make enquiries. A particularly awkward defendant was at the counter. We could hear him but not see him from our position and, equally, we would not have been visible to him. He was complaining to the lady member of staff who had the misfortune to be dealing with him that the level of maintenance he had to pay for the upkeep of his children and estranged wife was too high and more than he could afford. The patient member of staff explained to him that he could, if he wished, make an application to the court to vary the amount of his payments, and she helped him to fill out the appropriate form. At some point she had to ask him whether he wanted his application to be heard in the court at Chesterfield or at Renishaw. "Not Renishaw," he exclaimed - "That bastard Nevins is there." Without even looking up from the court register he was perusing, Mitch interjected: "Aye, and that bastard Nevins is at Chesterfield too!" The hapless defendant decided not to pursue his application and left the office in an embarrassed silence.

* * *

The members of the 'backroom' staff in the office were exclusively friendly and, almost exclusively, middle-aged women. The "legal" staff consisted of the Deputy Clerk to the Justices and the two court clerks, Royd and Ray.

I was often to sit in court to assist the Deputy, Geoff Clarke, and learnt a great deal from him over the next three years. His knowledge of criminal and matrimonial law and procedure was second to none, and I was often astonished by the level of deference accorded to him in matters of law and procedure by advocates in court, even though they were solicitors and barristers and Geoff's only qualification was his experience. He was also irascible and quick-tempered, however, and I witnessed many a heated exchange in court between Geoff and advocates, and on occasions he barely kept his composure with awkward chairmen of the bench.

Royd was also a very competent court clerk, which was no surprise to me. Ray, however, was less impressive. Another Yorkshireman, but younger than Geoff, flamboyant in manner and dress, his over-confidence sometimes ran away with him. The clerk should really be unobtrusive in court, as it is a "magistrates'" court, after all. Ray, however, had a tendency to try and take over. This was particularly evident in the courts held for fine defaulters, where defendants had to explain to the magistrates why they had not kept up their repayments or indeed, more often, why they had paid nothing at all off the fine. The examination of the defendant should have been carried out by the chairman of the bench; Ray, however, assumed this role for himself and conducted detailed and probing interrogations of defendants, often accusing them of extreme negligence or deliberate default and, as a result, often getting himself embroiled in angry exchanges with the person before the court. This was unseemly and the stronger chairmen of the bench had to intervene at this point and put Ray in his place; the weaker ones, however, allowed the embarrassing charade to continue!

* * *

The courts we covered sat at that time in three locations - Chesterfield, Renishaw, and Bakewell in the Peak District. Bakewell was very different from the other two and merits a chapter on its own!

Renishaw I went to on my first day and was to visit many times over the next few years. As well as the "Baptist Chapel" it had a second courtroom, about the same size as a standard school classroom, which it very much resembled. One could sit at the clerk's desk here and gaze out at the cattle grazing in the fields.

Chesterfield County Magistrates' Court was situated adjacent to Chesterfield Railway Station and also the *Trebor* factory, whose sickly smells were always very apparent! The courtrooms were ancient, shabby and in stark contrast to the palatial surroundings to be found in the brand-new courthouse that housed the Borough Magistrates'

Court up the road. The two courtrooms were of a similar size and were accessed from the public area by two sets of double doors, the inner pair of which were half-panelled like those to be found in western saloons. The acoustics were poor and the sound-proofing worse. It was almost impossible to make an entrance into the courtrooms without causing the 'saloon' doors to bang. One venerable local solicitor indeed always seemed to make a point of heralding his approach with a loud raised voice in the public area, and then completed his entry with a flamboyant sweep into the court, leaving the 'saloon' doors crashing in his wake, a la *Milky Bar Kid*.

* * *

The composition of the magistrates' benches at Chesterfield and Renishaw very much reflected the make-up of the local working populations. North East Derbyshire was at that time a heavy coal-mining area, and probably about 40% of the magistrates were, or had been, involved in some way in that industry, although few of them at the coalface. Most of the rest were professional people, housewives, shopkeepers, skilled workers in local industries, or retired representatives of the same sections of society. There were one or two farmers, but only a handful of what might be termed the landed gentry, the obvious examples being Sir John Renwick, a past president of the Law Society, who sat on the Renishaw bench, and Hugo Ernest Geldart Read, the agent to the trustees of the Duke of Devonshire's estate, who was then the chairman of the Chesterfield County Bench.

It became one of my tasks in time to ensure that each court sitting had an appropriate number of magistrates in attendance and, to this end, I spent a lot of time ringing round to persuade JPs to attend court where one or more of the rostered magistrates had cried off - something that happened with great frequency. I found most of them affable and easy to deal with, although there were one or two who stood on their dignity and clearly didn't expect to be contacted by a mere minion - nothing but the Clerk to the Justices himself would do! As it turned out, these were the same members of the bench that I was to encounter difficulties with when I later graduated to become a full court clerk in my own right.

This eclectic bunch of individuals, not surprisingly, consisted of persons with widely different character traits and idiosyncrasies. Some, with exaggerated personalities or eccentricities, stood out and were an endless source of amusement or irritation, as the case might be, to my colleagues and me.

There was, for example, the retired colliery deputy who, whatever the subject matter of the case, always knew "a bit about this". He invariably didn't, but this didn't stop him taking over conduct of affairs to the exclusion of his colleagues who were sitting with him. He would then go on to break what must be one of the most fundamental rules of conduct for a magistrate who is sitting as chairman of the bench on the day, by announcing to the court that: "I" am going to do this or that and "I sentence" you to this or that or "my decision" is this or that, completely failing to acknowledge the presence of his colleagues.

Another lady, who regularly sat as chairman of the bench, would repeat everything said to a defendant by the clerk of the court. Thus if the clerk said "Stand up" she would say "Stand up"; if he said "What's your address?" so would she straight after. "How are you going to pay the fine?" was followed by: "How are you going to pay the fine?" from the bench. Mitch Nevins always said it was like "having a parrot on your shoulder"! The habit was irritating, although the lady in question was otherwise an intelligent woman and an excellent magistrate.

There was the alderman who was on the bench, no doubt as a consequence of his aldermanic position, but who really never quite got to grips with how matters in court should be conducted. There was the most embarrassing occasion when, as chairman of a bench hearing a trial of a number of defendants charged with public order offences, he enquired, after a number of witnesses had given evidence for the prosecution, whether there were "any more witnesses for our side". This was not even *sotto voce*, but in open court for all to hear. It is still not clear to me why the defendants' solicitors did not ask for the trial to be stopped at this point and for the chairman to disqualify himself from sitting further!

There are many other such anecdotes from the annals of the Renishaw and Chesterfield County Magistrates' Courts. It is fair to say, however, that many of those on the bench conducted themselves with decorum and common sense, took the advice of their clerk, made sensible and correct decisions and passed condign sentences. As a body they were likeable and generally approachable. The most obvious exception was, and all of we clerks felt the same, the chairman of the Chesterfield bench. Hugo Read, as befitting a man in his position, was eloquent and charming. We discovered, however, that if you did something he didn't like, however trivial it might seem, he would not hesitate to make trouble for you. He could be quite vindictive. He became known to us as "The charming bastard".

* * *

Those who have practised in the magistrates' courts for many years as solicitors, probation officers, court clerks or in any other capacity, will often be heard to muse that "There are no characters any more, not like there used to be!" This is almost certainly not true - the passing of the years probably lends the description of "character" to individuals who may not necessarily have merited that description at the time. And the 'old-timers' who frequented the courts in the 1970s made the same sort of comparisons between my contemporaries and those who frequented the courts in their youth and earlier years. The passage of time distorts the memory and enhances the "character" of those one knew thirty or forty years before.

Allowing for that distortion, however, there was nonetheless, or so it seemed to me, a galaxy of unusual or larger-than-life characters who graced the courts, or otherwise, in the form of advocates at that time. They fell broadly into two groups, at least as far as the criminal courts were concerned: those who prosecuted and those who defended.

The prosecution of criminal cases in North East Derbyshire at this time was carried out almost exclusively by solicitors employed in the office of the County Prosecuting Solicitor (CPS) (there were no barristers then in his employ). These were mainly young men and women, fairly newly-qualified, who were, in effect, on the first step of the career ladder and used the experience as a stepping stone to a more lucrative career in the private sector. There were, however, some older practitioners and there were some who were to go on to become career prosecutors. The younger ones tended to be rather gauche, uncertain and not always very competent; there were, however, some highly competent and characterful individuals amongst the older and slightly more mature prosecutors.

The County Prosecuting Solicitor himself was an irascible Welshman called Colin Hill. He only appeared in court infrequently, but his appearances were invariably a treat for the onlooker. He had a 'history' with some of the defence practitioners, and the heated and eloquent exchanges that took place between them were a joy to behold.

He reserved his real venom, however, for barristers or high-flying solicitors from outside the county, attending to represent paying clients (i.e. those not on legal aid!). One such person who fell foul of Colin was a flamboyant solicitor from Leeds, the partner, in fact, of Barrington Black, a notorious criminal practitioner from that city and famed far and wide for the lengths to which he would go to secure acquittals (he would later become a Circuit judge - poacher turned gamekeeper indeed!). The unfortunate partner, no doubt thinking that his opponent in the impending trial was a malleable country 'hick', was heard to approach Colin in court but in the absence of the magistrates, and to say to him in a most charming and ingenuous way: "Of course, you will accept this piece of evidence, won't you?" (The piece of evidence in question was in fact critical, and to have "accepted" it would have seriously undermined the prosecution case and helped the defendant to assert his innocence!) The response was explosive - "Will I buggery accept it. Who do you think I am, you arsehole?!" Said in a lilting Welsh accent, it had particular impact. The poor solicitor was visibly and clearly shaken by the unexpected response and, not long after this, he indicated to the court that his client would be entering a 'guilty' plea to the charge he faced - there would be no trial.

Colin was also a master of cross-examination and of unsettling an opponent, on the rare occasion he exercised those skills. I remember in one trial, of a defendant charged with assault occasioning actual bodily harm, the accused was represented by a solicitor from Derby whose lack of experience in criminal trials was painfully obvious from the off. The poor man was probably put off for life by Colin's strategy of undermining the examination of witnesses and the accused by repeated, but perfectly legitimate, objections to the line of questions. Rather like a fielder sledging a fledgling batsman, the process of 'mental disintegration' eventually reduced the solicitor to an incoherent wreck. Just to rub salt into the wound, Colin then totally dismantled the defendant's account of events in a masterly and probing cross-examination.

Another master of unsettling one's opponent was the celebrated Dick Fletcher. Immaculately dressed and with a flowery handkerchief sprouting from his jacket top pocket, taking occasional pinches of snuff, Dick's technique often involved passing a note to his opponent whilst the latter was engaged in questioning his client in the witness box. Human nature and curiosity invariably meant that the defence advocate would feel compelled to break off his questioning to read the note. The note would say something like: "Isn't your client an ugly bastard?" or "Do you fancy a pint afterwards?" As far as I am aware no-one ever complained about this sort of thing (Dick was a very popular man), but it seemed to work wonders for breaking the concentration!

Of course there was a limit to how often Dick could get away with this trick, but it was by no means the only weapon in his armoury. He had a way of getting defendants and defence witnesses on his side and winning their trust by treating them with almost exaggerated respect. The person in the witness box would be addressed as "sir" or "madam"; there would be solicitous inquiries as to their health, and compliments as to how they were conducting themselves in the witness box and the clarity of their replies. Very often the witness, feeling very much at ease and feeling that Mr Fletcher was a very nice man indeed, would find himself agreeing with Dick that "perhaps he hadn't seen the incident" clearly after all or at least, in the case of the defendant, feeling uncomfortable about strongly asserting his innocence.

Tricks and softly-softly techniques aside, Dick was a highly competent and widely-respected advocate. He was also known as the "master of the late brief": the missing file that suddenly turned up in front of him in court, or the file for the prisoner who had just been charged and was about to be produced in court. Others would need time to read and acquaint themselves with the contents. Not Dick, who seemed to be able to get to grips with the case with a few casual glances and present the facts and the arguments as if he had been preparing for hours.

Then there was Fred Bates. Fred had been a policeman in Kenya and he brought to court the same techniques he had no doubt practised in interrogating errant Masai tribesmen. In those days defendants, whilst in police custody, invariably made "voluntary statements" - written statements taken under caution that may amount to a confession but were more often an innocent account. Fred's invariable practice in a trial was to take a defendant in cross-examination exhaustively through his statement and meticulously identify assertions which were, or appeared to be, at odds with what the defendant had said on oath when questioned by his own advocate. This approach did not always work and could be condemned as 'nit-picking', but sometimes the cumulative 'drip-drip' effect was to show the defendant's evidence to be unreliable.

Another senior prosecutor was one Keith Malkin, a cerebral individual and a most eloquent advocate. One of Keith's attributes was his ability to introduce clever humour into his advocacy without once attracting criticism or rebukes from the bench. This could enliven the most mundane cases. In the seventies a celebrated horseman called Harvey Smith had insulted the judges at a show-jumping event by giving them a V-sign as he left the arena. In describing the conduct towards police officers of a defendant charged with a minor public order offence, Keith told the magistrates that the accused had "made a gesture well-known in horse-jumping circles". This brought the house down!

The secret of the success of the likes of Fletcher and Malkin was, perhaps, that they endeared themselves to, and were trusted and respected by, the bench. It is a truism, as David Napley, no mean advocate himself, set out in his book on criminal advocacy, *The Technique of Persuasion*, that magistrates are more likely to accept what is said to them by advocates they like and respect.

Keith Malkin was cut out to be a prosecutor, but he left prosecuting and went into private practice in the mid-seventies. He was not a success here, however, and ultimately returned to prosecuting in the mid-eighties.

A notable feature of the CPS in Derbyshire at this time in the seventies was a heavy-drinking culture and indeed, I believe, one replicated in other such departments across the country where they existed. Eventually this took its toll and many of the older prosecutors at this time sadly did not reach retirement age - this included Hill,

Malkin and Fletcher, the latter dying at the very early age of forty-four.

* * *

Let it not be said, however, that competence, character and heavy drinking were the monopoly of the prosecutors! There were plenty of all those ingredients to be found amongst the ranks of the defence advocates who regularly appeared in the magistrates' courts of North East Derbyshire!

Most of the advocates who attended court on a day-to-day basis were solicitors from local firms; there were, however, occasional visits by solicitors from Derby, Sheffield, Leeds, Manchester and Liverpool, and also the occasional appearance from a member of the Bar!

As far as the latter were concerned, they came almost exclusively from the Sheffield Bar, there being no other local bar in the immediate area. The barristers tended to fall into two categories. The first category consisted of either young men or women starting out on their career at the Bar, or much older barristers who were there simply because they could not attract work in the higher criminal courts. The other category, and a much rarer bird, was the senior junior barrister or, even more rarely, the Queen's Counsel, who were representing wealthy, paying clients.

Both types were instantly recognisable: the former by their cheaper suits, sometimes frayed cuffs, and a generally impecunious air about them; the latter, by contrast, would appear in expensive, chalk-striped suits and dripping affluence from every pore. The former were either young, inexperienced and uncertain, or of late middle-age, not very coherent and uncertain - in both cases the standard of advocacy was not of great quality, although some of the younger brigade would go on to make the grade as advocates, whereas the older contingent never would. The latter group, as one might expect, would be, to a man or a woman, polished and eloquent advocates although sadly, in the case of many, patronising and supercilious, just to remind us mere mortals that they were 'slumming it' and that it was really beneath their dignity to appear before a bench of lay magistrates in a shabby courtroom!

The Bar, of course, has always regarded itself as much superior in every respect to the 'junior' branch of the legal profession, i.e. the solicitors. It was even more the case in the 1970s, when solicitors had few opportunities to appear in the higher criminal courts and break the virtual monopoly of the Bar in advocacy in serious criminal cases, and even fewer solicitors became judges, or even recorders or assistant recorders. The Bar I have always regarded as the biggest 'closed shop' of all, jealously defending its territory from outsiders and taking every opportunity to remind solicitor advocates that they were inferior and should not stray from their traditional hunting-ground in the magistrates' courts. In my experience the notion that barristers are better advocates and lawyers than a great many solicitor advocates is unfounded. Yes, there are some very fine advocates at the Bar and they will rise or have risen to the top of their profession and become Queen's Counsel or senior judges; to my mind, however, the best solicitor advocates have compared favourably with most of the rest of the Bar and have proved better lawyers and advocates than many barristers. The proposition that barristers are 'better' than solicitors when it comes to the practice of advocacy is, in my view, a modern myth, but one the Bar has always been keen to perpetuate! I shall return to this theme later in the book!

There were certainly some very able and skilled defence advocates among the local solicitors in the early seventies. There were nine or ten who regularly displayed a high degree of competence in representing their criminal clients, well-respected by the bench and their opponents alike. They are too numerous to name or identify separately. Some are, however, worthy of particular mention, either because of their excellence or because of their 'colourful' characteristics.

The most senior of the local solicitor advocates was one Colin Eagle. He was sixtyish, with wild, grey hair, enormous sideburns and a pronounced limp. He had the appearance of a large, shaggy dog, and even the most aggressive of his clients would invariably be cowed and intimidated by his physical presence. He would barge his way into court at Chesterfield through the two sets of double doors, chuntering and audibly complaining about his clients or the court listing arrangements, totally oblivious to the fact that the court was sitting and that he was disrupting the proceedings. It was presumably a tribute to his seniority and longevity that no-one ever sought to rebuke him or threaten him with contempt of court!

He had a very poor view of most of his criminal clients and often, whilst court was sitting, he could be heard outside on the concourse loudly abusing and remonstrating with them. They, however, would very quickly become in awe of him! I remember well one occasion where he had made a typically rumbustious entrance into court and taken his place on the advocates' bench. His client, whom he had only just met a few minutes before, was produced from the cells to face an application from the prosecution to be remanded in custody for a week. He was charged with Robbery. Before the prosecutor could begin his application, Colin stood up to inform the bench that there would be no application for bail by his client. Cue for a tirade from the prisoner in the dock - "This is a fucking stitch-up. Eagle, you're fucking useless. You're sacked. I want another solicitor and I want to apply for bail!" Colin threw his papers on the table and asked the bench to allow him "a few minutes" with the defendant. This was granted and he followed the accused down the steps to the cells below the court. He returned, indeed, within "a few minutes", with an obviously shaken defendant, who now sat quietly in the dock. "I have spoken with the defendant," Colin told the court, "And he now wishes me to continue to represent him and he does not wish to apply for bail." I was later told by the dock officer that the verbal battering issued by Colin in the cells was "something to behold".

The most successful defence advocate I encountered at Chesterfield didn't actually arrive on the scene until 1974 - a fugitive from a County Prosecuting Solicitor's office, as many of the local advocates were. Tony Taylor was then in his late twenties and he joined a local firm of solicitors that already boasted a couple of very able and respected advocates. He enjoyed success in a variety of defended cases, but his speciality was defending the middle-aged female accused of shoplifting. We worked out that, in a period of not much more than twelve months, he acted for such persons in twenty-three consecutive trials and secured acquittals in every one!

Tony occasionally sailed a bit close to the wind with his advocacy, but always got away with it. One example of this was a shocking and very disarming tactic he employed in prosecuting in trials where persons were charged with public order offences (because of Tony's pedigree and his success as a defence advocate, the local CPS often hired him to prosecute individual cases which they were unable to cover). Standing up to cross-examine the unsuspecting defendant,

Tony would look at him benignly and then would come his first question - "You fucking black bastard!" Pause for effect, and while his opponent and everyone else in the court picked themselves up from the floor. Then he would go on - "That's what you said to the police officer, wasn't it?" Many defendants would be too shell-shocked after this to put up much of a fight in the witness box.

Sadly, Tony fell out with his employers not long after and was lost to the defence cause. He went from strength to strength, however, returning to prosecuting, surviving serious illness, and ultimately becoming Chief Crown Prosecutor in Greater Manchester. I would meet him from time to time in later years and we would cheerfully reminisce about his time in Derbyshire.

Then there was Montagu J Martin, a solicitor in practice on his own in Chesterfield and another ex-prosecutor. Monty did not conform to traditional standards of court dress. He would appear in light-coloured suits, floral ties, and sometimes in checked trousers and a white linen jacket. With his light-sensitive spectacles and longish hair he cut a somewhat bizarre figure amongst the well-groomed and sharp-suited advocates that filled the advocates' bench in the magistrates' courts. He was a clever and very able advocate, but I suspect that his relative lack of success for his clients was, in part at least, as a result of the magistrates not altogether trusting him and being appalled by his appearance. Nor did he endear himself to his professional brethren when a number of "Monty Martin" beer mats suddenly began to appear in local pubs. Monty disappeared from the scene in about 1975, only to pop up again as Deputy County Prosecuting Solicitor in Humberside! Poacher turned gamekeeper?!

* * *

It would be wrong to leave the matter of local advocacy without mentioning the police. At this time in Derbyshire, and indeed, for some time into the late seventies, the CPS did not have the resources to prosecute in every magistrates' court in the county and, to fill the vacuum, they would instruct local defence solicitors to prosecute or, failing that, the police would prosecute their own cases! The job would usually fall to an experienced sergeant or an officer of inspector or chief inspector rank.

I have known and witnessed a number of police officer prosecutors over the years (and indeed, until 1986, as many police areas did not have a CPS presence until the advent of the Crown Prosecution Service in that year). It's fair to say that some were very good, not only in the quality of their advocacy and their courtroom presence, but also because they showed the kind of impartiality and objectivity that would be expected from a professional prosecutor. Many of them, however, were not really up to standard, gave painful performances, and simply failed to appreciate that they were "prosecutors" and not "persecutors". The English prosecutor, of course, should act like a 'Minister of Justice', be fair and even-handed, and not out to 'win' at all costs. It is surely difficult, however, to expect a police officer to take a neutral stance in a case which has come to court as a result of an investigation carried out by his professional colleagues. Try as he might, he has a 'stake' in the case and it is not surprising that many police officer prosecutors saw their function as purely to secure a conviction. This lack of independence, or perceived lack of independence, of course led to the investigative and prosecuting functions being severed by the creation of an independent prosecution service in 1986.

One extreme, if comical, example of a police sergeant prosecuting was the occasional appearance at Chesterfield court of an Irish police sergeant. He clearly had no empathy with, or understanding of, the art of prosecuting Apparently his 'briefs' would be drafted for him by another officer. He would read the 'brief' verbatim, without hesitation (even for full stops!), deviation, or repetition. The totally wooden performance was once, however, enlivened by an even more literal obedience of his instructions. Coming to the bottom of the page he failed to realise that "please turn over" was not part of the script and included the phrase in his recital of the facts of the case, to the muffled amusement of the rest of the court!

* * *

Although the main business of the magistrates' courts was the exercise of their criminal jurisdiction and, indeed, this is the main thrust of the book, a brief reference to the other business of the courts in North East Derbyshire would be appropriate here.

One day a week at Chesterfield the magistrates sat as Domestic Court justices. This involved hearing affiliation (or "bastardy") proceedings, matrimonial matters where spouses or ex-spouses sought orders against their estranged husband/wife on the grounds of adultery, desertion or cruelty, orders for custody of children, or variations of such orders already in force. Custody matters or adoption proceedings were often trying and heart-wrenching affairs and the other domestic cases often involved sordid details of peoples' private lives.

Every Tuesday at Chesterfield, one court would hear the purely matrimonial matters whilst the other would deal with applications for affiliation orders (i.e. orders asserting paternity of an illegitimate child and for support of same). As was our wont, we would find a humorous side to all this and, to reflect the nature of the cases heard, we would refer to "adultery in court one and fornication in court two"! Adultery was often admitted in court by the errant spouse and, if not, evidence would be heard from a private investigator. The regular witness was everyone's idea of a gumshoe or 'private dick' - seedy, cheap suit, nicotine-stained fingers, etc. He would testify as to his observation of clandestine trysts in cheap hotel rooms or late-night visits while the other spouse was away. It was never more than circumstantial evidence of adulterous activity, but it never seemed to be challenged or questioned!

There were many memorable moments in the domestic courts, but the most memorable one was the case of Trevor Birks. Mr Birks had been summoned to court because he had not been paying his maintenance to his ex-wife and he was also applying for the amount of maintenance to be reduced because of an adverse change in his means. I was in court at Renishaw when his case was called.

Through the court doors strode a tall, blonde lady, fairly short skirt, high heels, and complete with handbag. Or was it a lady? What perhaps gave the game away was the suspicion of five o'clock shadow and the unpractised walk to the front of the court. The Deputy Clerk to the Justices who was clerking the court was not deceived, but went through the motions of identifying the defendant. "Are you Trevor Birks?" "Yes," replied the defendant, "But I prefer to be called Judith." The chairman of the bench, late sixties, retired manager of the local *Co-op*, pillar of the church, appeared to be having an apoplectic fit. Eventually he regained the power of speech - "For God's sake, man, pull yourself together!" He decided it was appropriate at this point to adjourn the court sitting so that he could regain his equilibrium and for sanity to prevail!!

Needless to say, the defendant did not "pull himself together". He was a legitimate candidate for a sex-change operation and he/she became a familiar sight around that court as he/she continued to fail to pay his/her maintenance. Changing sex was not an escape from one's liability to one's ex-spouse!

This was our 'light relief' from the endless diet of criminal matters!

The magistrates also sat several times a year to deal with matters relating to liquor licensing and gaming licensing (these days dealt with by local authorities). And the beginning of every criminal court also saw local licensees queuing up to apply for extensions of licensing hours for "special occasions". We on the court staff were always very helpful to local licensees, helping them sometimes to draft their applications and reminding them of the need to apply for renewal of licences, for example. Our assistance was often rewarded at Christmas by the arrival in the office of a box of chocolates, or a bottle of sherry, or even whisky.

We were also responsible for the processing of applications for criminal legal aid, and local solicitors often also came bearing gifts at Christmas. Such would probably be construed as corruption these days, and I think the practice died out many years ago!

* * *

As I have said, the principal business of the magistrates' courts was the hearing of criminal matters. All criminal cases started in the magistrates' court and most were finalised there, although the more serious cases and those where a defendant had a right to elect for trial by jury were sent on to the Crown Court at Derby or Nottingham. For the first three months of my career at Chesterfield, the Crown Courts did not exist. The higher criminal courts initially were the historic courts of Quarter Session and Assize. As a result of the Beeching Commission, however, the Courts Act 1971 was passed and on 1st January 1972 the Crown Court came into being as the court for trying serious criminal cases and Assizes and Quarter Sessions were consigned to history.

Most defendants whose cases were finalised in the magistrates' court had pleaded 'guilty' to all or most of the charges they faced. The ones who pleaded 'not guilty' faced a trial in which all the evidence was presented and heard. Any suggestion that these were 'police courts' and that the magistrates rubber-stamped prosecutions brought by the police, or always accepted evidence given by police officers, is entirely wrong - many defendants were acquitted after trial and rightly so.

Cases that were destined for the Crown Court were sent there in a simple, formal procedure although the defendant and, indeed, the prosecution, could opt to have the prosecution evidence called at this stage. This may be because the defence thought there was insufficient evidence to even provide a case to answer for the defendant, or the prosecution had doubts about their witnesses and wanted to see if they would a)turn up at court and b) come up to proof when they gave their evidence in the witness box. All the evidence had to be recorded as it was given by the clerk of the court on a 'noiseless' typewriter and then read back to the witness for him to sign his deposition. Such arcane and long-winded procedures have been largely obsolete for many years, much to the relief of the court staff!

In those early years in North East Derbyshire there were many criminal cases that stir the memory and many more that can only be described as mundane. Shoplifting, assaults, public order offences and drunk & disorderly were rife. The area, of course, was in the middle of the Derbyshire coalfield and, when there was a miners' strike in 1972 or thereabouts, cases of petty theft rapidly increased, as did house burglary. There were quite a number of cases of robbery, albeit not with firearms and, every now and then, a murder. There was not a high incidence of serious sexual offences, and this was well before the time when child abuse cases abounded, as these offences were just not reported by the victims at this time. It was also well before the age of drug use and trafficking - I cannot remember a single case involving drugs at this time, or one involving solvent abuse. Excess alcohol was behind the majority of offending and it was as powerful an influence on offending as it is today. If alcohol became much less readily available or prohibitively expensive, then the key to reducing crime may have been discovered! We are, however, today no nearer to solving the alcohol problem than we were then!

Some cases do particularly stand out in my memory, for whatever reason.

My first "murder" occurred before I had been in the area for a month. A lorry driver called James Francis Knight strangled a prostitute on the moors outside Chesterfield going towards the Peak District. He was acquitted of murder on the grounds of provocation, I recall, as the unfortunate woman had been foolish enough to scorn his sexual inadequacy with predictable and violent results. He was sentenced to eight years' imprisonment for manslaughter.

Three very different and reasonably rare sex cases come to mind. One involved a Polish labourer who chose to commit buggery with a pig in a farmyard in the small hours of the morning. The squeals of the animal brought the farmer to his bedroom window with his shotgun, which he discharged at the fleeing perpetrator, without managing to hit him. The Pole was caught and prosecuted for an offence which reputedly would have gone unremarked in some rural areas, and was put on probation. The farmer was not prosecuted!

Colin Eagle represented an elderly man who was charged with an indecent assault on his granddaughter. The defendant was on the verge of senility and in denial as to his culpability. Colin took a step the like of which I have never seen since. He asked to address the bench in the absence of his client and explained, in a nutshell, that they should not believe his client when he gave evidence!! This was surely in breach of the Solicitors' Rules for conduct of advocacy, but no-one questioned this approach, which is unlikely ever to be repeated!

The young girl, aged five, gave her evidence unsworn standing in front of the clerk's bench, clutching her doll. Nowadays, of course, her own account would have been videoed and she would have been on a TV link from a room separate from the court. No such refinements then! The young male prosecutor proved quite unequal to the task of eliciting her evidence from her, and Mitch Nevins intervened to take over the questioning - it was skilful but involved a number of questions that could only be described as leading. There was, of course, no objection from the defendant's solicitor! The elderly defendant himself gave evidence on oath and categorically denied the offence. Colin's last question to him was: "Did you interfere with this little girl?"

"No sir," was the reply. Colin turned towards the bench and, in an act of pure farce, nodded his head several times. He thus rendered purely superfluous any cross-examination of the defendant! Conviction, of course, followed.

The other memorable sex case involved a young man who was charged with "flashing" (indecently exposing his penis) to a female attendant in a petrol station. He pleaded 'not guilty' and his defence was one the like of which I have never heard since. He had been, he said, at his girlfriend's house in Wakefield. They had had such a night of passionate and prolonged lovemaking that when he left her house at six o'clock in the morning he was quite "numb" and did not realise that, as he drove fifty miles down the motorway, his flies were undone and he was 'exposed', and continued to be as he filled his car with fuel and went to pay the forecourt attendant. The magistrates did not swallow his story, but he showed little surprise when they convicted him!

The most notorious case in Chesterfield in this period was that of Billy Hughes. Hughes was a man with a very violent past - amongst other serious violent offending he had once killed a police dog with his bare hands. He had been charged with a particularly nasty rape in Chesterfield and had been remanded in custody awaiting committal to Nottingham Crown Court. It seems remarkable to us now but in those days, very often, prisoners were brought up the motorway from Leicester prison to court in a taxi with three members of the prison staff as escorts! It didn't prove exceptionally difficult for Hughes, on one such trip, to overpower his guards and escape onto the moors as the taxi came into the outskirts of Chesterfield. What happened thereafter is the stuff of infamy. Hughes came across an isolated dwelling - Pottery Cottage - between Chesterfield and Baslow, and proceeded to murder the four inhabitants (or allegedly, as he was never tried) - all members of the same family. He then fled across moors and fields in the snow until he met his predictable end, shot and killed by a police marksman, a fifty-year-old detective constable from Buxton.

* * *

So much for those early days in the north-east of the county. Just fifteen miles down the road from Chesterfield, however, lay

Bakewell. It might have been on another planet, and it's there we must go next!

CHAPTER TWO

The Bakewell Experience: Toffs and Tarts

Bakewell is a small market town in the heart of the Derbyshire Peak District. It has, and had then, a population of just under four thousand, but in the seventies it boasted a police station and a magistrates' court. The magistrates' court, as with many of the smaller rural courts, has long gone, but in those days it sat regularly as a criminal court every Friday in the Town Hall. There were two courts which sat - one downstairs in the main hall and one upstairs in the Council Chamber. Both had separate "retiring rooms" for the magistrates to conduct their deliberations. The Clerk to the Justices, Mitch Nevins at this time, had an office in the same building where a small staff carried out the same sort of work as was carried out in the Chesterfield office, albeit on a much smaller scale.

The court served a geographically large but thinly populated area of the Peak District, including many villages with such evocative names as Stoney Middleton, Ashford-in-the-Water, Stanton-in-the-Peak, Monyash, Youlgreave, etc. There were twelve local magistrates, drawn from this area, and their composition could not have been more different from that of the Chesterfield and Renishaw benches. There was not one who could remotely be described as "working class", and several of them were definitely of aristocratic stock.

One of the biggest employers in the area was the Chatsworth Estate. Chatsworth was the ancestral home of the Dukes of Devonshire, and Chatsworth House and Park employed scores of workers, household and otherwise - there were even "Mole-catchers" employed in the Park. In addition, of course, there were a significant number of tenant farmers who held leases from the Estate. The Comptroller of the Duke's Household, Captain Dennis Fisher, was on the bench, and there was at least one other JP at any one time connected with Chatsworth.

Other aristocratic and landowning members of the bench included Sir Humphrey Davey-Thornhill, proprietor of the Stanton

Estate, Lady Huddy, and Lieutenant Colonel Olivier, who was the brother of the eminent actor and film star! There was also George Kenning, a magnate of the motor industry. The rest of the bench consisted of local professional people.

The chairman of the bench at this time was a local headmaster, Harry Schofield. Out of court he was an affable, intelligent, quiet-spoken sort of man; on the bench, however, he became bombastic and autocratic, and often seemed to lose control of his reason. He had a frequent tendency to open his mouth and 'put his foot in it'.

Mitch Nevins had been Clerk to the Bakewell Justices for only a year or so in 1971 and, although he would often have his head in his hands when he sat in front of Harry, he made no serious attempts to restrain Harry's outspoken and sometimes outrageous statements from the bench. Prior to Mitch's tenure, there had been a part-time clerk who acted as the legal adviser. He was the managing clerk of a local firm of solicitors and so not a qualified solicitor himself. He was, however, a personal friend of Harry's and not in the least afraid of speaking his mind when appropriate. Rumour had it that he would routinely stand up after one of Harry's inappropriate statements and tell him, not very *sotto voce*: "You've opened your fucking mouth again!" Thus he was perhaps able to exercise a degree of restraint on his wayward chairman, but, having thrown off these shackles, Harry was once again a 'loose cannon'.

The most obvious example of Harry Schofield's gaffes was fortunately one that was rectified before it could lead to an appeal. Following a trial, and after their deliberations, Harry brought his bench back and announced to the defendant: "We think there is a doubt in this case but, on the balance of probabilities, we find you guilty." In a criminal trial, of course, guilt can only be established "beyond reasonable doubt", and the "balance of probabilities" was well short of this standard! Mitch Nevins rose wearily from his chair and 'suggested' to Harry that he might like to retire again and reconsider the decision after hearing his (Mitch's) advice. Fortunately Harry agreed to do so and, a little later, re-emerged to inform the defendant that there had been "A slip of the tongue," and that, of course, the case against him was "dismissed". The day was saved but, of course, had Harry taken advice from his clerk at the appropriate time, he would not have fallen into this trap. Fond hope! One would like to have thought that a lesson was learnt here. Regrettably not!

It would have been only a few weeks later that Harry was hearing a case brought by the Trading Standards Department against a butcher, for supplying defective meat to a local Italian restaurant. The evidence in the trial was overwhelming against the defendant but, nevertheless, he strenuously denied the allegation. I was not present but we heard from Geoff Clarke, Mitch's deputy, that in the retiring room, after hearing all the evidence, Harry was making it loudly very plain that he was "not having the word of an Englishman being impugned by a couple of dagos." He prevailed over his two colleagues and was not for heeding the advice of his clerk. The case was dismissed. Not surprisingly, the Chief Trading Standards Officer asked for the court to give reasons for its decision for the opinion of the High Court. This is known as an Appeal by Way of Case Stated and involves the magistrates setting out in writing their reasons for the decision by reference to the facts of the case and the law. For "magistrates", of course, read "the clerk", and poor Geoff had to attempt to justify a decision which was completely indefensible and which, furthermore, was totally in the face of his advice. He did a sterling job but was making bricks out of straw, and the inevitable outcome was that the High Court sent the case back to Bakewell Magistrates' Court with a "direction to convict" and to impose an appropriate sentence. Harry made sure that he sat on the reconvened case and had the last word by persuading his colleagues to impose a purely nominal sentence! Not for a moment did he show any regret or embarrassment!

Another area where Harry consistently brought himself into conflict with the law was in relation to applications by licensees for gaming permits - for a licence to have on their premises a gaming machine that paid out small cash prizes - "One-armed bandits" in common parlance. Although these may have been commonplace by this time in pubs in towns and cities, they were only just appearing in rural areas. It was Harry's proud boast that he knew intimately every pub on his 'patch'. It was no idle boast, either, as he made a point of regularly sallying forth of an evening, and at weekends too, and taking a drink in wayside inns from Youlgreave to Hathersage, and from Baslow to Ashford-in-the-Water. He knew every licensee by name and they knew him too! Harry genuinely felt, as probably did many others at this time, that gaming machines in rural pubs were incongruous and anti-social, and he felt that he had a moral duty to do something about it. Hence he embarked on a crusade to persuade his fellow JPs that all applications for the infernal machines should be refused out of hand! Whether they shared his distaste or not, the other magistrates, as ever, or most of them anyway, appeared to be in thrall to Harry and he got his way again and again.

Harry would listen patiently to every application for a permit and would then launch into the same prepared speech, which began something like this: "We are justly proud of the character and traditions of our wayside inns and our rural public houses, and we on the bench, as the guardians of those irreplaceable virtues..." and would end thus: "We cannot allow that character and those traditions to be besmirched by the intrusion of machines which are, to our mind, totally incompatible with the maintenance of that character and those traditions...;" and so the applications would be consistently refused.

It was, however, always a Pyrrhic victory and a pointless stand against the march of progress. The licensees would always appeal against the decision and would always succeed since there were, in reality, no legitimate grounds for refusing the applications. Harry would, however, be quite unfazed by each reversal and would continue on his merry way, refusing each application as it arose. By the same token, the licensees did not hold it against him. They seemed to respect his stance and were content to indulge him, in the certain knowledge that they would win out in the end!

* * *

Whilst Harry was the overall chairman of the Bakewell bench, on occasions Sir Humphrey Davy-Thornhill would sit as chairman in one of the courts, and sometimes one or two of the other magistrates. They showed, all of them, a remarkable degree of consistency in how they dealt with particular kinds of crime. Poaching was regarded as a heinous offence and one got the impression that, had the power to order transportation to the colonies still existed, it would have been exercised. On the other hand, there was a strange reluctance to deal harshly with other offending where the offender was local, whereas people who came out of Sheffield or out of the county to commit crime locally were hated and despised. Woe betide the travelling poacher!

Sir Humphrey, as a chairman, would veer from wanting to "hang 'em and flog 'em" to a strange compassion. Sometimes he simply failed to grasp the point of a case; at other times he showed remarkable perception. He could be an asset or a liability. On one occasion, chairing a matrimonial court where the wife was alleging physical cruelty by her husband, he leaned over to his male colleague and remarked: "Her trouble was he wasn't fucking her enough." Had this observation been made in the larger courtroom downstairs, it might have remained inaudible to everyone in the courtroom except the clerk; unfortunately we were in the much smaller council chamber upstairs, and it was quite apparent that all present heard the remark! There was a stunned and embarrassed silence. Somehow, however, and to their great credit, the parties and their respective solicitors (and the clerk - me!) managed to conceal their feelings, regained their collective composure and just got on with the case. It was a remarkable show of restraint to spare judicial blushes. Not that the chairman of the bench appeared for a moment to recognise his *faux pas*, although his two colleagues looked distinctly uncomfortable. Neither of the solicitors made any complaint about the conduct as far as I am aware although, in anticipation of such an event, I did mention the matter to Mitch. Whether or not Sir Humphrey was spoken to I do not know but, in my time at least, he did not feature again as the chairman of the bench in a matrimonial court.

⋆ ⋆ ⋆

The local solicitors in Bakewell were of the same patrician stock as many of the magistrates. Whilst there were occasional appearances of solicitors from Chesterfield or Matlock, most of the defendants before the court were represented by one or other of the local advocates.

There was Michael Brooke-Taylor. He was one of five brothers, all of whom were solicitors, and four of whom were solicitors in Derbyshire. The fifth was then the Clerk to the Justices in Northampton, but he retired in the late seventies and came to work for one of his brothers in the Matlock 'branch' of the family empire. The brothers were also the cousins of the comedian, radio and TV personality Tim Brooke-Taylor who, I believe, also had connections with the law in his early days.

The Bakewell firm was also joined in the mid-seventies by Keith Malkin, who had left the CPS, and he became a regular defence advocate at Bakewell and Matlock. This did not have a happy ending, however. Keith was imbued with the hard-drinking culture of the local CPS, apparently fell out with his new employers, and then set up on his own in Bakewell. It came as no surprise that this did not work out either. By a strange coincidence, in 1984 I had the task of interviewing Keith when he applied to rejoin the CPS, this time in Cumbria. He appeared then as a somewhat sad and forlorn individual, clearly having fallen on hard times. He wasn't appointed, although he did eventually manage to get a job with the CPS in Kent. Like many of his contemporaries at Derbyshire CPS, however, he died in harness before reaching sixty years of age.

The other prominent local solicitor also, in due course, came to grief. Vernon Colhoun at this time was in his early thirties, public school, suave, and eloquent. He was widely tipped to be the next Conservative parliamentary candidate in West Derbyshire. In the event, he never did attain those heights and years later he was struck off the roll of solicitors and imprisoned for nine months when he became implicated in a fraud which involved the forgery of a conveyancing document.

⋆ ⋆ ⋆

A regular feature of Fridays at Bakewell was "number three court". This was, in fact, the back bar of the *Wheatsheaf Hotel*. The real courts invariably finished by lunchtime and the local solicitors, the prosecutors, the court staff and sometimes the probation officer, would meet in the bar with Harry Schofield and some of the magistrates. Whilst the convention was that only 'halves' would be drunk, the session would last a couple of hours in a free-and-easy and convivial atmosphere. On occasion, police officers would stray in as well: Sir Maurice Oldfield, at that time the head of MI6, lived nearby at Over Haddon and when he was out of the area the two police officers assigned to protect him when he was at home often came into the bar, noticeable bulges under their armpits! (Sir Maurice was reputedly Ian Fleming's model for "M" in the *Bond* novels, although the more likely scenario was being Le Carré's model for George Smiley in *Tinker, Tailor, Soldier, Spy*).

This type of post-court gathering was probably common-place in days of yore, when rural courts were often to be found located next to a hostelry. They were less common by the later 1970s, particularly after the advent of the breathalyser and, no doubt, more stringent guidelines from the Magistrates' Association and the Lord Chancellor as to how magistrates should conduct themselves! I did, however, come across other such examples later in one or two of the rural courts in Lincolnshire, but not since. "Number three court" was still going when I returned to Bakewell as a prosecutor in the late 1970s; it would have ceased to exist, however, when Bakewell court itself became history and, as the rural courts slowly disappeared, so this pleasant activity would have died with them.

* * *

In many ways Bakewell was in a time-warp, a throwback to much earlier times. In his book *Town without Pity*, local newspaper editor Don Hale described the social structure as "feudal". The composition of the local bench reflected this. An example of the workings of 'privilege' was to be found in the way, it is said, that the man who ran the local Magistrates' Clerk's office in Bakewell came to be 'appointed'.

In about 1970 there arose a vacancy for the job of managing Mitch Nevins' office at Bakewell. Mitch had apparently set in motion the necessary steps for the post to be advertised, no doubt believing that he would be interviewing suitable applicants with appropriate qualifications for the job, and that the post would be filled as usual by "open competition". Rumour has it, however, that no such interviews ever took place.

Tom Wright had recently retired as a chief superintendent of police in Derbyshire. He was known to many of the 'dignitaries' in Bakewell and West Derbyshire. He had no doubt made it known that he was looking for a 'little job' to supplement his not insubstantial police pension. Whether or not he actually submitted a written application for the job, however, and this is what I later learnt, before Mitch had had time to consider the applications that had been submitted, he received a telephone call from his then 'boss', the Clerk to the Magistrates' Courts' Committee, informing him that a "decision" about the vacancy had been made and that ex-Chief

Superintendent Wright would be "starting on Monday" - and so he did!

I wouldn't say that Tom Wright was entirely unsuitable for the post, or that he made a bad job of it once he had learnt the ropes. But that is scarcely the point. The allegation is that he was not appointed on merit but as the result of some sinister, clandestine process that completely subverted the proper procedures and offended against all principles of openness and fairness. Whether freemasonry was involved or simply 'knowing the right people', I do not know but, if the tale is true, Mitch had to roll with the punches and accept the *fait accompli*!

A humble clerk he may have been, but Tom Wright certainly did not regard himself as such and did not act as such. He had an inflated opinion of his own importance and would let you know it. Geoff Clarke, who was, of course, Mitch Nevins' deputy, recounted how, when he met Tom and his wife in Bakewell, he was introduced by Tom as "Mr Nevins' assistant at Chesterfield", completely failing to acknowledge that Geoff had any authority at Bakewell!

It is one of the more beneficial developments of progress since 1970 that public appointments could never be made in such circumstances now!!

* * *

My reference above to Don Hale and his book brings me quite nicely to what is probably the most notorious event that has ever occurred in Bakewell - the "Bakewell Tart murder". This description may be a play on words but it is, in fact, absolutely nothing to do with the cake that originates from Bakewell (itself not to be confused with "Bakewell Pudding", another local delicacy!). It refers to the brutal murder of Wendy Sewell, a thirty-two-year-old local woman, who acquired the unfortunate tag "Tart" as a result of a reputation, deserved or not, of being highly promiscuous. By coincidence, Wendy had at one time worked in Bakewell Magistrates' Clerks' office, although before my time, and was well known to Geoff and the other court clerks (purely as a colleague, I hasten to add!). In 1973 she was bludgeoned to death in the local churchyard. Only one arrest was made - that of Stephen Downing, a seventeen-year-old labourer who worked in the churchyard and the council's parks and gardens. What then followed has become the longest-running "miscarriage of justice" case in English legal history.

Stephen Downing was subsequently charged with Wendy's murder. The principal evidence against him was a 'confession' he made to the killing whilst in police custody. The other evidence against him was circumstantial and, indeed, would not apparently have sustained a prosecution against him on its own. Looked at from this distance in time, the confession was obtained in such circumstances that it seems unlikely that nowadays Downing would have ever been charged and, certainly, the confession evidence would never have been allowed to go to the jury. Since 1985 there has been a substantial body of law that governs the detention and interviewing of persons in police custody – i.e. the Police and Criminal Evidence Act 1984, aka PACE. PACE would have ensured that the police quite simply would never have dealt with the defendant in the manner they did in 1973. He was interviewed late at night, denied the services of a solicitor, and not cautioned at appropriate times, to name but a few actions that would have constituted a breach of PACE. Prior to PACE the situation was governed by a loose, non-statutory set of provisions called the "Judges' Rules". Even then, in Downing's case those rules were breached in more than one way, but it was less likely that any "confession" obtained following such breaches would lead to the trial judge excluding it from evidence than would be the case where PACE applied.

In this instance one of the most amazing things about the confession was that the defendant had been initially interviewed by CID officers, who would always be the category of officer entrusted with that function in a case of this seriousness but, when they had not obtained a confession, the defendant was briefly and informally interviewed by a uniformed police officer, in effect the local 'village bobby', Ernie Charlesworth. It was at this point that the "confession" was suddenly made, and then confirmed when the CID officers picked up the reins again. The modern criminal lawyer would say that the situation 'stank' and that the "confession" could never in these circumstances be regarded as reliable. I don't know how strongly the defence team contested the admissibility of the confession at the trial at Nottinghan Crown Court, if they did at all, but the confession was allowed to stand by the judge and Downing was duly convicted.

Sentenced to life imprisonment, the defendant had served twenty-seven years in custody by 2001. He never became eligible for parole because he would never acknowledge his guilt, always maintaining that his confession was untrue. This is the longest period anyone has ever served before his or her conviction has been overturned.

Don Hale was, from 1995, the editor of the *Matlock Mercury*. He started a campaign to secure Downing's release after he had been contacted by the defendant's father, Ray, and after he had carried out his own exhaustive investigation into the circumstances of the crime and the police investigation. Hale was quite scathing in his book about the social hierarchy in Bakewell - the gulf between the 'haves' and the 'have-nots', the culture of privilege and secrecy, and the total inadequacy of the police investigation. He saw conspiracies, police cover-ups and other suspects under every stone, and catalogued a number of sinister phone-calls and incidents received by, and directed at, him which were, he said, designed to discourage his investigation. There has been some evidence since that Hale's account was exaggerated and even inaccurate in some respects but, nonetheless, he did highlight the obvious weaknesses in the case against Downing and ultimately was able to persuade the Criminal Cases Review Commission to look at the case and refer it to the Court of Appeal. At a first hearing in the Court of Appeal the Crown, significantly, indicated that it no longer sought to uphold the conviction. The Court agreed that the confession evidence was unreliable and should have been thrown out by the trial judge and, consequently, the whole case should have failed. Stephen Downing was released from prison and, in early 2002, his conviction was formally quashed. The Court of Appeal judges, however, did not go as far as to say that he was "innocent".

For Stephen Downing, however, there was not a satisfactory or very happy ending. The police re-opened the case, considered the evidence against all the potential suspects identified by Don Hale, and found that there was no evidence to suggest that any of them could have committed the crime. Their closing position was that they "were not looking for any other person", and the case was closed. They were still clearly very much of the opinion that Downing was the guilty party.

As for Stephen Downing, although he was compensated for his imprisonment, at fifty-seven years of age he is on benefits and has been unable to hold down a regular job. His father was himself imprisoned for offences of historic child abuse and then died. Stephen has said that he still feels a "prisoner" because of the constrained and isolated life he has been forced to lead since his release from custody.

Hindsight is, of course, a wonderful thing but, whatever the truth behind this grisly crime Stephen Downing was wrongly charged and convicted. In this sense alone, there was a very grave miscarriage of justice and for this the police, the legal profession and the judiciary must share the blame!

CHAPTER THREE
1974 And All That

1974 was the year of substantial local government reorganisation: new counties and new councils were created, and some old counties changed their name. Cumberland and Westmoreland disappeared into a new "Cumbria"; Shropshire, for a while at least, became "Salop"!

The changes also impacted on the magistrates' courts. Amongst other things, a new West Derbyshire court area emerged and we said goodbye to Bakewell court, which now came into the jurisdiction of the Clerk to the Justices at Buxton. Some of the smaller courts began to disappear too - an insidious process which continued until recently (there are now only three magistrates' courts in Derbyshire).

The real change for us at Chesterfield was that the Chesterfield County and the Chesterfield Borough benches merged. There were several ramifications of this, some good, some not so good. Mitch Nevins became the Clerk to the Justices for the combined bench. The "acting" Clerk to the former Borough Justices became his deputy. This meant that, in effect, there was no job for Geoff Clarke. Fortunately for him there was a vacancy for a Deputy Clerk at Rotherham, and he was appointed to that. Rotherham's gain was our loss! Ray also left us to take up a court clerk post at Sheffield. All the other staff from the two offices remained in place, but the plus was that we moved to the relatively new and palatial building previously occupied by the Borough staff and magistrates, which housed not only three new courts but also a suite of offices big enough to take all the combined staff. The new courthouse also had a library, and car-parking spaces for all staff who required them - luxury!

* * *

In the new set-up, as well as Mitch and his deputy, there were four other permanent court clerks and one who was peripatetic (i.e. he went to courts all over the county as required). I soon became the fifth clerk - I had completed my articles and, although I was still some way off qualifying as a solicitor, there was a vacancy which I was invited to fill. There was no open competition to fill the post, but I believe the view that was taken was that I was by this time supernumerary, was sufficiently qualified by experience to fill it and, otherwise, I wouldn't have been gainfully employed!

The court clerks were an interesting bunch. Royd we have met before. Ron, despite not being thirty, had worked in half a dozen different court areas in his time. He had a delightful, dry sense of humour and was completely unflappable. The other two clerks and the peripatetic, however, merit a fuller description!

What is it about lawyers that, despite the experiences they must encounter in their professional work, they seem to have a remarkable propensity to be susceptible to 'distractions' - be they alcoholic excesses, extra-marital activity, or even criminal conduct? Or perhaps they are not alone amongst the professions in this? I have encountered many examples of this amongst my professional brethren throughout my career.

Robin was the peripatetic court clerk. He was in that role not by choice but by virtue of his own professional misconduct. He was an ex-policeman, had been Deputy Clerk to the Justices at Ilkeston, was a very good lawyer and legal adviser and had been, for all the world, a highly respectable family man and pillar of the establishment. A Conservative councillor, no less! He had, however, been caught with the female usher *in flagrante delicto* by his boss at Ilkeston, one lunchtime in his office. The latter felt compelled to resign; Robin was, for some reason, rather more fortunate. The Magistrates' Courts Committee created for him a special post which, presumably, they felt would keep him on the move and away from the distractions he might find in an office-based job. As the peripatetic clerk, he travelled round the county, sitting in courts from Derby to Glossop.

One might have thought that after this experience he might have kept a low profile and might have learnt the lesson. Not a bit of it! He travelled round the county bewailing his lot to anyone who would listen, and the general impression he created was that he regarded himself as "very hard done by". To compound the felony, within twelve months of leaving Ilkeston he was conducting a not very clandestine affair with a female magistrate on the Chesterfield bench and, indeed, one who had been on the bench only a very short time. Had he been more discreet in the matter he might have got away with it, but it was only too obvious what was going on! He was 'spoken to' and, presumably, warned that he was sailing close to the wind if he wanted to remain in his employment. On the face of it he heeded the advice this time and broke off the affair, or at least publicly. He was still around when I left the county in 1979, so perhaps the penny had dropped…?

Another one who found himself in hot water was Henry, the principal court clerk. He was the victim of what in modern times would be referred to as "stalking". He had allegedly been conducting an adulterous affair with a married woman, but unfortunately her husband found out, and he proved to be extremely jealous and, potentially, very violent. He discovered where Henry worked, having followed him from home one day, and he took to turning up at the office and demanding to see Henry, threatening staff on the reception desk in the process. On more than one occasion, Henry felt obliged to absent himself from the office, and eventually he took an enforced 'holiday' to see if the dust settled. Fortunately for him it seemed to do so. Nor did it have any adverse effect on his career and, in due course, he became a Magistrates' Clerk in his own right.

The other court clerk, Alan, had been an articled clerk like me and, like me, was having trouble in passing his professional examinations (in fact, like Royd, he never did pass them!). His 'difficulties', it turned out, were rather more serious and he was very fortunate to a) keep his job and b) not be prosecuted. Alan regarded himself highly, was very status-conscious, and saw himself as a member of local 'society'. He was engaged to a girl in the office who clearly shared his aspirations; their forthcoming wedding was in the planning for a year and the details were repeatedly and ostentatiously broadcast round the office and, indeed, there was not a solicitor or local magistrate who did not know those details. This was to be "the society wedding of the year"!!

The wedding came and went in a blaze of self-publicity. Within twelve months, however, Alan found himself in extra-marital hot water of a different nature than those alluded to above. The matter was 'hushed up', but some of us became aware that Alan had been caught twice in police operations targeting homosexual activity in certain public lavatories in the town. At the time, this was criminal behaviour. For whatever reason, however, there was no prosecution, although he may well have been cautioned. Given his previous hubris about the "wedding of the year", there were those in the know who felt not a little *schadenfreude* at his fall from grace! Be that as it may, he continued in his job, albeit he was noticeably more subdued thereafter. As far as I am aware, his wife stood by him, but I do not believe his career ever progressed much beyond this point.

The Deputy Clerk, Ken, was also an interesting character - a man with hidden depths. He was a quiet, almost taciturn, Yorkshireman, pleasant and easy-going, and quite unobtrusive when in court. He had no 'difficulties' regarding alcohol, women or anything else! Put him behind the wheel of a car, however, and he was a totally different man! All his repressed inhibitions were cast to the wind when he drove to Renishaw Court. For anyone unfortunate enough to be a passenger in his car, it was a 'white-knuckle' ride. Whilst he would pay lip service to most speed limits, he would pull out of junctions in front of other vehicles and overtake at speed in the face of oncoming traffic, leaving in his wake hooting and fist-shaking fellow motorists. It was a frightening experience, and the more so considering that it was so flagrantly out of character!

Not that long after the amalgamation of the benches, the post of Clerk to the Justices at Buxton arose. Ken applied and got the job. A richly deserved promotion, but bad news for regular travellers on the A6 between Buxton and Bakewell!

* * *

Local government reorganisation also impacted on the CPS. The County Prosecuting Solicitor's office was a department of the County Council, and it would seem that heads of departments were having to reapply for their corresponding jobs in the new County Council. This was an opportunity, I suppose, for the authority to get rid of 'dead wood' or troublesome employees.

It also gave an opportunity for some heads to retire early, and with a compensation package to boot! The head of the CPS in Derbyshire, Colin Hill, was one such, reapplying for his job but ensuring in the interview that he made himself unsuitable for re-employment. He left with a handsome redundancy package and, after a short dalliance with the private sector, retired to his native Wales.

His successor was Colin's erstwhile deputy, David Robin Kersley Seddon, who was four years older than his newly-appointed deputy, thirty-two-year-old Roger Exley. I have already mentioned the drinking culture in the CPS, and more of this later, but suffice to say at this stage that Messrs Seddon and Exley led from the front in preserving the culture!!

★ ★ ★

It was about this time that some of the smaller rural magistrates' courts began to be abolished. Courts that had existed for centuries, with such evocative names as Wirksworth, Melbourne, Repton, New Mills and Chapel-en-le-Frith, and followed not long after by Long Eaton, Heanor and Ripley. Their work was transferred to larger court centres - Matlock, Derby, Buxton or Ilkeston. This process was to continue piecemeal over the next thirty-five years, for better or worse. Many would say for worse, because it meant that magistrates sitting in urban centres were dealing with matters arising in localities for which they had no 'feel'. 'Local justice' also meant that local criminals really were being tried by their peers and that they did not have to travel vast distances to court, at great expense and often on antediluvian roads or on irregular public transport. This applied equally, of course, to witnesses, who were at least reimbursed to some extent for their inconvenience. The arguments for more and more centralisation are admittedly strong - massive financial savings and the ability to provide vastly better facilities at court for all court users. The development was inevitable, but one cannot help feeling that something was lost with the replacement of the quaint rural charm of the little local courts by the soulless utility of the teeming urban centres.

★ ★ ★

By June 1976 I was starting to look to the future. I had finally passed my professional exams in April 1976 and in June that year I was admitted as a solicitor. I had more or less decided by then that I did not want to spend the rest of my career in the magistrates' courts service. I had also married and acquired a mortgage, and sorely needed to boost my earning power!

Being a magistrates' legal adviser had its moments, and there were some challenging times but it was often, too often, routine and mechanical. I yearned to play more of a part in the court process.

I also found dealing with some of the magistrates rather trying, to say the least. I am not one of those who disparage lay magistrates. In my time in the court service I found most magistrates, individually and collectively, to be sensible people and, in over forty years in magistrates' courts, I disagreed only rarely with their decision-making. Certainly, when it came to trials, I found magistrates a more reliable and predictable decision-making body than juries!

Between 1974 and 1976, however, there were some magistrates on the benches in North East Derbyshire I simply couldn't get on with. These tended to be those from the former Chesterfield Borough bench rather than those whom I had known and become accustomed to over the previous three years. There were two in particular.

Wing-Commander Lumsden was, I believe, the proprietor of the *Derbyshire Times*, the local 'rag'. He was a small, rotund, self-important man who tended to make it rather obvious that he had little respect for any legal advice he was receiving from a 'youth' of twenty-five years of age who did not share his extensive experience of people and life in general. He wouldn't take it from me, but invariably wanted to see chapter and verse when I advised him what the law said. And then there were the occasions that he had "made a special study" of the area of law in question and he knew better than I, even when he was wrong! Fortunately he didn't sit as chairman of the bench at any time and his two colleagues on the bench were able to outvote him and save me from the perils of having to justify an indefensible decision to the High Court!

If he was bad, Henman was even worse. He regularly sat as a bench chairman and was able to 'bully' his two colleagues on occasions into decisions with which they seemed uncomfortable. Like Lumsden, he seemed to regard me as a callow young upstart and he was another one who wanted to see the law in written form rather than take my word for it! He seemed to want to make a point of going against my advice, and it was fortunate that he usually favoured the defence in this regard and the prosecutors were pragmatic enough not to want to make an issue of the decision. Matters came to a head in a trial where the defendant was pleading 'not guilty' to Driving with an excess of alcohol. It was his case that, following an accident in which he was involved, he had fled the scene and had consumed a very small amount of alcohol at home before the police arrived to demand a breath test from him. He was clearly over the prescribed limit at the time of the accident, but the law at that time was that post-accident consumption of alcohol in effect provided the defendant with a complete defence to the charge, however little the amount consumed. The prosecution weren't able to contradict his assertion that he had consumed alcohol after the accident and I advised the bench that they would have to find him 'not guilty', however unacceptable they might find that position. Henman, siding with the prosecution on this occasion, was outraged and, even when I showed him the case that laid down the law in these circumstances, he wasn't going to have it. His two colleagues seemed too cowed to overrule him. I stood my ground, however, knowing that the defence were bound to appeal if the defendant was convicted and "muggins" would have to draft the hopeless case for the opinion of the High Court. My final attempt to save the day was to say to Henman: "Well, if you won't take it from me, perhaps you will from Mr Nevins." He agreed to speak to Mitch on the phone. He of course got the same advice and very grudgingly backed down.

I used to dread being clerk of the court when either of these two was sitting on the bench, which seemed more often than I would have liked, and this, as much as anything else, made me determined to look elsewhere for employment in the law when the occasion presented itself.

I had always wanted to be an advocate and, even in 1976, I dreamt of appearing in front of a judge and jury - something not possible at that time, or for more than twenty years thereafter. I hated the idea of being in private practice as a "fat-arsed conveyancer", or doing probate or personal injury claims. Nor did I particularly want to be a defence advocate, dealing with unsavoury and mendacious clients. The clear course of action for me was thus to join the CPS! I also quite envied the lifestyle of the CPS lawyers - I was attracted by the idea of the flexible working arrangements and long lunches, and I was by no means averse to the drinking culture! There just happened to be a vacancy for an assistant prosecuting solicitor in Derbyshire in August 1976.

I had no qualms about being able to do that job. I had sat in court for five years watching prosecutors with varying degrees of ability and I was arrogant enough and confident enough to believe I could do the job as well as at least some of them! I made my intentions known to our regular CPS lawyers at court and waited for the advert to appear.

In the event I didn't have to apply, but was invited to come and have an interview with Messrs Seddon and Exley. The 'interview' was as about as unchallenging and informal as you could get and they offered me the job on the spot. I accepted. I learnt afterwards that I was well thought of by the CPS advocates and that the job was mine unless I insulted the interviewers or seriously blotted my copybook before the interview!

So much for the notion of open competition, but at least there was an interview of sorts and I was as qualified for the job as most applicants would have been!

Thus on 1st October 1976, exactly five years after I had started out in the Magistrates' Clerk's office, I started my thirty-six-year career as a prosecutor.

CHAPTER FOUR
1976 to 1979: Learning the Ropes

Unlike many solicitors (or barristers) who joined the CPS at the start of their career as a fully qualified lawyer, I had had, in effect, five years' introduction to the art of prosecuting. I had sat in court watching it from the front row and had picked up the terminology and the processes. I had, moreover, a fair bit of experience and acquaintanceship with the law of evidence, I was more than familiar with the criminal law, and I knew more than most about procedure in magistrates' courts. Nonetheless, I was not thrown in at the deep end on my first day in the CPS, as my practising certificate had not yet been issued and I was obliged to travel round the county for a month, shadowing other prosecutors, and champing at the bit more and more as October wore on.

Finally, at the beginning of November, I was ready and able to make my debut! My first appearance was to be in the second court at Matlock, prosecuting a full list of cases, which included the trial of a defendant charged with an offence under the Public Order Act. I spent hours preparing and, when I stood up in court for the first time, I was just as nervous as I was twenty-five years later when I first appeared as an advocate in the Crown Court. I found, however, that I quickly warmed to the task and by the end of the court I had recorded my first 'victory' in a trial. The latter was not a particularly difficult task, as I had three police officers giving first-hand evidence of the offence as against a not-very-convincing defendant who was able to call no witnesses himself. Speaking to the most senior of the officers afterwards, I confessed that this was my first day in court as a prosecutor. His response was flattering - he would never have guessed, he said, and he could see that I had "a flair" for prosecuting! Perhaps he was being disingenuous, but I was happy to take him at face value anyway!

My first 'beat' for the next twelve months or so was to cover the courts at Alfreton, Matlock and Belper, as part of a team of three lawyers. Alfreton was a purpose-built court, but Matlock and Belper courts were the town hall and an old school respectively. Matlock closely resembled Bakewell court, with a large hall downstairs and the council chamber upstairs. The acoustics downstairs were notoriously bad, but when I left Derbyshire in 1979 the local newspaper saw fit to pay me the apparent compliment of having proved that one could make oneself perfectly audible despite the acoustics. Whatever other qualities or failings I might have had as a prosecutor, I never had any problems with voice projection in any court, and no-one ever asked me to "speak up"!

The Clerk to the Justices for the three courts at this time was one Kenneth Allwood Round, a rather intimidating, bloodless, humourless individual, but a first-rate lawyer. His deputy, Fred Westmoreland, was an entirely different character - open, friendly and supportive, as well as being an equally sound lawyer.

Over the next two and a half years I also did an eighteen-month stint in the north-western courts - Buxton, Glossop and Bakewell - but also from time to time visited the other courts in the county. I was told at the start that I would not be permitted to prosecute at Chesterfield or Renishaw - not surprisingly, perhaps; but there was no such prohibition as far as Bakewell was concerned - presumably it was felt that, as I hadn't 'clerked' there for a couple of years, I had served the 'sentence'?!

The Clerk at Buxton was Ken Wormold, who had briefly been the deputy at Chesterfield, and he had responsibility for Glossop and Bakewell as well and later also for Matlock (and much later for Ashbourne too). Buxton was a purpose-built court, but Glossop was just a large assembly-room with a partition down the middle to create two courts. If the voice was pitched at a certain level it was possible to cause the partition to rattle - one former prosecutor had apparently been banned from appearing there because he so regularly disrupted the proceedings!

There was a series of bad winters in the late 1970s in Derbyshire and the snow would lie for weeks, making travelling to Buxton and Glossop (which was in the High Peak) at times very difficult. There was one year when those prosecuting in the north-west just couldn't get back to the office in South Darley for several days and had to put up at a pub in Peak Forest. As long as they could still get to court, however, they were able to use the police files to prosecute as the CPS only kept copies of these.

Bakewell Court I found to be just as I remembered it - nothing had changed. Harry Schofield was still Chairman and "Court Three" was still going strong.

South Derbyshire, outside Derby city, was the bailiwick of the Clerk to the Derby County Justices, Jim Exley. He was a genial, grey-haired man and the father of our own Roger Exley. Outside Derby his courts were situated at Ashbourne and Swadlincote. I only went to the latter once and my only memory is of the clock over the bench, which bore the inscription "Time the Avenger". Ashbourne court sat on Thursday, which was market day in the town. The composition of the bench was similar to that of Bakewell, with a significant element of local gentry. CPS lawyers rarely got to appear at Ashbourne as there was only one court and it was regularly prosecuted by an appointed "agent", Jack Cleaver who, as I recall, was a consultant with a well-known firm of Derbyshire solicitors. I was never quite sure why this arrangement persisted when there were always sufficient CPS lawyers to cover the court and it would therefore have proved an unnecessary expense. It may have had something to do with the fact that the admin clerk in the CPS office who was responsible for allocating lawyers to courts was a personal friend of Jack - but then I don't know! Jack was an unusual case as he had had cancer of the throat and his voice-box had been removed and replaced by an artificial device (the same operation that the actor Jack Hawkins had had). This didn't seem to present any obstacle to Jack, who was a very well-respected prosecutor in that court.

I also went occasionally to Ilkeston Court, where the Clerk was Harold Westhead, a swarthy little man and, again, a very accomplished lawyer. The courthouse was relatively new and expensively furnished with rosewood tables and plush benches. The courtrooms, however, were windowless and it was like prosecuting in some subterranean cavern. Give me the old-fashioned courts and the town halls and the schoolrooms anytime!

The last of the Clerks was Arthur Exton at Derby City Magistrates' Court. I had never met him before his retirement in 1978, except when he appeared as a defendant earlier at Bakewell court! He was being prosecuted for driving without due care and attention. He insisted on appearing in person, which he needn't have done as he was pleading guilty, and he did his best to upstage the court clerk, who on this occasion was Royd, by taking every possible opportunity to make pedantic points about the procedure, the way the charge was put to him, etc. I was present and I thought Royd dealt with the situation admirably, remaining respectful but unflustered and in control!

Arthur used to wear a wig in court. I am not sure if he was entitled to do so or whether it was just an affectation. However, the Clerk of the Peace and the Clerk to the Assize at the old Quarter Sessions and Assize Courts used to wear wigs, and the clerk who sat with a High Court judge in the Crown Court also, and these persons were not solicitors like Arthur but middle-grade civil servants, so one can hardly criticise him for his choice of court apparel!

* * *

Derbyshire CPS was based at a rural office in the village of South Darley, near Darley Dale. There were in 1976 some thirteen or fourteen prosecuting solicitors, excluding the County Prosecuting Solicitor and his deputy. These were split up into four teams, each team routinely covering courts in a particular area of the county and dealing with casework arising on each of those areas. You could go days without seeing some of the lawyers, because the teams covering Chesterfield or Derby tended to work from local police stations rather than returning to the office.

Most of the solicitors at this time were under thirty-five and the average age was probably no more than thirty. Despite this collective inexperience, however, there was not one of the lawyers who could be branded as incompetent and some of them were, to my mind, very able indeed, and I benefited considerably in my first year from the wisdom of many of them. Although by the time of my arrival some of the more notorious 'boozers' had moved on, there was still a heavy-drinking culture in the office, particularly amongst some of the senior lawyers, and the reputation of the department was and had been tarnished by one or two alcohol-related incidents.

The County Prosecuting Solicitor, David Seddon, was a clever and able lawyer but scarcely a fine example of mature behaviour. On one occasion he purported to suspend himself from his post after an incident on a country road one night when he lost control of his car and ran into a dry stone wall, then leaving the scene in a taxi. By the time the police arrived at his home address he had consumed alcohol for "medicinal purposes" and so any breathalyser test would have been pointless. Judging from his earlier movements that evening, he would no doubt have been over the limit at the time of the accident and he thought so himself.

On another occasion he was drinking in a pub in Matlock after work instead of going home for his tea, when his young wife came into the premises and thrust their very young child into his arms and then marched out, leaving him holding the baby - this in front of a pub full of customers. The incident came to the attention of a local journalist, who gleefully arranged publication in a local newspaper together with a photograph of him holding the baby which David thoughtfully provided! He had no embarrassment whatsoever about the incident – indeed, he always seemed to relish any kind of personal publicity, good, bad or indifferent!

Another example was the occasion of Princess Anne being prosecuted for speeding on the M1 in Derbyshire. She clearly had no intention of appearing in person and a solicitor was to enter a 'guilty' plea on her behalf. Nonetheless, a special court was arranged at Alfreton with no other cases listed, and the press attended in great numbers. David insisted that he must prosecute the case himself and he went out and bought new suit and shoes for the occasion. The whole proceedings took ten minutes, David's part amounting to less than 90 seconds but, much to his disappointment, there was no photo opportunity afterwards!

On two other occasions of which I was aware he brought derision on his head. At a national conference of the Prosecuting Solicitors' Society in York, he managed to get himself thrown into the lake on the university campus by two lawyers from Essex CPS. At a similar event at Churchill College, Cambridge, he "fell" down a flight of stairs and broke his jaw. He took his food through a straw for a week or two after that. Did he fall, or was he pushed…?

By the time I left Derbyshire in 1979, there was scarcely a soul to be found in the local criminal justice system or, indeed, in Derbyshire CPS who had an iota of respect for David Seddon. This was a very sad state of affairs, but he was the author of his own misfortunes. He must have been at least a borderline alcoholic but he managed to survive as head of the Derbyshire CPS until a national reorganisation of the Crown Prosecution Service in 1993 abolished his post and he was given the chance, I believe, a little later, to leave with a voluntary redundancy package. I never heard what happened to him after that.

David's deputy, Roger Exley, shared his fondness for the 'sauce' but perhaps that was where the resemblance ended. Roger was gregarious and utterly charming. He had an easygoing approach to life and, indeed, to prosecuting – he had a natural style of advocacy. He seemed to be universally popular, outside the CPS at least, and appeared to know people all over the county.

In my first month I spent a good deal of time with Roger, going round the county in his MG soft-top. He always seemed to contrive to finish his court by lunchtime and invariably we would stop at various hostelries on the way back to the office. He seemed to be known in every pub we went in, not only by the landlords, but also by the locals! He also knew a lot of CID officers and seemed to know in which pubs to find them at lunchtime, wherever we were in the county.

He seemed to have little regard for, or fear of, being stopped and breathalysed, although he must have 'run the gauntlet' on an almost daily basis. Like Seddon, he did have one close-run thing when he was involved in a road traffic accident outside Matlock Fire Station one night. Almost inevitably, however, he had friends in the fire station and they provided him with a shot of something to recover from the shock! As with Seddon, there were consequently no criminal repercussions, although I always wondered why, in both cases, the police did not contemplate seeking a prosecution for Attempting to Pervert the Course of Justice, since that was always an obvious avenue where persons sought to frustrate the breathalyser procedure!

Roger was not so popular with his lawyer colleagues in the office. He was regarded as idle and with an obvious distaste for paperwork. He often put the rest of us in difficult situations. He was responsible for reviewing and advising on every case in the county where a death had occurred in a road traffic collision, and where he advised proceedings for Causing Death by Dangerous Driving he should have kept control of the case and prepared the evidence for service on the defence and court. Time and again one would find that one would have a case of his in court the next day and that no papers had been prepared or served. Roger, of course, would not be available to go to court to explain the failure or to make a humble application for the case to be adjourned, so that what should have been done could now be done! If you approached him the day before the hearing he would say: "You'll be all right, I'll square it with the court and the defence." You found when you got to court, however, that he had not "squared it" with anyone and you were left to face the music. I cannot remember the courts ever refusing to adjourn such cases, even where it was not the first time in the proceedings, but we all resented being put in a position where criticism from court and defence was both inevitable and justified.

He was charming and had a charmed life. His luck did eventually run out, however. He fell ill on a holiday in Greece and died ignominiously and without dignity on a trolley in a hospital corridor. He was not yet sixty.

Jerry Purser was out of the same mould as Roger Exley. All the same epithets applied - he was charming, laid-back, gregarious and equally fond of the 'amber liquid'. He was an extremely intelligent man. Apparently, as a schoolboy, he had appeared on the TV show *Junior Criss Cross Quiz* and had broken all the show's records by beating challenger after challenger for many weeks.

He also was not a lover of paperwork and much preferred spending his time after court 'networking' with police officers in one pub or another. Jerry was my immediate superior for the last fifteen months or so that I was in Derbyshire, and both my co-assistant solicitor and I on his team found that we were reviewing most of the cases and preparing most of the paperwork for the Crown Court, as Jerry would only pick up files in "selected" cases – i.e. ones which took his fancy for whatever reason. He contrived to avoid coming back to the office in South Darley any more than occasionally; after court his preference was to visit various watering-holes between Glossop and Buxton, in Buxton itself, and between Matlock and Ashbourne. He lived in the north-west of the county so, on many occasions, there was no incentive for him to drive back to the office and, after closing time, he might call at Buxton police station but then head home. He was 'getting away with murder' but made no secret about it, and Seddon and Exley were not the ones to do anything about it!!

Like many of the heavy-drinking brigade in the CPS, however, his lifestyle eventually caught up with him. After three marriages he ended up, I believe, unattached and quite ill after contracting stomach cancer. He, too, never lived to collect his pension, dying in his late fifties.

The rest of the lawyers in the CPS were either totally abstinent or avoided the worst excesses of the heavy-drinking culture (I include myself in the latter category!). The other lawyers I got to know well. I liked them all and some, but not all, were excellent role models for the young and inexperienced prosecutor.

My immediate superior and team leader for my first twelve months was Martin Howard. He was enormously supportive and encouraging and I came to admire him greatly. He ended his career as the Chief Crown Prosecutor for Leicestershire.

The other persons I much admired were the other two most senior lawyers in the office. Fred Bates I have mentioned before; Roger Furness was an equally competent lawyer and eventually departed to join the ranks of the Crown Prosecution Service in North London in the late eighties. He never moved from his home in the north and acquired some fame by living on a houseboat on the Thames during the week. He left the CPS in the nineties, a loss they could ill afford.

Probably our most controversial prosecutor at the time was John Calvert. He had joined the CPS at the age of forty-seven, having been a public health inspector in Egham before qualifying as a solicitor. Out of court he was affable, generous and good company. As a prosecuting advocate, however, he had rapidly become feared and disliked in equal measure by his opponents and court clerks across the county. He was forever taking procedural and legal points and constantly objecting to lines of questioning. He was never off his feet. He would take issue with advice given to the magistrates by their clerk. What's more, his constant interventions, and interruptions of his opponent's questioning of witnesses, would be voiced in a strident and aggressive fashion. Some of the clerks and some of the more acerbic defence advocates would lock horns with him and there would ensue a loud and unseemly exchange.

Unfortunately, many of the points that John took were fatuous or misconceived and served only to irritate the court. This was not a good plan since, even when he was on sounder ground, he had by then so queered his pitch that the court was set against him. I am quite convinced that decisions went against him and he lost cases that he should have won because he had got everyone's back up.

Magistrates, of course, should always be dispassionate and set their feelings and prejudices aside when making decisions. The reality, however, may well be different. In his book *The Technique of Persuasion* the eminent solicitor advocate David Napley was firmly of the opinion that getting the court to like and trust you was very important and that magistrates would tend to accept the arguments and assertions of those they liked as against those they did not. This may be cynical or wishful thinking but, in grey areas and in situations where there was a narrow dividing line between one decision and another, I am quite sure that this theory proved correct! Certainly I always strove as an advocate to be fair and even-handed as much as possible and to keep the court 'onside', and there have been times when I have felt that I have got the benefit of the doubt in circumstances where decisions would have been marginal because my opponent has been overly partisan, or has conducted himself or herself in a manner not calculated to find favour with the bench.

* * *

I have to admit that prosecuting in Derbyshire in the late seventies was an agreeable and often leisurely pursuit. There were not the same pressures that beset the job after 1986 and, certainly, from the nineties onwards. One might be in court three or four days a week, but on the other day or days in the office there would be long, leisurely 'lunch-hours'. Regularly, the five or six of us in the office at any one time would decamp at 12.30 pm to *The Red Lion* at Birchover, a village about three miles away, and spend two to three hours playing darts or dominoes or just 'chewing the fat' over lunch and a few pints. There was usually one person who would volunteer to drive, if not two.

Even on court days there was invariably opportunity for lunchtime recreation if there was no afternoon session. One of the CPS' favourite watering-holes was *The Sycamore Inn* on Matlock Bank. The pub at this time was kept by Arthur Bassett, an ex-Welsh international rugby union player. David Seddon seemed to spend a couple of hours in there most lunch-times, and we often went there from Matlock Court on a Tuesday or a Thursday and indulged in a long, leisurely 'lunch-hour' playing dominoes with the Deputy Clerk Fred Westmoreland and the court usher. Rumour had it that Arthur would also provide an early-morning service at the back door of the pub to those who required a 'hair of the dog' or a pre-court dram. I believe Exley and Purser may have availed themselves of this service from time to time.

A common occurrence was the Thursday 'away-day'. This involved those lawyers who were not in court or who had finished their court duty setting off at lunch-time and heading towards Ashbourne, where it was market day and the pubs would be open until 4 pm (in those days lunch-time licensing hours would otherwise finish at 3 pm). There might be five or six of us, invariably including Jerry Purser, and driving duties would fall on the most abstinent or, failing that, a volunteer. The journey to Ashbourne would involve taking in the *Knockerdown Inn* and the *Red Lion* at Hognaston and usually the *Barley Mow* at Kirk Ireton. More often than not Roger Exley would also be in Ashbourne, and sometimes David Seddon as well. More pubs in Ashbourne then home.

Visits to Glossop and Buxton, if in the company of Jerry Purser, would also involve calling in at various hostelries on the way back, assuming one was not caught up in an all-day court sitting. As far as Buxton was concerned this usually involved just the *Bakers Arms* in the town; between Glossop and Chapel-en-le-Frith, however, there were several isolated pubs which Jerry favoured. For me the trick was somehow to contrive not to drive that day or, otherwise, to make sure that I restricted my intake of alcohol - no easy thing! Jerry, on the other hand, made no concessions to the perils of exceeding the prescribed limit!

* * *

It may be thought by the reader that lawyers in Derbyshire CPS spent more time at play than working, and abused the trust reposed in them by their employers and the ratepayers who paid their wages. Despite the picture that might be portrayed by what I have described above, however, this was far from the truth.

The job involved not only prosecuting at court but also providing written advice on case files submitted by the police and preparing case papers for service on the court and the defence where cases were destined for hearing at the Crown Court. One might add to that carrying out correspondence with the court and defence solicitors and sometimes preparing submissions to counsel in cases where the opinion of the High Court on a magistrates' decision was being sought.

Whilst it was comparatively rare for courts to finish later than 4.30 pm, one would invariably be in court the following day and any preparation for the next day often had to be done or concluded at home or by staying late in the office. I found that I would spend, on average, two to three hours a night working at home on probably three days a week, and the same sort of time on a Sunday afternoon or evening (this is a working pattern I have in fact followed all my working life as a prosecutor).

If one went back to the office after court, there was always a pile of files that had come in from the police that required reading and advice providing. If one didn't go back then the pile would mount. Normally there would be one day a week for most of us where we didn't go to court and could make inroads into the backlog. Some files necessitated only a brief endorsement, but others may have required a detailed letter setting out the law, applying the law to the facts of the case and justifying the advice that was being given. In addition, a lawyer would bring back from most courts he prosecuted files relating to cases that had been decided would go to the Crown Court, and he or she would be responsible for putting them in a suitable format for service on defence and court. There were always deadlines to be met and, I have to say, most of the lawyers didn't think twice about taking files home to work on where the allotted time in the office proved inadequate. From my point of view, I would spend another five or six hours a week working at home on such cases, over and above the time at home referred to above preparing for court.

This was no nine-to-five job and, whilst we 'played hard', any time spent in working hours on non-work pursuits was completely dwarfed by the time spent after working hours in ensuring we were prepared for court or deadlines were being met. There were, of course, one or two who didn't contribute to this work ethic and the reader will have deduced from what I have said before who these exceptions might be! I found that being a prosecutor was far more demanding and challenging than being a court clerk, but not for a moment did I ever regret my decision to change my career path.

* * *

Whilst as lawyers we were obliged to be objective and dispassionate in the conduct of prosecutions and to give impartial advice to the police, nonetheless we worked closely with police officers. Prior to 1986 we had, in effect, a solicitor/client relationship with the police - they sought our advice, we gave it. They didn't have to accept it and, in the last analysis, it was a police decision whether a prosecution should continue or not and on what charges. The reality was that, more often than not, our advice would be accepted, although at times not without an argument! To bring about this state of affairs, it was essential that we maintained a close working relationship with the police and that there was mutual liking and trust.

In those days a sergeant or inspector would accompany the prosecutor in the main court at each court centre and there was thus someone available to consult about decisions that often needed to be made in court - do we accept the 'guilty' plea the defendant is offering to a lesser charge, for example? These officers were attached to the police department that was solely responsible for dealing with prosecutions, and we were in daily and constant contact with these departments. There were exceptions, but most of these officers were excellent to deal with - they were realistic and pragmatic and we rubbed along very well indeed. I remember one inspector in particular, "Budgie" Williams at Buxton, who came to court every day with us and who never disagreed with a proposed course of action and, indeed, sometimes even suggested it before we raised it. The usual decision to be made was: do we drop the existing charge and accept the plea offered to a lesser one? "Cuff it" was Budgie's stock phrase.

We also had, and were encouraged to have, very close contact with CID officers. Inevitably this involved most of all drinking together. This might be after court in *The Sycamore Inn* in Matlock, the *Bakers Arms* in Buxton, *The Wheatsheaf Hotel* in Bakewell, or a myriad of other hostelries. Or it sometimes involved a gathering in some rural inn on an evening, or just before Christmas. Or there were leaving or retirement parties in police clubs. It will come as no surprise that most CID officers were as fond of drinking as most of us, and there is no doubt that our 'common interest' was responsible for forging a very close relationship with the detectives. This facilitated the process of persuading them to accept our casework opinions (and occasionally vice versa!). I have always thought that when the CPS became an 'independent' body in 1986, and lawyers were expected to have a more arm's-length relationship with the police, that something valuable was lost and it was to the detriment of our working relationship.

The quality of work we got from the police was very good, on the whole. The files were always typed and well presented, and most of the evidence that needed to be gathered was present. The standard of the officers themselves, particularly CID, was as high as I have ever encountered since. It will always be the case, I suspect, that many police officers will have a more optimistic view of the prospects of conviction in any given case than we will. This is only to be expected since, as the investigators, they have a vested interest in the outcome of the case and they will often know the defendant well enough to be certain of his guilt (he may even have admitted his guilt to them in 'off the record' conversations!). On the other hand, we are trained to look at the evidence objectively and dispassionately and without any preconceived notions (not as easy as all that when you yourself know the defendant from previous dealings and know his criminal record!). As I say, however, it was usually the case that, if we had contrary views about the likelihood of success of a potential prosecution, then our view would be accepted.

* * *

Over the thirty-two months I was with Derbyshire CPS I encountered many defence advocates from across the county. Some I already knew from Chesterfield days, as solicitors from that town also on occasions got out to Bakewell and Alfreton. There were, however, solicitors from Buxton, Stalybridge, Bakewell, Matlock, Belper, Alfreton, Ilkeston and Derby that I met regularly at the courts I covered over that period. There were some very good advocates amongst them and, if I am labouring the point I apologise, those who compared favourably with many barristers I have come up against or witnessed in court over forty years!

There were many impressive solicitor advocates from Derby I met from time to time, too many to mention perhaps, although the best of them I always thought was Alan Moore - low-key, no flamboyance at all, but quietly effective. The most effective from Alfreton was John Turner - a reluctant advocate, I think, but very organised, well prepared, knowledgeable and again, not an ounce of flamboyance! I remember very well one of his clients leaping over the dock at Alfreton after being remanded in custody and fleeing from the courtroom. He needn't have done, but John immediately set off in pursuit, leaving dock officers and other police officers in court stumbling in his wake. John was an ex-amateur England football international and his client was no match in the running stakes - he brought the fugitive down within a hundred yards along the street with a beautifully-timed rugby tackle.

The Chesterfield and Bakewell solicitors I have mentioned before. There were also, however, some decent advocates from Buxton - one in particular, John Bunting, who I believe is still going strong today!

The Matlock solicitors were perhaps the exception to the rule. David Brooke-Taylor was affable but unimpressive. Then there were the terrible twins - Keighley and Cotman. They were disciples of what one might call the "school of irate advocacy". They were to the defence what John Calvert was to the prosecution and, indeed, watching Calvert and one of them go hammer and tongs at each other was something to behold. It was not an edifying experience being involved in a trial with one of these characters. Cotman in particular seemed to regard defending his client as a personal crusade and believed that police officers were engaged in some sinister conspiracy to fabricate evidence against his clients, whose version of events he seemed to believe implicitly. I have often found it to be the case, however, that those advocates who make the most noise in court are not necessarily the most competent and that their sound and fury cover up a lack of legal knowledge. Certainly the case with these two!

The more disagreeable moments, however, tended to be when one ran into certain solicitors from Manchester and Liverpool, which did happen sometimes at Buxton or Glossop. I don't want to identify any in particular, although I have encountered some of them in later years. They seemed to regard prosecutors from Derbyshire, especially younger ones, as novices or second-rate, lacking in knowledge, competence and experience. They were invariably from large, criminal practices which no doubt dealt regularly with heavy-duty professional criminals from those cities, and 'slumming it' in the sticks was really beneath them. They were slick but sinister and, quite honestly, they were difficult to trust. I have not found the same attitude from solicitors in other cities, and I include the East End of London here, and Sheffield and Newcastle as well. It seemed to be something peculiar to Manchester and Liverpool. I have on occasions in later times read of solicitors from there being the subject of criminal proceedings themselves, and I can't say that I have ever been wildly surprised!

Appearances by members of the Bar were less frequent in the courts I covered than they had been in Chesterfield (and much less, I believe, than they were in Derby), but nothing I witnessed in this regard had cause to make me review my previous opinions about barristers in the magistrates' courts! Nor have I had such cause since.

* * *

After the first couple of occasions, I found appearing as an advocate before benches of lay magistrates a comfortable experience. My background and earlier experience no doubt helped in this regard.

The composition of the benches was broadly the same in the courts I covered - some local gentry (more so at Ashbourne and Bakewell, of course), professional people, wives of professional people, skilled 'working class' and, in the Alfreton and Belper courts, some ex-colliery employees, which reflected the importance then of the mining industry in that part of Derbyshire.

At Matlock we had one lady chairman of the bench who rather tended to wear her prejudices on her sleeve - we tended to refer to her as "batting first wicket down" for the prosecution. Fortunately not something I have encountered too often over the years! Most magistrates are quite inscrutable when sitting on a trial, and give nothing away! One chairman at Matlock, a retired major, used to quite ostentatiously fall asleep in the longer trials – no-one ever complained, but you wonder what contribution he was able to make to the bench's deliberations!

I was particularly fond of the Alfreton bench, most of whom were friendly and down-to-earth. What particularly endeared them to me was an incident which happened one morning after court. I had prosecuted two trials that morning, both alleged offences of driving without due care and attention. In the first one the evidence, to my mind, was very strong and I had confidently expected a conviction. To my surprise (and indeed that of the clerk) the case was dismissed. The second trial I had no illusions about - it was not a strong case and it got less strong as it proceeded. There could surely be only one outcome? Again much to my astonishment, the same bench came back from their deliberations and announced that they found the defendant guilty! As I headed across the court car park a little later, the chairman of the bench hailed me from across the other side of the parking area. I went to meet him, wondering what was about to transpire! "Mr. Binstead," he said, "We should have thrown that second Due Care out, but we didn't want to see you go away empty-handed." I couldn't think of an appropriate response, so I just smiled...

* * *

Most of the casework I was involved in during my time in Derbyshire was routine or "volume" crime, as it became known and, as befitting my learner status, I did not have much to do with anything particularly serious. I prosecuted and advised on cases of Driving without Due Care and Attention, assaults, public order offences, Shoplifting, Drink Driving, Theft and Taking Motor Vehicles without Consent. This was enough, however, for me to learn the rudiments of my trade. Nonetheless, by mid-1979 I was ready to move on to greater things and face new challenges. Before I move the story on, however, it is time to pause and digress and provide the reader with an idea of what "prosecuting" was all about....

CHAPTER FIVE
The Art of Prosecuting

Whilst I was far from being the finished article in 1979, and indeed probably never would be, I felt that I knew enough and had learnt enough to be able to say that I had acquired the necessary basic skills to be a prosecutor. So what were those skills?

"Prosecuting" wasn't just about what went on in court. There was far more to it than presenting facts, examining and cross-examining witnesses and addressing magistrates on the law, although clearly this was a very important aspect of the art. As a prosecutor it would always be the case that you would spend a great deal of time perusing case files submitted by the police, evaluating the evidence, deciding whether there was sufficient evidence to proceed and, if so, on what charges, and advising accordingly.

In Derbyshire, in every criminal case except those involving minor traffic offences, the police would submit to the CPS a file containing the evidence that had been gathered, a summary of that evidence, and the charges or proposed charges. I say "proposed charges" because, in some instances, the police had already preferred charges against a defendant before we became involved, usually where there were reservations about granting bail and a remand in custody was to be sought - and even here the police might have sought oral advice from us before charging. Otherwise, one of two things would happen - either the defendant, having been arrested and interviewed, would be released on bail and advice sought from the CPS before charging took place, or he would simply be released and told that any proceedings would be by way of a summons to court, again the file of evidence being submitted to CPS before any proceedings commenced.

The result was that significant quantities of copies of police files would arrive at the office every day and would be allocated for advice to the appropriate team leader, who would in turn divide them up amongst the lawyers on his team.

Having read the file, the lawyer would first of all have to determine whether there was sufficient evidence to proceed with the case. This was the most important decision he or she had to make. The standard we applied at that time was one handed down to us by the Director of Public Prosecutions, a standard his office applied in all criminal cases. This was, quite simply: "Is there a 51% chance of conviction on this evidence?" The corresponding standard applied today is: "Is there a realistic prospect of conviction?" I.e. "Is conviction more likely than not?" Given that last phrase, and by definition, it has always seemed to me that the test was the same then as it is now!

The test, of course, is quite subjective and no two lawyers would necessarily reach the same decision on the same case, although we would discuss cases between ourselves and, probably more often than not, we would agree. Over a period of time a lawyer would develop an instinct as to whether a case was a 'winner' or not - this would be based on his experiences in court as to when cases succeeded and when they failed. Sometimes decision-making was not clear-cut, sometimes it was very difficult. Where, however, the decision was a marginal one, my inclination and, I believe, that of most of my colleagues, was to advise that the case should proceed. We were, of course, looking at cases 'on paper'. There was no telling in many cases how witnesses would shape up in the witness box or, indeed, if they would actually turn up at court if required. There was no guarantee that even the strongest case on paper would succeed! But the paper case was all you had to go on!

It was inevitable that we prosecuted some cases that failed, either because the lawyer's initial judgment was wrong or because of matters outside our control. The important point, however, was that we were weeding out the cases that were weak and had no prospect of success. Over and above that it was something of a lottery!

Sometimes we might consider that the evidence as it stood was insufficient to afford a 51% chance of success, but that this could be rectified by obtaining more evidence. It was important that, where we thought it might be feasible to reinforce the case, we advised accordingly and gave the police the opportunity to gather more evidence before any final decision was made.

It is important to be aware that at this time the final decision as to whether cases proceeded or not was one for the police, not the CPS. They might ignore our advice and ask us to prosecute the case, and we would do so, whatever our reservations. I have already said that this did not happen very often and our advice was routinely accepted.

In today's CPS, the test as to whether there should be a prosecution, or whether a prosecution should continue, is not confined to the sufficiency of the evidence. It has also to be considered whether the public interest requires a prosecution or whether some disposal of the case other than by prosecution may be more appropriate. In the 1970s, however, the CPS was not really required to apply a public interest test when advising whether a case should proceed or not. This was regarded as being solely a consideration for the police. We might venture to suggest that a caution might be more appropriate than a prosecution in an individual case, that any penalty might be nominal, or that we might be criticised for taking a case to court. Essentially, however, the police did not want to hear this and such comments would likely be met by a gentle reminder that this was their province!

* * *

Having advised that a case could proceed, we then had to consider whether the charges or proposed charges were the correct ones. This required a completely different kind of expertise and one that was gained only by experience.

Charge selection was sometimes easy, as there might be only one possible offence that was made out by the evidence, and no alternative lesser or greater charge was possible. Theft from a shop or driving with excess alcohol, were obvious examples. The challenge arose when there was a multiplicity of offending or when more than one type of charge could be supported by the evidence.

Assaults presented regular difficulty (and even more in modern times with the introduction of a purely summary offence of "common assault"). Where an assault resulted in infliction of a "wound" or "grievous bodily harm" there was going to be a decision to be made as to whether Assault Occasioning Actual Bodily Harm was preferred, or Causing GBH/Malicious Wounding. The two distinct offences attracted the same maximum penalty in both the magistrates' court and the Crown Court. Defendants, however, tended to regard the latter as more serious than the former and were often reluctant to plead 'guilty' to, say, Malicious Wounding when the injury also amounted to Actual Bodily Harm. The tendency would therefore be to choose Assault Occasioning Actual Bodily Harm to charge, unless there was a bad cut or a broken limb, when the other charge would be considered much more appropriate. In later years there would be "Charging Standards" handed down which gave guidelines as to which offence should be chosen but, at this time, there was no such guidance.

The even more difficult challenge was the situation where wounds or grievous bodily harm had been inflicted with a weapon - typically a bottle or a glass in a pub or nightclub incident. The issue was then whether the defendant "intended to cause grievous bodily harm" and, if this could be proved, then there was an offence which carried much more serious penalties - a maximum of life imprisonment, indeed. This was the offence contrary to section 18 of the Offences Against the Person Act. The dilemma for the prosecutor was: "Do we charge section 18," or "Do we take the line of least resistance and charge the lesser offence of Causing GBH/Malicious Wounding or even Assault ABH?" Defendants would rarely be prepared to plead 'guilty' to the more serious offence, for obvious reasons but, if that were charged, would often offer to plead 'guilty' to the lesser offence. The decision then was to either accept what was offered or stick to one's guns and have a trial before a jury on the more serious charge. It was always tempting, except in the most obvious cases of section 18, to take what was offered - although sometimes this incurred the wrath of the judge if he/she thought the more serious charge should proceed!

It was never an easy decision but, in practice, we tended to adopt a rule of thumb which could apply in many cases. If the defendant was alleged to have thrown an unbroken bottle or glass at another, or thrust an unbroken bottle or glass into another's face, then we inclined to the view that a jury would probably not find an "intention to cause GBH", and we would not charge the more serious offence, or, if we had, would accept the 'guilty' plea offered to the lesser offence. On the other hand, if it were alleged that the bottle/glass had been broken by the defendant first, or, indeed, was already broken before being used by him, then we would advise the police to charge section 18 and would continue to trial on this charge. Judges have always tended to accept this factual distinction as being relevant to charge selection, although it was not always as clear-cut as this.

An even more difficult situation was where the injuries inflicted were very serious and potentially life-threatening. Although this was never a decision I had to make in my formative years as a prosecutor (I did many times in later years), consideration had to be given as to whether a charge of Attempted Murder should be preferred. This is one of the hardest offences in the criminal calendar to prove - it required proof of an "intent to kill", not just to cause GBH. The defendant had certainly inflicted grievous bodily harm in these cases, but the challenge was to convince a jury that he or she had intended to do more than what was actually achieved, i.e. to kill! Ironically, it is easier to prove a charge of Murder itself since, if the victim actually dies, then the prosecution only need to prove an intent to cause grievous bodily harm and not an intent to kill!!

Not surprisingly, defendants would rarely plead 'guilty' to Attempted Murder and in my experience we would rarely go to trial on such a charge and, if it had been charged, there was always a strong imperative to accept a 'guilty' plea to section 18 Wounding/GBH. This knowledge tended to influence our charge selection at the outset.

The real test to be applied in charge selection is whether the charge reflects the criminality of the case, and thus does it give the court adequate sentencing powers in the event of a conviction? Many judges in particular get quite irritated if they feel that we have "undercharged" and that their sentencing powers are not as great as they would have liked. On the other hand, courts, and judges in particular, won't hesitate to criticise the prosecution if they feel we have "overcharged" and if we are going to trial for an offence which they consider is 'over the top'. Charging selection can, therefore, be a very fine balancing exercise and is rarely entirely straightforward at the best of times!

Another fairly common situation is the defendant who has committed a multiplicity of offences or has, for example, been stealing money from his employer regularly but over a period of time. Until fairly recently the rule was that, if specific individual offences could be identified, then they had to be charged as such, even if one couldn't be precise about dates, for example. Thus, if it could be proved that a defendant had indecently assaulted an identifiable child on a number of occasions over a five-year period, the correct approach was to charge individual counts of indecent assault on a day between two dates at intervals over the five-year period. It is always important not to charge too many offences, or "overload the indictment" in the Crown Court (the "indictment" being the schedule of charges drawn up by the Crown). How we would deal with this, then, was to charge, say, two offences for each of the five years involved, even though there may be many more offences committed over the period. This strategy of charging "specimen offences" has always proved acceptable to the courts and does give the sentencer adequate sentencing powers.

There is also always the back-up position in multi-offending cases of drawing up what is called a "TIC Schedule" – i.e. a list of all the other uncharged offences which a defendant will be invited to have "taken into consideration" by the sentencing court. This might be usefully employed where there have been a lot of burglaries, for example, and where it may be important not to offend individual victims by appearing to ignore their case, or where compensation may be sought. It is, however, a cumbersome procedure and, if the defendant doesn't admit any or all of the listed offences on the TIC sheet when they are put to him at court, then that is the end of the matter unless he is then charged with them, which will usually be after he has been sentenced for the charged offences. The procedure is really largely unnecessary and seems to have fallen out of favour in the last ten years or so.

In very recent times the rules have been changed to permit the prosecution to 'roll up' a number of offences into one charge where they are similar - a number of thefts committed against the same person, for example. This has simplified matters and has given the prosecution another option in multi-offending cases, although judges don't always like this approach and it has, therefore, to be used sparingly.

Where it is not possible, or it is difficult, to identify specific offences, then it has always been acceptable to roll up offending into one charge. Thus, where a man has been stealing from his employer over a period of time, but it is not possible to say when or how much on each occasion but the total is £X, then one can charge theft between two dates of £X. This is known as a "general deficiency" charge.

Sometimes charge selection needs to be tactical, subject to the overall caveat that the court must have adequate sentencing powers in the event of conviction. If, for example, there is a large incident of public disorder in which police officers are assaulted, threatened and abused, there is always, to my mind, more mileage in keeping the matter in the local magistrates' court to be heard by local magistrates rather than in a Crown Court, which may be out of the area and where the case will be heard by a jury whose members may be from another part of the county. The magistrates, of course, will no doubt have read about the incident in the local paper and will doubtless share the common local sense of outrage! Furthermore, and I will say this again, the evidence has always shown that there is a higher rate of conviction in the magistrates' court than before a jury. This is scarcely surprising, in my view: magistrates are case-hardened and have heard it all before, and are unlikely to be swayed unduly by the blandishments of advocates; members of juries, however, are men and women taken off the street, who have probably never been in court before, and are far more likely to be susceptible to the urgings of the last advocate they hear from, defence counsel, who will be repeatedly reminding them that they cannot convict unless they are "sure" of a defendant's guilt. In this sort of situation, therefore, it may be good tactical sense to charge offences which can be tried only in the magistrates' court - e.g. Assault on a Police Officer rather than Assault Occasioning Actual Bodily Harm, and offences under the Public Order Act of Threatening Behaviour.

This may be regarded by some as a rather cynical approach to charging, but it is entirely legitimate. I took this approach in what turned out to be the longest trial I ever had in court, and with complete success, both in terms of convictions and adequacy of sentencing. Had I chosen charges which could have gone to the Crown Court, by the defendants' election that is, I am not sure that the result would have been as favourable, not least because the judge may have been persuaded to exclude some of the evidence. As it was, none of the defendants appealed against their conviction or sentence, which they could have done (see next chapter for this case in more detail!).

★ ★ ★

The most obvious aspect of prosecuting, of course, and the part that is conducted in public, is courtroom advocacy. To do this is why most of us went into prosecuting in the first place. It is the most challenging part of the job and the part that I have always found the most fulfilling. I have never been able to understand how people who join the CPS can later give up this part of the job in favour of becoming a full-time manager in the same organisation, but then I have never been able to understand why anyone qualifying as a solicitor should want to spend their life conducting conveyancing transactions or applying for probate!

One can divide courtroom prosecuting into essentially three activities - bail applications, 'guilty' pleas and trials. I am dealing here with magistrates' court advocacy - whilst the same basic principles apply to Crown Court advocacy, the whole business of prosecuting before a judge and jury is a different ball game and is the subject of another chapter!

If conducted properly, opposing an application for bail in the magistrates' court should provide a real test of a prosecutor's skills in advocacy and the "technique of persuasion". (More later but, in the Crown Court, bail applications are often non-events!). The keys are proper preparation and presenting a structured argument. Preparation is often difficult for the simple reason that, in many cases, one will not have seen the necessary paperwork until just before court starts, or even whilst court is progressing. Where the police charge a defendant and are not prepared to release him on bail, he has to be brought before the court as soon as possible. A short file will then have to be prepared by the police containing the charge sheet, a case summary, possibly some witness statements if there are any at this stage, details of previous convictions, and details of why bail should be opposed. By the time this file is ready to be given to the prosecutor it is likely to be just before court starts, or while the court is already sitting.

When I prosecuted in the East End of London there would often be fifteen or sixteen such sets of papers to be read before the start of court. Often more would arrive during the court sitting. It would always be a lot fewer than this in the shires but, nonetheless, one had to make time to read them and prepare one's arguments, often whilst one was in the midst of prosecuting other cases before the court. There would be pressure from the court and from the defendant's solicitors to get the case called on, and the temptation for many would be not to prepare properly and try to 'wing it'. This is something I was never prepared to do. It is unprofessional and, indeed, a breach of the solicitor's Advocacy Code. It can create a very bad impression, as it is likely to be obvious if preparation has been skimped. I have always dug my heels in and refused to proceed with the case until I have properly prepared.

Almost since I started prosecuting, the question of bail has been governed by the Bail Act 1976. Apart from other considerations, this sets out the grounds on which bail can be refused by the court and the sort of reasons the court may find to apply one or more of those grounds if bail is to be refused. The prosecutor, who has to address the court first and has therefore to justify the application to oppose bail, must identify which grounds apply and identify material to support those grounds. Bail may thus be opposed on the ground that there is a substantial likelihood that the defendant will reoffend and, to support that, it can be shown that the defendant has offended whilst on bail in the past, is already on bail now and, perhaps, because the nature and seriousness of the offence are such that it points to a likelihood of reoffending. Other grounds for refusing bail are the substantial likelihood of absconding, or interfering with the course of justice, or for the defendant's own protection.

Often, on television programmes, prosecutors are seen to be opposing bail simply because of the "seriousness of the offence", and I have seen and heard prosecutors in court, usually where unprepared, oppose bail on this basis alone. The "seriousness of the offence" is not, however, in itself a ground for refusing bail! It may be a factor in establishing one of the grounds referred to above, but that is all.

The police will often suggest that bail should be opposed on several grounds. I have always made a point, however, of opposing bail on only the strongest ground or grounds, since it only detracts from the application to the court if one is trying to 'splatter the target' with too many grounds, some of which are weak. I have always found it beneficial, indeed, to make a point of telling the court if the prosecution is not relying on a particular ground - "We are not saying that the defendant will not answer his bail, as there is no evidence to support this contention," for example. This is the prosecutor being fair and even-handed, which is likely to put him in a good light with the magistrates and, indeed, is likely to enhance the strength of the ground or grounds on which he does rely! This has always been my experience.

It is also important to set out, in summary at least, what the nature of the evidence is against the defendant. If one fails to do so or fails to set out that there is a reasonable case against the defendant, then this will be exploited by any competent defence advocate. It is always the case that, at this stage, the defence will say that the client will be pleading 'not guilty' and that the trial will be many months off. If it is apparent that the case against him is weak, the defence will highlight this and they are then halfway at least to getting bail for the client. (I wish I had £10 for every time the defence said at the first hearing that the defendant would be pleading 'not guilty', only for him to plead 'guilty' further down the road!)

All this, I believe, needs to be put together in the form of a structured application: one starts by indicating that bail is opposed, then sets out the 'headline' grounds on which it is opposed, outlines the allegations, then sets out the grounds one at a time, each supported by the material on which each of these grounds may be found. By so doing, the prosecutor is clearly and logically identifying why bail is opposed and is giving the bench the evidence on which to find grounds to refuse bail. This approach also pushes the defence into dealing with each ground individually and specifically, something they might not always be able to do with equal force.

I have opposed bail on hundreds of occasions over the years and have succeeded far more often than I have failed. There have been occasions, however, when I have decided not to oppose bail, even though the police have clearly felt that bail should be opposed. Whilst as a young prosecutor I might have been reluctant to do so, certainly after a few years I started to be much more selective. I learnt from experience to identify the cases where bail was likely to be granted, and did not see any point in those cases in making an application that was almost certain to fail. Much better again to take the moral high ground by pointing out that, although the police refused to grant bail I felt, subject of course to the magistrates' own views, that bail could be safely granted with "appropriate conditions". I would have already canvassed those conditions with the defence and they would gratefully go along with them. Such conditions might, of course, be quite stringent and sometimes too stringent for the defendant who would, in time, be back before the court for breaching them. The prosecution would, of course, be in a much better position to oppose bail at that time!

The magistrates would almost always endorse this approach and grant bail with the conditions suggested. They too, of course, would be grateful for the fair and enlightened approach taken by the prosecutor and would, no doubt, be receptive when he was opposing bail in another case! The overall "technique of persuasion" strategy means, of course, that the court will be more likely to heed the arguments of those it likes than those it does not!

It has to be said that magistrates were much more likely to remand defendants in custody even ten years ago than nowadays. They have, in recent years, come under a lot of pressure to keep people out of prison because of overcrowding, and this has certainly had an impact - even more important nowadays, then, to be very selective about the cases in which one opposes bail.

* * *

The "technique of persuasion" applies just as much, to my mind, in situations where a defendant has entered a 'guilty' plea in the Magistrates' Court and the prosecutor is called upon to outline the facts of the case against him and to refer to his antecedent history.

Most files supplied by the police come with a summary of the case as well as any witness statements that have been taken and details of the content of any police interview with the defendant. It is tempting often just to read out the case summary to the court and, indeed, this is probably what the sloppy and unprepared prosecutor will do! I learnt early on, however, that to rely on the police summary was dangerous. It has been prepared by a police officer, probably the "officer in the case", and is his subjective view of the evidence in a case which he may have investigated. It is quite likely to be inaccurate or exaggerated, and unbalanced. It may make one a hostage to fortune to rely on it. That is not to say that some summaries may not be very good. However, in my view the only reliable and professional way to prepare to present the facts in a 'guilty' plea case is to read the evidence that has been gathered, and prepare one's own "summary".

This, of course, increases preparation time quite substantially, especially where some witness statements are handwritten and sometimes illegible! I have known one prosecutor who would laboriously write out exactly what he was going to say to the court. This isn't necessary, however, and, over time, one becomes quite adept at identifying and highlighting the parts of the evidence that need to be presented - the advent of the yellow highlighter pen has been very beneficial!! In this way one can present an accurate and balanced outline of the evidence. Familiarity with all the file contents also enables one to answer any questions posed by the magistrates, something that may not be possible if one has only read the summary, and there is nothing worse than to be seen scrabbling through the file in open court to try and find the answer to a question that has been posed. Familiarity with the whole case and proper preparation, I have always believed, are the keys to a professional presentation. As will be seen, this is particularly important in the Crown Court, where judges are always going to be much more probing and inquisitive than lay magistrates, and the prosecutor who doesn't know his case is going to be cruelly exposed!

Unfortunately magistrates' courts can, in my experience, be guilty of double standards in this respect. The situation will often arise, too often in fact, where there are two courts sitting in the same building at the same time and one finishes its business before the other. In order to make the best use of magistrates' time, the 'finished' court will want to take business from the other court. This creates an unsatisfactory situation for the prosecutors in both courts - one has to give up cases which he may have spent a good deal of time preparing, and the other will now have to spend time preparing the ones he has inherited. The latter will inevitably come under pressure to be ready as soon as possible, so that the magistrates are not sitting around waiting for something to happen. With the best will in the world, the transferred cases are likely to be less well-prepared than they were originally! Although courts are insistent, and rightly so, on proper presentation of cases, there is often, in my experience, a lack of appreciation on their part in this situation of how long it takes to prepare a case to an acceptable standard and that the prosecutor cannot just pick up a case and prosecute it from 'cold'. There are those, of course, and I have known them, who can do this and without giving the impression of being unprepared (the celebrated Dick Fletcher was a case in point), but they are few and far between!

Most of my time over the years prosecuting in magistrates' courts has been spent on "list" prosecuting. This means having all the criminal cases that are listed in the court on that day - this will be a mixture of cases for plea, sentence, for adjournment, bail applications, and possibly even a trial to do when all the other business is over. This may be anywhere between fifteen and forty cases. Some of these cases, and indeed, in all likelihood at least 30% of them, will end up being adjourned for one reason or another, probably at the behest of the defence or for the preparation of a report on the defendant by the Probation Service. One can never know for certain, however, when and if this is going to happen, so the reality is that most of the cases have to be prepared as if they were going to proceed to sentence that day. It goes without saying that this may involve many hours pre-court preparation, much of it probably in the prosecutor's own time, and that inevitably some of that preparation is going to be wasted because cases don't proceed. One learns to accept that and live with it. It doesn't help, however, when preparation time is wasted or created by cases being transferred from one court to another! I cannot see this situation ever being any different!

Going back to the issue of "presenting" a case on entry of a 'guilty' plea, it is important that the case is presented in a fair and even-handed manner. I have known, and have heard of, prosecutors who haven't done this - who have embellished, exaggerated or over-stressed the case against the defendant and failed to make any points in his favour. I even heard of one person, nameless, who was forever informing the court that: "This is the worst case of... I have ever come across." This is wrong. It is also unnecessary. The English/Welsh prosecutor is not a "persecutor". He is supposed to be Minister of Justice, setting out the case against the defendant fairly and impartially and without trying to score points against the defendant, and, indeed, drawing attention to any points in favour of the defendant where those points exist.

There is, indeed, no need to 'go in hard' against the defendant. The magistrates will be experienced and sensible enough to see the case against him for what it is. Presenting the case in an unbalanced way is likely to offend the court rather than assist the prosecution. At the same time, drawing attention to the fact that the "defendant was very frank with the police," for example, or underlining that his previous convictions are for different sorts of offences, is something that is clearly noted by the magistrates and appreciated. I was always pleased, too, when the defence advocate publicly thanked me for my "fair and balanced presentation of the facts." Part of the "technique of persuasion" again. To gain a reputation as a fair and impartial prosecutor, I firmly believe, stands one in good stead when one wants the court to find favour with one's arguments in other situations.

★ ★ ★

Prosecuting a full trial, in any court, is something I always found to be the most challenging and, if successful, the most rewarding part of prosecuting. It is surely what any criminal advocate aspires to and I have never understood those prosecutors or, indeed, defence practitioners, who shy away from getting involved in trials. It is also the opportunity for the prosecutor to show off the full range of his advocacy skills.

Over a period of about 30 years I prosecuted many magistrates' court trials for a variety of charges, ranging from minor motoring offences to more serious driving offences, public order matters, shoplifting, receiving stolen goods, assaults and sexual offences. I was involved in hundreds of trials lasting in length from an hour to six days. Many more than this, however, did not proceed as trials. By this I mean that there were a lot of cases which were listed for trial and I would turn up at court ready and prepared to deal with the case as a trial, but then either the case would "crack" or it would be ineffective for one reason or another.

A "cracked" trial arose, for example, when on the day of the trial the defendant would decide at the eleventh hour to plead guilty, or he would offer to plead 'guilty' to a lesser offence or to, say, a number of the offences with which he was charged, and the offer was acceptable to the prosecution. These scenarios were the most common reasons for trials to crack. Other reasons may be the prosecution deciding not to proceed with the case because the witnesses fail, or a witness fails to turn up at court, or the victim approaches the prosecutor at court and says he doesn't want to go ahead with giving evidence.

Trials may be ineffective that day because, for example, the prosecution witnesses fail to attend but the prosecutor still persuades the court to adjourn the case so that an attempt can be made to get them to court next time; or, the defence persuade the court to adjourn the case so that they can get a missing witness to court, or for a variety of other reasons. Sometimes the court simply finds that it doesn't have sufficient time that day to hear the case because other matters have taken longer than expected.

Criminal courts have striven for years to reduce the number of cracked and ineffective trials. They are bad news for courts because they will often result in unnecessary attendance of magistrates and wasted time. They may be bad news for witnesses who turn up and find their attendance has been unnecessary (although sometimes they are grateful that they haven't had to go through the ordeal of giving evidence!). It may be bad news for prosecution and/or defence advocates who have had to spend a good deal of time in wasted preparation. Whatever has been tried, however, has failed significantly to reduce these phenomena.

It will always be the case, I believe, that many defendants will offer to plead 'guilty' on the day of the trial, either to the existing charge or something else they think acceptable. They may plead 'not guilty' originally because they hope something will go wrong - for example the prosecution witnesses will not turn up at court, the prosecution will lose the file, or the prosecution will lose faith in the case and drop it! When none of this happens and defendants are now confronted with the prospect of having to give evidence, be cross-examined and possibly receiving a tougher sentence if they are convicted after a trial, then many of them lose heart! The imminence of the trial does tend to concentrate minds!!

Whatever measures are taken, whatever strategies are pursued, I feel sure it will also always be that there will continue to be cases where witnesses will not turn up at court or will not want to give evidence when it comes to it. Let's face it, most people do not like being in court in any capacity, let alone standing in a witness box and being cross-examined and accused of being mistaken or worse! Some witnesses are scared of reprisals from violent defendants. Others, when it comes to it, simply do not want to testify against their violent husband or boyfriend who has allegedly assaulted them.

I firmly believe that courts should recognise that it is useless and forlorn to spend hours in meetings with other criminal justice agencies, and hours conducting monitoring exercises year after year, in the vain hope that cracked and ineffective trials will go away or, at least, wither on the vine. They have always been with us and will continue to be so – let's just accept that!

★ ★ ★

Whatever happens on the day of trial, the prosecutor must beforehand prepare as if the trial is going to take place. As ever, preparation is the key and failure to prepare is unprofessional and a breach of the Advocates' Code. I have known those who either do not prepare at all or try and get away with the absolute minimum of preparation. It doesn't work. It shows and it will be apparent to the court. There have been CPS lawyers who don't read their files until an hour before court - most in my experience, however, have been diligent in their preparation. In more recent times, however, I have often seen barristers, who have been hired by the CPS to prosecute in a particular court on a particular day, turn up at court half an hour before court starts to look at the files for the first time. Needless to say, magistrates I have known tend to form a very bad opinion of many of these "agents", as they are known, and they do their branch of the legal profession no credit at all.

I have always believed in good preparation for trials and would be mortified if I had ever been accused of lack of, or inadequate, preparation.

It should go without saying that one should be totally familiar with the content of the statements made by the witnesses who are to be called to give evidence, and what the defendant has said in interview with the police. One should be very aware of the strengths and weaknesses of the case. Also, one should have carefully researched and considered the law which is applicable to the case and how it relates to the evidence. Advocacy training courses teach that the prosecutor should have a detailed case plan, in writing, setting out what has to be proved, how we are going to prove it, etc., and a clear case 'theme' – i.e. what 'line' or 'angle' are we going to adopt in presenting the case and in examining the witnesses.

I have never, either in the magistrates' court or in the Crown Court, prepared a case plan as such, but I always have firmly in mind a case 'theme', and I use this to inform my opening address to the court and to guide my examination and cross-examination of witnesses. If, for example, in an assault case the defendant is clearly going to claim that he believed that he was just about to be struck by the victim and that he acted purely in self-defence by getting a blow in first, then the theme may be that the degree of force he used was unreasonable. In reading the witness statements I would note what additional questions I might have to ask the witness to draw out this theme, and I would highlight any part of the defendant's interview with the police that might support this line.

At court, and before the trial begins, I have always made a point of seeing the prosecution witnesses, assuming they've arrived, trying to put them at their ease as far as possible, and making sure they have an opportunity to refresh their memories from their statements. Most witnesses will want to reread their statements at this stage, as the events they describe may have been many months before, but I always tried to encourage the most confident witness to do so, because it is not uncommon for a witness to claim that there is something in the statement which he didn't say or which has been recorded inaccurately. The statement will almost certainly have been written by a police officer as he is interviewing the witness, and sometimes what he has recorded doesn't accurately reflect what the witness is telling him. The witness is supposed to read his recorded statement through before signing it, but many simply won't take in everything that has been written and will just want to get the process over with. To me this pre-trial meeting with witnesses is very important - you get some idea of how they are going to shape up in the witness box, you can at least try and allay their fears about the 'ordeal' that lies ahead, and you can be forewarned about any discrepancies in their statements. Clearly, the advocate who arrives at court half an hour before court starts and needs to read his files then, may well not get the chance for this pre-trial process, with possible adverse repercussions for himself and the witness when the case gets under way.

These days there are volunteers at court who have been trained to deal with witnesses - they will meet them when they arrive, keep them apart from defendants, show them the courtroom, and generally look after them and put them at their ease. We did not have this facility in the 1970s - the witness' only 'friend' was the prosecutor!

Still on the subject of witnesses, the prosecutor will need in his preparation to decide which witnesses he is going to call to give evidence and in what order. This may be obvious in many cases and there will be a logical order to call them in – e.g. victim, anyone who has witnessed the incident, arresting officer, interviewing officer. Often, however, there will be a statement from a witness which contains evidence which is not favourable to the prosecution. If the statement is wholly unfavourable then this is easy - he/she is really a defence witness and you don't have to call him and you can tender him to the defence so that they can call him if they wish. The difficulty comes with the witness whose statement is broadly favourable to the prosecution but contains material which supports the defendant's version of events. The rule is that such a witness should be called by the Crown, warts and all! However, I have to say that in circumstances where the other witnesses I propose to call are sufficient, in my view, to prove the case, then I have tendered the witness to the defence. I have generally found that the defence have not insisted that the witness be called by the prosecution. There are obvious advantages to this course: the defence may not call the witness as he is not wholly favourable to their cause - so the witness then is not undermining the prosecution case; on the other hand, if the defence decide to call him, then the prosecutor has a fine opportunity, in cross-examining him, to draw out the evidence in his statement which supports the prosecution case!

Another issue which may arise on occasions with witnesses is how many to call. In a public order incident, for example, there might be a number of police officers who have witnessed the defendant or defendants committing the alleged offence or offences. There may be a number of them whose statements are identical or similar, and who are going to give the same evidence. Technically they should all be called to give evidence. In practice this may be neither necessary nor desirable. After a certain point, calling the same evidence does not strengthen the prosecution case and there is always the danger that it may dilute it if subsequent witnesses turn out to be weak or do not perform well in the witness box. Far better to draw the line somewhere and tender the remaining witnesses to the defence; not that the defence, of course, will wish to call them. When calling a number of witnesses who are giving evidence about the same offender or offence, it is always best to call first those who appear on paper to be the stronger witnesses. Strategically, I have always found it is better to establish a strong prosecution case early on, even if later witnesses tend to weaken it, rather than trying to retrieve a case which has been undermined by poor early witnesses!

* * *

Having, hopefully, prepared the case to a decent standard the trial, if effective, now begins. For the prosecutor the first step is to make an opening address to the bench. This is optional but, in my view, and this is what I was taught, it is a mistake not to do an "opening". I have known some prosecutors, albeit not often, not to open and simply begin by calling the first witness. This is not calculated to impress the magistrates - they need to get a flavour of the case, they need to know what's coming. It is unsettling for them to have to find out about the prosecution case as it goes along. I have always made an opening speech.

Essentially the purpose of the prosecution opening is to outline to the court what the evidence against the defendant is. I stress the word "outline". Unlike the Crown Court, where one is addressing a jury, the opening address, in my view, should be brief and concise. To go too far into detail of what the witnesses will say may be unwise. It makes one a hostage to fortune, as the witnesses may not say what one wants them to say! This then gives the defence advocate a significant weapon at the end of the case, when he or she is addressing the court after all the evidence - "The prosecutor told you that Mr X would say that....He didn't say that!" Given that the burden on the prosecution is to prove the case against the defendant "beyond reasonable doubt", the defence are already likely to be creating that doubt if they can do this!

In opening I always had my case theme in mind, but I tended to be wary about setting it out in opening. Rather, I preferred to work it up in the course of the evidence. I preferred to 'keep my powder dry' at this stage as far as possible. Thus, to give a simple example, in a shoplifting case the defendant may be saying that when he got to the checkout he "forgot" that he had a joint of meat in his shopping bag and this is why he did not offer it for payment. The prosecution theme here may be that the joint was so heavy that he must have been very aware of it in his shopping bag. In opening, however, I might simply state that: "The prosecution allege that the defendant was perfectly aware that he had goods in his possession that he was not offering for payment...," without going into "why". This is tactical. The defence may not appreciate what the prosecution 'line' is and this gives the prosecutor the opportunity to raise it for the first time in cross-examination of the defendant, hopefully to good effect!

I also tended in opening not to dwell too much on any weaknesses or inconsistencies shown by the defendant in interview with the police. There is always the possibility that these have not been spotted by the defence, or they have not appreciated their significance. Again, by 'keeping one's powder dry', there may be a good opportunity to highlight these to good effect in cross-examination of the defendant.

Another issue is whether the prosecutor should raise any points of law in opening. In the Crown Court the convention is that one doesn't at this stage. Unless the whole case turns on the interpretation of the relevant law, my inclination was always to do likewise in the magistrates' court. Again this is tactical as much as anything else. If I felt that there was a point of law that supported the prosecution case, I would tend to keep it to myself at this stage. Again, the particular point might not have occurred to the defence, and it could then be raised by the prosecutor at the end of the case in an address to the court on an issue of law, and at a time when it likely to have most impact. Until comparatively recent times, the prosecution did not have the right in the magistrates' court to address the court on the "facts" of the case after the evidence was over - only the defence could do this. There was, however, always a right for the prosecutor to address the court on the law at this stage of the proceedings and I often found it beneficial to keep this ace up my sleeve!

Despite what I have said above about brevity and conciseness, it was also important in opening for the prosecutor to leave the bench with the impression that the prosecution case was a strong one. So, as well as being brief and not over-specific, the opening should be robust and assertive. Important, as this was the only chance in those days for the prosecutor to address the court on the facts of the case. Nowadays he can do this at the end of the case as well, however, albeit with the defence still having the last word in this respect. This change in procedural law, to my mind, makes it even more desirable to keep it brief in opening.

⋆ ⋆ ⋆

Having made his opening address, the prosecutor now goes on to call the prosecution witnesses. He or she will already have decided which witnesses to call and in what order, although very occasionally one may decide to change the order as the case proceeds, for whatever reason, or not call a witness, depending on how the case has gone.

Eliciting the evidence from one's own witnesses is known as "examination-in-chief". The witness will go into the witness box (unless he or she is giving evidence by way of live TV link - see later) and will be asked to take the religious oath. If the witness is non-Christian, or has no religious beliefs, then he or she may take an oath based on their particular religious beliefs or, in the latter case, may "affirm". At the end of the day the nature of the oath or affirmation is not significant - what is important is that the witness regards himself or herself as bound by the oath or affirmation to tell the truth.

In my view it is very important then to tell the witness what is going to happen next and who he or she should be addressing. One may have already done this in the pre-court meeting, but I believe it is important to remind them and to put them at their ease as far as possible. The witness should be told that the prosecutor will be asking them questions first of all, then there will be questions from the defence advocate and then, possibly, questions from the magistrates (or judge), but that their replies to questions should always be directed towards the magistrates (or, in the Crown Court, to the jury). Most witnesses will prefer to remain standing but, if they appear frail or unsteady, it is always a good idea to ask them if they wish to sit down, and the court will never refuse such a request in appropriate circumstances. It may also be necessary to remind the witness to "speak up", and this is something I have always done. For most civilians, giving evidence is an experience they have never had before and for many of them it will be something of an ordeal. There is not much one can do to mitigate the unpleasantness of it, but at least one can take the minimum steps I have referred to above.

The witness having been "sworn" and put at ease as far as possible, he or she is now asked to identify himself or herself, after which the prosecutor will seek to elicit their evidence. If the witness has earlier refreshed his memory from his witness statement, then, hopefully, his evidence will correspond with the content of his statement. Civilian witnesses may expect the prosecutor to tease out their story by use of leading questions but this is not how it is done in normal circumstances and the witness must tell his story in response to a series of 'open' questions - "What happened next?"; "What colour was the car?" etc.

A 'leading' question is one which suggests the answer required - "Is it right that the defendant hit you with the bottle?" It should be apparent that this type of questioning in examination-in-chief is unacceptable and would almost certainly result in an objection from one's opponent. There are, however, occasions when at least part of a witness' evidence is uncontroversial and where one can secure one's opponent's approval to "lead" the witness through this part of his evidence in order to expedite the proceedings.

Sometimes, despite having re-read his statement comparatively recently, a witness will not give the answer 'required', or will forget details, or will become uncertain where he was sure of a fact in his statement. Basically, you are then stuck with this and left hoping that it hasn't damaged the case too much. Attempts to try and 'prompt' the witness or slip in a leading question are calculated to lead to objections from the defence advocate, and rightly so! It does, however, demonstrate the importance of getting your witness to refresh his memory from his statement before court starts, no matter how confident he is about being able to remember his evidence!

More of a problem is the "hostile" witness - the witness who goes "bandit", as we say. This is the witness who is quite deliberately departing from his statement, and in an obvious fashion, because, for whatever reason, he no longer supports the case. He will either show complete amnesia about crucial events, or he will even go as far as exonerating the defendant from any criminal activity! This may be because he has been 'got at' by the defendant or his friends and is scared of reprisals, or, more likely, because he was never more than a reluctant prosecution witness anyway and has always really been in the defendant's 'camp'.

What to do about the "hostile" witness? The conventional approach is to ask for leave from the court to treat him as "hostile". The court will allow this if it is apparent that the witness, by his demeanour and his answers to questions, is showing himself to be manifestly hostile to the party that has called him as a witness. The prosecutor will then confront the witness with his statement and, having confirmed with him that it is his statement, will then put the content of that statement to the witness in order to destroy his credit. In effect, the prosecutor is permitted in these circumstances to cross-examine the witness and ask him leading questions, even though he was originally a prosecution witness.

Until about ten years ago the result of treating a witness as hostile was simply to neutralise his testimony. It was rendered worthless and of no account and the court would disregard it. For the prosecution, however, it might prove fatal, if this was the only evidence against the defendant or if the remainder of the evidence didn't provide a case against him on its own. If this was going to be the outcome, then there was little point in going through the hostile witness procedure anyway, and one would abandon the case as soon as the witness had gone "bandit". Now, however, the hostile witness may not get away with his stance in the witness box. Recognising, perhaps, that it is likely that the content of his statement is more likely to be the truth than what he is asserting in the witness box, the law has changed to allow the jury (or the magistrates) to consider both his statement and his sworn evidence, and to accept the former as the truth if they so wish! The defence advocate, of course, will say: "Well, how can you possibly tell what is true and what is not? How can you attach any weight to anything said by this witness?" But at least it gives the court the opportunity to weigh up the opposing accounts, something it couldn't do in times of yore!

In practice, the hostile witness shouldn't come as a surprise, because it will be evident from the pre-court meeting with the witnesses that the particular witness is going to go "bandit". He won't read his statement, or he will even make it clear to you that his statement is wrong, or he will tell you that he is not going to give evidence. He may turn up at court late, or, even more obviously, not at all. There are sanctions for refusing to testify - imprisonment! Usually the witness will be persuaded to testify, but you know what's coming when you get him in the witness box!

As well as civilian witnesses, there will invariably be police officers to give evidence in a trial, and sometimes "experts" such as doctors, forensic scientists, etc. These should all be reliable and predictable witnesses. Police officers will be allowed to refresh their memory of events from their pocket notebooks, and experts will have the records of their examinations. Having said that, there are many younger police officers these days who rarely give evidence in court, for whatever reason, and often don't appear to have had any training as to how to give evidence and, as a result, they can be as hard work as some of the civilian witnesses. I have, however, over the years seen a lot of older officers who have shown great accomplishment in the giving of evidence - firm but undemonstrative, not unsettled by cross-examination, polite and reasonable.

TV dramas, apparently heavily subject to American influences, portray the examination and cross-examination of witnesses as being constantly interrupted by advocates leaping to their feet to make objections to individual questions or a line of questioning, and the judge "sustaining" or "overruling" the objections, or inviting counsel to "approach the bench". The reality is rather different. In the Crown Court in particular, objections are fairly rare and hardly ever made to the judge - if an advocate steps over the line and tries to ask an inappropriate question, all he is likely to get from his opponent is a *sotto voce* demand not to "lead" the witness and the question is withdrawn or rephrased! The judge rarely gets involved and I have never heard an objection being "sustained" or "overruled", let alone a demand that counsel "approach the bench" or come into the judge's chambers!

If one is uncertain about a course of action one is proposing to take, or an intended line of questioning, then usually one will sound out one's opponent in advance and, if the latter intimates he is against you, then the matter can be raised as a preliminary issue with the judge in the absence of the jury, or in the magistrates' court, with the legal adviser (or the District Judge if one is sitting). Advocates were probably more 'objectionable' in the magistrates' court in the 1970s or 1980s, but far less so these days and, as I say, it is almost never seen in the Crown Court in my experience!

* * *

After examination-in-chief, of course, there will be cross-examination by the defence advocate. This will be the most unsettling time for civilian witnesses. Their version of events may be challenged, called into question; they will be accused of being mistaken or, worse, being untruthful. It is bound to be an unnerving experience even for the most robust witness and inevitably some will react badly, becoming indignant or even angry. On the other hand, some will wilt and end up being less certain about what they had witnessed. Cross-examination can be a real test of the mettle of a witness. Having said that, in my experience the majority of witnesses will 'hold up' and come through relatively unscathed.

Following cross-examination, and after any questions from the judge or the bench, the prosecutor has the opportunity to "re-examine" the witness. The rule is that this should be confined to clarifying matters that have arisen unexpectedly in cross-examination. In practice, however, it is sometimes used as an attempt to repair any 'damage' that might have been caused in cross-examination, as 'damage limitation'. Personally I rarely asked questions in re-examination. If the witness had been undermined to any extent in cross-examination, then really the damage is done, and trying to retrieve the situation is only likely to make matters worse or, at least, simply underline and draw attention to the 'defect' in the witness' evidence. Better to leave well alone!

* * *

There will often be some evidence that the defence will not challenge. One example is the evidence of, and surrounding, the recording of the police interview with the defendant. Once upon a time the defence would, quite often, challenge the admissibility of any 'confession' made by the defendant whilst in police detention, on the grounds that it had been obtained by oppression or some other impropriety on the part of officers, or had been made as a result of an inducement. This then required the prosecution to call the officers who had interviewed their prisoner and, indeed, sometimes others who may have dealt with him whilst in police detention. This would often take place as a 'trial within a trial' - the *voir dire*, as it is known. This could lead to the confession being excluded from evidence if the court found that it had been obtained improperly. This sort of challenge, however, seems to have long gone out of fashion. With detailed records being maintained of the defendant's stay at the police station, the regular presence of legal representatives at critical stages of the process, and the tape-recording of interviews, it is now fairly rare for such challenges to occur and the "interview evidence" will usually be presented without any defence questioning.

Invariably, there will be no need for the prosecution to call the interviewing police officers and the record of the interview can simply be read out by the prosecutor. Judges, in particular, tend to be insistent that such officers are not called to court to give evidence when there is going to be no challenge to their testimony. As a prosecutor, however, I would usually try to find some reason to have at least one of the officers present. There would be two reasons for this. Firstly, I always found it very useful to have at court a detective, as they usually were, connected with the case, so that I could discuss any issues that arose with him - if the defendant was offering to plead 'guilty' to a lesser offence, for example. Secondly, for the prosecutor to read out the record of interview, which may be many pages long, was not necessarily calculated to retain the attention of the jury or the bench. I always believed the interview evidence was likely to have far more impact if the reading out of the record of interview was carried out as a 'double act' - with the officer playing the part of the defendant and giving his replies in the interview, for example, and the prosecutor the part of the interviewing officer, reading out the questions. I always felt this brought the interview much more to life than a sterile monologue from the prosecutor!

To shorten the proceedings and avoid the calling of unnecessary witnesses, there are two other devices available. If the defence (or indeed the prosecution) do not wish to question a particular witness, then his or her statement can be simply read out to the court. This is known as a "section 9" statement - a reference to section 9 of the Criminal Justice Act 1967, which created this procedure. This is often used for purely formal evidence but can be used for any uncontroversial statements. It is not supposed to be used, however, for evidence that goes to the heart of the case and sometimes, as a prosecutor, I would prefer to call a witness to give 'live' evidence, even if there is going to be no cross-examination, simply to make the evidence more impactive. Suffice it to say courts, and judges in particular, do not like or encourage this!

As well as section 9 of the Criminal Justice Act, there is also section 10. This allows for the parties to make formal admissions about the truth of parts of the evidence. Particularly in the Crown Court, the fashion these days is for the parties to draft sometimes quite large paragraphs encapsulating chunks of the evidence which are not in dispute. These are then read out to the court during the proceedings. Judges, needless to say, love this!

The only real difference between the section 9 and the section 10 procedures is that in theory the court can decline to take account of section 9 statements, whereas a section 10 admission creates conclusive evidence that cannot be challenged or ignored by anyone. In reality there is no practical difference between the two procedures, although the section 10 procedure allows the content of several witness statements possibly to be reduced to one paragraph.

★ ★ ★

At the end of the prosecution case, the defence may submit to the court that the defendant has no case to answer. The court will accede to this submission if either the prosecution has failed to call evidence of a particular element of the offence charged, or the prosecution evidence has, in the view of the court, proved to be so manifestly unreliable that no bench or properly directed jury could convict on that evidence. Usually what has happened is that the prosecution witnesses, or at least the critical ones, have been so discredited or undermined in cross-examination that they are no longer believable. More often than not the prosecutor will be very aware of this and will make no attempt to oppose the submission. The more difficult situation is where there is still <u>some</u> evidence that has held up, even though other important witnesses can no longer be considered as reliable. Whilst technically there may still be a case to answer in these circumstances, I have seen judges, if not magistrates, take a robust approach and still accede to the submission, no doubt on the basis that the prosecution case has been 'holed below the waterline' and the jury is not going to convict!

In my career I have been met by submissions of "no case" on perhaps a dozen occasions and certainly, in 75% of them, I have not resisted the application as the submission was clearly right. I have known one advocate, however - Malcolm Dodds from Carlisle - who did not often run trials but, when he did, seemed to regard it as *de rigueur* to make a submission of "no case" at the end of the prosecution evidence, even though there was no prospect of success. When he tried it in front of Judge Brown in the Crown Court at Carlisle, he was told to "sit down and don't be ridiculous", or words to that effect!

Assuming the prosecution case survives any 'half-time' submission as above, it will then be the turn of the defence to present its evidence. The defendant, of course, is under no obligation to give evidence himself (until one point in the 19th century he was not permitted to testify!). It is very rare these days, however, for the accused not to go into the witness box, as his failure to do so may now lead to the court being able to draw an 'adverse' conclusion – i.e. that he has not given evidence because, for example, he has no defence to the charge!

Much has been written about cross-examination and there are some 'dos and don'ts' - such as "never ask a question to which you don't know the answer" (a rule which is, nonetheless, regularly breached by most of us!). Some advocates have a pre-prepared list of questions to ask. For my part, although I will always have my "case theme" in mind, I have never done much preparation for cross-examination prior to the defendant testifying. Although you may have a good idea of what he is going to say, you can never be quite sure what he is going to come up with, so I often used to be mentally formulating my final approach whilst the defendant was still in the witness box. Cross-examination, in any event to me, was always something largely spontaneous, instinctive and pragmatic.

Over the years, however, I did develop a number of techniques for dealing with specific kinds of cases. Most of the trials in which I was involved in the magistrates' court were of offences under the Public Order Act, Theft (mainly from shops), Assaults, and motoring offences (mainly Driving without Due Care and Attention). Burglaries and sex offences tended to end up as Crown Court trials.

Public order charges tended to be amongst the easiest to prove, as the incidents were often late at night and there were several police officers giving evidence against defendants who were invariably the worst for drink at the time of the alleged offence. More often than not, the prosecutor had to do little more than establish that the defendant or defendants had consumed a significant amount of alcohol at the time. In this one was very often aided by the defendant himself. Although they always claimed they were not drunk and had a clear recollection of events, I found that I could usually extract from them that they had consumed seven or eight pints of beer or lager. It always seemed to be a source of macho pride or a 'badge of honour' for the defendant to acknowledge that he was able to drink copious amounts. This would usually be his downfall, as most middle-aged magistrates would readily believe that someone who had consumed that much alcohol would be more than capable of doing what was alleged against him! The defendant's witnesses, if he had any, would rarely help him much either. They would have, by their own admission, drunk similar amounts and it wasn't difficult to highlight inconsistencies in their evidence with that of the defendant. They may have rehearsed their stories with the defendant prior to court, but they invariably found it difficult to stick to them!

Shoplifting trials in those days often involved middle-aged women who had "forgotten" to pay at the checkout for some of their goods. Some of these may well have been genuine and the 'genre' proved a fruitful one for defence solicitor Tony Taylor in Chesterfield, who enjoyed a long run of success in trials of such matters (see Chapter 1). In my experience, however, the fact that the thefts came to light was because the individual had drawn attention to themselves in the first place because of their furtive behaviour, spotted by alert store detectives, who would then witness the secretion of an item in the person's own shopping bag rather than the store's wire basket or trolley. Whilst many magistrates were prepared to accept that older people may have an aversion to using wire baskets, or at least putting all the selected goods in the basket, I often found that there were ways of undermining the claim that the defendant had "forgotten" that he or she was in possession of goods that were not offered for payment at the checkout. Very often one could point to the fact that the undisclosed item, often a joint of meat, was heavy, and surely the defendant must have been aware of it? Or again, very often the item in question was by far and away the most expensive item selected in the store, and how could you forget it when paying for cheaper items? I also got into the habit of checking the defendant's custody record, compiled from arrival at the police station following arrest - it was by no means unusual to find that, when searched, the defendant wouldn't have had the means to pay for the offending item anyway!!

Despite Tony Taylor's successes, I rather think that there were more convictions recorded in shoplifting trials than acquittals. Such trials seem to have long gone out of fashion, however. I suspect that, with the proliferation of police cautions and other out-of-court disposals, many people are content to accept such disposals rather than have a court appearance.

I must have conducted trials for Driving without Due Care and Attention almost every week. We weeded out the weaker cases when giving advice but, nonetheless, there were still many trials, mainly of men who, perhaps, found it difficult to accept that there was anything wrong with their driving skills! The typical scenario was the defendant who pulled out of a side road or a junction into the path of another vehicle which would have had right of way. The defendant would claim that the road was clear when he pulled out and, ergo, the other driver must have been driving at excessive speed. Again and again the technique I employed here was to refer the defendant to the arithmetic. They would almost always agree that less than two seconds had elapsed between pulling out and the collision occurring and that, therefore, it followed that the other vehicle had covered the visible distance in that time. The defendant would then be surprised to discover that this meant the other vehicle must have been travelling at more than 100mph if it was not visible when he pulled out! Even the most obstinate defendant would then be obliged to agree that this was unlikely, since he would not be here to tell the tale if that were the case!

Over the years I could probably count the number of "Due Cares" that I lost on the fingers of two hands, and it was no different for my colleagues!

Another common occurrence was the Assault trial. Again many such cases never got to court because we advised against proceedings. The usual defence would be "self-defence" and, if there were no independent witnesses to the incident then it would often be very difficult, if not impossible, to shake such a claim. In law the defendant had only to raise that issue for the prosecution to "disprove" it beyond reasonable doubt. This often made it hard to proceed with cases of domestic violence - because of the 'nature of the beast', such offences would invariably occur behind closed doors and without witnesses. In later years the CPS would come under severe pressure to pursue domestic violence cases, which became a political 'hot potato', and I often felt we were pursuing cases which, for evidential reasons, we shouldn't have been. The other perennial problem with assaults by men on wives or partners was that, even where we did proceed, in many, many cases the complainant would want to retract her complaint before the matter got to trial because she was now reconciled with the defendant or, for the children's sake, she didn't want to see him go to prison!

There were, however, many assault trials in the magistrates' court in which I became involved. More often than not it was plain beforehand that the defendant would be claiming "self-defence", and so it turned out. He was defending himself against the aggression or feared imminent aggression of the 'victim'. If one was lucky there would be witnesses to the incident and, if one was luckier still, they, or at least one, would be "independent" rather than in the camp of the complainant. But failing that, there were sometimes other deficiencies in the self-defence claim that could be exploited.

I always carefully scrutinised what the defendant had said in interview with the police, as evidenced by his written voluntary statement or, later, in the record of the tape-recorded interview. There were sometimes chinks of light to be found. Often a defendant would be claiming self-defence in circumstances where he had struck the first blow - a pre-emptive strike, as it were. He would assert that he believed the victim was about to hit him so he got in first before he could be struck. Fair enough! But sometimes in interview the defendant would fail to establish any real grounds for the belief that the victim had aggressive intent towards him. He "looked at me in a funny way", for example. It was then possible to work on this in cross-examination and, in effect, establish that the defendant in fact had no legitimate reason to believe he was about to be struck. His self-defence claim then went out of the window!

The defendant claiming self-defence was also only entitled to use "reasonable force" in his defence. Whilst he was not obliged to 'weigh up to a nicety' the degree of force necessary to defend himself from imminent attack or further attack, there were occasions when the prosecutor could show that the degree of force used was entirely disproportionate. If the defendant saw the victim coming towards him, with obvious menacing and violent intent, he may be entitled to throw a blow with his fist towards the victim's face - he would not, however, be entitled to pick up a bottle from a table and hit the complainant around the head with the weapon, causing facial cuts. This would be excessive and unreasonable use of force.

Many defendants would not appreciate that there are limits to a claim of self-defence. Many would believe that, having thrown a blow in self-defence, they could continue to throw blows and even kick a victim who has fallen to the ground. The points that self-defence must be proportionate and reasonable and that it doesn't apply once the 'danger' is past, may not be known to many defendants. This may well be the reason that some accused, when interviewed by the police, claim, possibly quite genuinely, that they were acting at first in self-defence, but then inadvisedly go on to admit "taking the fight to the other person" in the belief that this is within the range of self-defence! Mileage here for the prosecutor, of course, and it may well have been his case "theme" that the possible use of force in self-defence was not reasonable and proportionate, or went beyond the need to defend oneself.

Even if the defendant has not made such admissions in interview, it is still sometimes possible to lead an unwary defendant into this trap in cross-examination. His solicitor may have explained the ramifications of self-defence to his client, but it is not necessarily an easy concept for the lay person to understand in its totality.

These techniques, of course, will not always be applicable and will not always work, but they are, nonetheless, worth knowing! But, at the end of the day, although the CPS will weed out unworthy cases, there will always be those which, after the evidence, rightly end in an acquittal. I have already stated that I was rarely surprised by any verdict returned by a bench of magistrates. Things do go wrong in trials - the witnesses are not as good as they may seem on paper, or the defendant himself is a compelling witness! Given the criminal standard of proof, the burden on the prosecution, I believe it is hardly surprising that many trials do not result in a conviction. Having said that, in the many, many trials I have conducted in the magistrates' court over thirty years I have won more than I have lost. I put this down to preparation rather than skilful advocacy!!

Jury trials are another thing, and I will come to these in another chapter!

⋆ ⋆ ⋆

After all the evidence, the advocates have the opportunity to make a final address to the court. Until fairly recently only the defence could do this - apart from dealing with issues of pure law (see before). I have not prosecuted a trial in the magistrates' court where I had a chance of a final address on the facts of the case (as opposed to the Crown Court - see later). It seems to me, however, that there would not be a lot to be gained for the prosecution case by this second address. The case will probably have lasted not much more than a couple of hours and the magistrates will have the evidence still fresh in their minds. I find it unlikely that the prosecutor making a final address is ever going to make any difference to the decision that the bench is shortly going to make!

★ ★ ★

So much for the case review and advocacy functions of the prosecution lawyer. There is just one more regular duty he or she has to discharge. That is the preparation of a set of papers to be served on court and defence in cases that are bound for the Crown Court. This job is considerably more onerous and time-consuming nowadays than it was in the 1970s and early 1980s, and the modern equivalent can best be described in a later chapter. In my early days it was a fairly straightforward task. Basically, it consisted of bundling-up a copy of the charge with a paginated copy of the witness statements and the documentary exhibits that one had on one's file. There was an order which statements had to follow, but this was no more than a logical and chronological order - the order one would call them to give evidence, in effect.

One consideration was which statements to include in the bundle. One would tend to include all of them apart from those which assisted only the defence. Nowadays it would be imperative to disclose the latter to the defence, but in 1976 I don't believe it ever occurred to any of us that this should happen! They would just be left on the file and might never see the light of day! I say this although none of us CPS lawyers had any real idea of what went on at the Crown Court. We had a body of clerks who sat behind counsel there and it seemed that there was rarely any feedback as to what had gone on in individual cases (including the sentence, if any) and we never went to the Crown Court ourselves. Our only real contact with counsel was with those we met in the magistrates' court. It may be then that prosecuting counsel in the Crown Court did disclose such statements to his opponent.

Although there is much more interaction between CPS and prosecuting counsel now (and indeed, prosecuting counsel may be a CPS lawyer), there is still a residual culture amongst CPS lawyers that, once a case has been despatched to the Crown Court, they have little interest in or involvement with its final progress. To me this has always been most regrettable and hard to understand, but our systems and the attitude of senior management have never encouraged this interaction and involvement!

CHAPTER SIX

1979 to 1982: Little Old Boys and Little Tin Gods

By early 1979 I was contemplating a change. I was very happy with my lot in Derbyshire CPS, but I was very aware that I was in a 'comfort zone' and I needed to move on and seek new challenges if I was to get out of the easy-going rut I was in. The need for change was also precipitated by a domestic tragedy in February 1979, when my second child died at eight weeks of age from cot death syndrome. Derbyshire was now the place of bad memories as well as happy ones and I needed to draw a line under this part of my life.

More in hope than expectation I responded to an advert for a Senior Assistant Prosecuting Solicitor in the Lincolnshire CPS office. I had less than two and a half years' experience as a prosecutor and this was, on the face of it, a substantial promotion, so I was not optimistic. To my surprise, however, I was called for interview and, to my even greater surprise, I was offered the job! Not without a little regret, I accepted the post and took up my new responsibilities in May 1979.

Lincolnshire was different from Derbyshire in many ways, but there were similarities as well. The county was geographically much larger, stretching from the Wash almost to the Humber, from the Fens almost to Scunthorpe, from Stamford almost to Grimsby, and from the Nottinghamshire border to the North Sea. Prior to 1974 it had been larger still, stretching to the banks of the Humber and including Grimsby and Scunthorpe, before part of its territory was taken to create the county of Humberside. The population was diverse - city-dwellers in Lincoln, seaside-dwellers in Skegness and Mablethorpe, London overspill in Gainsborough, and the "little old boys" of the fenland and dyke country in the south-east of the county.

The county was predominantly rural and the incidence of criminal activity less than in Derbyshire. The CPS was correspondingly smaller, with only eight lawyers when I joined (although this expanded to ten 18 months later). There were again great distances to be travelled to court, but even greater than in Derbyshire, the journey to Long Sutton Court on the Wash being a round trip of 120 miles! Unlike in Derbyshire we were not organised in teams, or not to start with, and all of us, except the boss, spent a lot of time driving round the county with different venues every day.

Otherwise, the working pattern was the same - case review/advice, advocacy, preparation of cases for the Crown Court. Also much the same was the drinking culture, the leisurely lunches and the need for out-of-hours court preparation!

* * *

Of the eight lawyers in the department, four of them were called Richard, as was one of the four clerks who attended the Crown Court. With the exception of the County Prosecuting Solicitor and his deputy, I found that I was, indeed, the most experienced lawyer in the office! I also soon found, however, that there were no weak links - all the lawyers were very able and very motivated.

The County Prosecuting Solicitor, Brian Coase, had been the deputy with the Thames Valley CPS and had only just joined Lincolnshire CPS shortly before myself. He was an affable and sociable man and always very supportive of his staff. Unlike his counterpart in Derbyshire, he was only a moderate drinker, however! He had inherited from his predecessor (also called Richard!) a legal executive called "Fred". I have never encountered such an animal before or since, but it seemed Fred's role had been to act as the "legal adviser" to the former boss. I have no idea why a qualified lawyer should want or need a legal executive (not a qualified lawyer) to "advise" him, and certainly Brian Coase did not need him, but he was stuck with him. Rumour had it that Brian's predecessor spent a lot of his time doing conveyancing for his friends and had no time to look at cases himself - this, however, may be apocryphal! Fred had never, of course, been an advocate in a magistrates' court and had no real conception of what cases would succeed and what cases would fail. Nonetheless, he spent much of his time looking at cases submitted by the police for advice and probably did more such work than any of the lawyers. It's fair to say that he had a decent knowledge of criminal law, but there were a not insubstantial number of cases that he had reviewed which were later quietly dropped by one or other of the prosecutors!

The Deputy County Prosecuting Solicitor was our old friend Dick Fletcher (see Chapter One). He had moved from Derbyshire shortly before I joined CPS. Like his opposite number in Derbyshire, Roger Exley, he was an accomplished advocate, popular with police and courts, and rather too fond of the amber liquid. I have already listed his special talents and qualities as an advocate. Wherever he went round the county he was greeted with enthusiasm in police stations and courtrooms. He did his fair share of travelling, but his regular Thursday haunt was Bourne Magistrates' Court in the south of the county, where at lunchtime he would hold court to the magistrates, the clerk and defence solicitors in one of the local hostelries. The chairman of the local bench seemed to hold him in very high esteem and always expressed deep disappointment if Dick didn't make it for any reason on a Thursday!

Tales about Dick were legendary, and particularly about his drinking exploits. For the first couple of weeks in the county I 'shadowed' Dick for much of the time and he introduced me to the courts, etc., as well as the 'watering holes'. I remember on my first visit to Grantham court, despite the fact that he had a trial to conduct in the afternoon, we went to the *Barley Mow* next door to the court and I watched him down five pints of bitter at lunchtime. He successfully negotiated his afternoon's business without there being any obvious effect on his performance or, indeed, on his bladder. Then on the way home he insisted we call in at *The Bell* at Coleby for another couple of pints. If you were in the office on a day when Dick was there, you knew you wouldn't escape a long lunch 'hour' in one of the pubs in Lincoln or, indeed, a post-work visit to the *Morning Star* in the city. He had an intimate knowledge of many pubs in Lincoln and seemed to be well-known by many landlords. One of his favourite pubs in the city was the *Roebuck Inn*, which tended to be frequented as well by some of the regular customers of Lincoln City Magistrates' Court. Not surprisingly, he seemed to be well-known by some of the local villains but, perhaps surprisingly, as equally popular with them as anyone else! I remember later being told by one defendant in the city court with some pride that he had last time "been prosecuted by Dick Fletcher"!

Inevitably perhaps, Dick's days were going to be numbered if he ever had a less easy-going and indulgent boss than Brian Coase. It was well after my time, but Brian moved on (as Chief Prosecuting Solicitor in West Mercia), in 1984 I think, and was replaced by Dick Williamson (yes, another Richard!), from Greater Manchester. Williamson had been a senior lawyer there and was a fearsome and intimidating character and expected high standards in all respects from his staff. He and Dick Fletcher were on a collision course from the outset, and "Fletch" eventually gave up the unequal struggle and left the CPS to go into private practice.

Perhaps equally inevitably, Dick's lifestyle also caught up with him and he died, tragically young at forty-four, in 1988 after a cerebral haemorrhage from which he never recovered consciousness.

Of the other five lawyers in the office in 1979, Dick's closest ally and protegé was Andy Donaldson. He and I lived in the same village and became good friends. Andy was a very affable and generous guy, as well as being a very competent lawyer and advocate. He was one of life's lost causes, however. From public school and patrician stock, he always felt he had to pursue a lifestyle which was commensurate with his background and upbringing, but was way beyond his means. A sort of lesser version of Lord Lucan, but without the murderous ambition and gambling addiction! He was always in great debt and his wife eventually decamped to Cumbria with the children. I lost touch with him after I left Lincolnshire, but I heard that he had left the CPS and started up a practice in Lincoln with another refugee from the Thames Valley CPS. I heard that they had a well-appointed office in the city, furnished lavishly with *objets d'art* but no clients!! The practice, needless to say, did not apparently last long and I have never heard of Andy since.

The other 'interesting' case amongst the lawyers was Nick Wise. Probably the most unlikely prosecuting solicitor I have ever come across. He was bearded, with longish hair, and drove a green 2CV with CND stickers plastered across the back screen and bodywork. He lived in a country cottage out in the 'sticks' - called "Wasps Nest". The police made several representations to Brian Coase about his suitability as a police prosecutor. To his credit, Brian defended him stoutly. He was right to do so, because Nick was a very professional lawyer and advocate and always conducted himself impeccably. The police had nothing to complain about as far as his performance and conduct were concerned. He was a very good prosecutor. He was never cut out to do the job for the rest of his career, however, and he eventually left to set up on his own, working from "Wasps Nest" and no doubt earning a very modest living representing underdogs and the underprivileged!

⋆ ⋆ ⋆

Unlike in Derbyshire, most of the magistrates' courts that existed in 1979 have survived to the present day. This is remarkable, bearing in mind the tendency, accelerated in recent times, to close down rural courthouses and move the jurisdictions to urban centres. This may, in Lincolnshire, be because there is a shortage of urban centres, and what there are are widely scattered.

What have changed, however, are the numbers and types of the clerkships. I believe there are now just three clerkships in Lincolnshire. In 1979, however, there was a plethora of Clerks to the Justices, many of them part-timers who doubled up their clerking responsibilities with being a solicitor in private practice.

In the north-east of the county the clerk was a Grimsby solicitor, Dennis Jebb, whose jurisdiction covered the small rural courts of Market Rasen and Caistor - the latter still exists. Dennis Jebb is another of the seemingly inexhaustible catalogue of solicitors who have fallen from grace following conviction of criminal offences. Jebb was convicted of laundering drug money, sentenced to eighteen months' imprisonment, and struck off the roll of solicitors. At his trial at Newcastle Crown Court in 2000 the judge described him as a "drug-dealer's lackey"

There was a separate part-time clerk at Gainsborough, a man called Oliver. Gainsborough was different from the rest of the county as the town had been populated previously as a London overspill settlement, so there was a significant London element in the town.

Lincoln City Magistrates' Court itself, as the busiest court, was in permanent session and had a full-time clerk. There were, however, two other courts that sat perhaps once a fortnight in a building in the grounds of the Castle in Lincoln (the Crown Court sat in the Castle itself). These were respectively Lincoln (Lindsey) and Lincoln (Kesteven). As I recall, these covered the rural areas immediately around the city and reflected the time when the county was historically divided up into three areas - Lindsey, Kesteven and Parts of Holland. The latter was in the south-east of the county. The three areas had their own county councils until these were abolished in 1974 and they were merged in Lincolnshire. As I recall, the Kesteven court was covered by the Lincoln City Clerk, but Lindsey had a part-time clerk to the justices who was also a partner in the solicitors' firm Sills and Betteridge - he was also Clerk to the Justices at Sleaford. These two latter courts have now disappeared.

In the south-west there were courts at Sleaford, Grantham, Bourne and Stamford. There was a full-time clerk covering the last three, Brian Foster. He was a tall man with a military bearing, quite intimidating at first acquaintance but easy to deal with once he realised you knew what you were doing. He had a particular dislike of barristers in his courts and made little attempt to disguise it! I once prosecuted a trial of a defendant at Bourne Court for driving with excess alcohol. He was represented by young junior counsel from London who clearly hadn't entirely acquainted himself with all the procedural minutiae of that offence. Brian quickly realised this and proceeded ruthlessly and humiliatingly to expose the poor chap's lack of knowledge. I might have felt sorry for him if the man hadn't been such a condescending bastard!

Bourne was a pleasant market town and Stamford was a delightful and historic place. Grantham, however, was not. It has since gained the reputation of being the most boring town in England, and there was really very little about the place to upset that reputation. It was also, of course, the birthplace of Margaret Thatcher, but that fact has done nothing to enhance the town's standing! The courthouse was a ramshackle building with few facilities. Many of the 'regulars' were from a local housing estate and all of them seemed to be refugees from a particular area of Glasgow.

One of the most embarrassing episodes of my professional life occurred in Grantham Court and on this occasion I was entirely blameless! I was prosecuting in court number one. The chairman of the bench was a local farmer called Chadburn. Chadburn was one of those magistrates who suffered from what we called "judgitis" (a more common complaint in judges, as the name suggests - see later!). He may have been a perfectly reasonable gentleman in private life but when on the bench, where he regularly sat as chairman, he seemed to feel the need to be loud, aggressive, rude and irascible. The only redeeming feature was that he didn't discriminate when selecting his 'victims', and solicitors and defendants alike were subjected to his tyranny.

What happened to me was that the court clerk called a case on that involved a man in custody charged with a number of dwelling-house burglaries. The defendant had been charged only that morning, and his file had been brought over to court by a detective constable whilst the court was already in session. He slid the file in front of me whilst I was addressing the court on another matter. I had the opportunity only to glance at it and could see that the paperwork was in the spidery, almost indecipherable hand of the said detective, who had by now craftily exited from the courtroom. I knew that I was going to need some time to get to grips with the file before I was ready to deal with the case. There was nothing unusual with this type of situation and, normally, the court would allow such preparation time; normally, in fact, I would have quietly briefed the clerk as to my requirements and the case would not be called on until I was ready. For some reason I didn't get the chance to brief the clerk on this occasion and, within five minutes of my receiving the file, the case was called on.

I stood up at this point and began to make my perfectly reasonably application for the case to be put back for a short period until I had had the chance to assimilate the details of the file. I had only just started speaking and had not got on to the reasons for my application, when Chadburn cut me off and launched into a tirade about prosecutors being unprepared and unprofessional, and I had clearly just "jumped into the car" this morning without having read the files beforehand. I was incensed. The poor clerk, who, of course, knew the situation, was trying to intervene but without success (had it been Brian Foster it might have been different!). When this torrent of abuse finished, Chadburn would not allow me to respond, but at least the clerk at this point did manage to persuade him to retire and went out with him to explain the real situation. When the bench came back I expected an apology, but didn't get one. Chadburn's two colleagues on the bench looked distinctly uncomfortable. The case was put back and I presented it later in the day. The clerk apologised to me later but shrugged his shoulders, as if to say: "Well you know what he's like!" Before I left Lincolnshire I heard that Brian Foster had received complaints from defence solicitors about Chadburn and had apparently persuaded him to stand down as a chairman. At least then he was no longer in a position to bring the court into disrepute again!

What was the most embarrassing aspect of the incident for me was that my sister, who had been stopping with us, was in court to witness my humiliation! This was the only time she ever saw me in court!!

At Sleaford Court there occurred one of those bizarre coincidences which bore out once again that old cliché "it's a small world". Whilst living in Derbyshire, a man called Keith Mugglestone, from Chesterfield, used to service my car. He continued to travel over and do this even when he moved to Antons Gowt near Boston, Lincolnshire in 1978. One day in 1981 I arrived at Sleaford court knowing that I had a case in my list which involved a charge of Driving without Due Care and Attention on the A17 against the same Keith Mugglestone, and that I would have to approach the court clerk with a view to the case being adjourned to another date so that another prosecutor could deal with it. (There was only one court sitting at Sleaford, so the case could not be transferred to another court in the same building.) I spoke to the clerk, who was the Deputy Clerk to the Justices, Peter Smith, before the start of court and explained why I could not prosecute that case, because the defendant was well-known to me. "Yes," said the clerk, "I have the same problem. He's well-known to me also. He's my cousin."

* * *

In the south-east of the county there were courts at Boston, Spalding and Long Sutton. All these courts, I believe, still exist. This was a long time before Boston became a magnet for East European migrants, and many of the defendants were from the fenland country that lay round about. They were a different sort of folk from those in other parts of the county - "little old boys", as they were known. This was a reference to how they alluded to all other males. In police interviews, defendants referred to men and youths of any age as "little old boys". They tended to share a common accent and dialect with the indigenous population of neighbouring North Cambridgeshire and North-West Norfolk - typified in the ditties of the local sixties' folk-singer, "*The Singing Postman*".

This area was littered with villages with evocative names such as Mavis Enderby, Antons Gowt, Terrington St Clement, Quadring

Eaudike, Tumby Woodside, Whaplode Drove, and Cuckoo Bridge. Many of these names presented a verbal trap to the unwary prosecutor, as I quickly learnt, as many of them were not locally pronounced as they were written!!

Spalding and Boston courthouses had clearly been designed by the same architect, as each was an exact replica of the other. Both had part-time clerks, the clerk at Spalding also being the clerk for Long Sutton.

At this time Boston Court had two magistrates who sat as chairman of the bench on alternate Wednesdays. One was called Day, and he was cast in the same mould as Chadburn at Grantham, if perhaps to a lesser degree. He was, however, fond of pontificating and tearing defendants and others off a strip. He finally came to grief, however, when one day he was busy castigating a defendant for making what he regarded as a derisory offer to pay off his fine at 50 pence a week. "Not good enough," said Day; "When are you going to pay this fine in full?" "Well," retorted the defendant, "As soon as you pay me what you owe me!" It turned out that Day, a local businessman, owed a not-inconsiderable unpaid debt to the defendant, who had done some work for him. Day ceased to sit as chairman after this incident!

Jack Francis was a different kettle of fish. He was affable and courteous most of the time, but had the unfortunate habit of being unable to sit in silence for more than thirty seconds. Prosecuting (or defending) in front of him became a staccato affair, with interruptions coming at regular intervals. It would go something like this:

PROSECUTOR: "This burglary occurred in commercial premises on the 15th February…"

JACK: "What time of day?"

PROSECUTOR: "I was just coming to that, sir. The burglary was between 3pm and 5.30pm."

JACK: "Was it dark at the time?"

PROSECUTOR: "It would depend, sir, whether the burglary took place earlier or later within that time frame. We can't be certain about the precise time."

JACK: "Why is that?"

PROSECUTOR: "Because the premises were secured at 3pm and the burglary was not discovered until 5.30 pm. A large quantity of goods was stolen..."

JACK: "What sort of goods?"

PROSECUTOR: "I was just coming to that, sir. Fifty boxes of cigars..."

JACK: "Were they *King Edwards*?"

And so it went on! The technique I learned was to try and cut off the interruptions and attempt to anticipate, to second-guess, the inevitable questions and to get the answer in before he had a chance to ask the question. I was only ever partially successful.

The thing that has always struck me about the Jack Francises, the Days, the Chadburns and the Harry Schofields of this world is that they seemed to regard the bench as their personal fiefdom, and to take no account of the fact that they were sitting with two colleagues who might be exasperated by the utterances of their chairman and might wish sometimes to be consulted by him! It is often the same type of chairman who uses "I" rather than "we" when addressing court-users, e..g. "I do not accept what you say...", etc. - failing to acknowledge that he or she has colleagues on the bench and that any such decision should be a 'corporate' one! I encountered such chairmen not only in Derbyshire and Lincolnshire, but throughout my career in other court centres as well. The best chairmen were those who were largely unobtrusive during the proceedings, spoke only when it was necessary and after obvious consultation with colleagues, and refrained from lengthy diatribes!

There were no such maverick chairmen at Spalding and Long Sutton. I did not often go down to Long Sutton, situated on The Wash, as Dick Fletcher was a close mate of the Deputy Clerk there and was also well-known in the local hostelries! I did, however, conduct the longest trial there I have ever prosecuted (and I include the Crown Court in this). This was a case involving about eight defendants, as I recall, involved in a brawl in a ballroom in a local motel, the *Anglian Motel*, where a concert fronted by *Gerry and the Pacemakers* was taking place. There were about fifteen witnesses, mostly police officers, and the trial lasted six days. It then took another half-day to sentence the defendants. The defendants were all "little old boys" from Wisbech and were pretty amiable characters, taking their convictions and custodial sentences philosophically.

⋆ ⋆ ⋆

The biggest challenge for us prosecutors was in the east. Not at Horncastle Court, which sat once a week and still exists, and where the part-time clerk, local solicitor and coroner, Ian Mitchell-Smith, was a delightful character. He always relished lunch-times, when he would prevail on all the solicitors still at court to join him for a convivial hour in *The Kings Head*.

East of Horncastle, however, lay the land of the "Little Tinn God". The courts of Alford, Spilsby, Louth and Skegness lay within the full-time clerkship of John Tinn. (Alford closed while I was still in Lincolnshire and Spilsby later, I believe, but the other two still exist).

Out of court John Tinn was an amiable, self-effacing sort of man, who physically resembled "Corky" from *The Beano*. In court he was a totally different personality. None of the magistrates fell into the Chadburn/Francis category - they never got the chance. They did and said what they were told by John Tinn. He did most of the talking in court, controlled the proceedings entirely, and quite audibly told the magistrates what sentence to pass in individual cases. If the magistrates retired to consider anything, he retired with them; he didn't wait to be invited. And this included when they retired to consider their verdict after a trial. We called him the "Little Tin(n) God".

I remember once having prosecuted a trial at Spilsby on an occasion when John Tinn was not present and one of his assistants was clerking the court. I forget the precise details now but it was a case of a defendant obstructing the police by disposing of incriminating evidence before he was arrested. He was convicted. A day or two later, John Tinn was quizzing me about the case and the nature of the evidence. It was a case which turned entirely on whether or not the court accepted the prosecution version of the facts - there was really no controversial issue of law involved. I related to him the prosecution version of the facts. Tinn's response was: "I would have taken some persuading to accept that." I would dearly have liked to point out that the finding of fact was for the magistrates and not for their clerk, but I thought better of it. I have no doubt that, had he been the clerk on the day, it would have been him I would have had to convince and not the bench, and the result might well have been different!

Just so we are clear, the role of the clerk is to advise the magistrates on points of law. He should take no part in the decision-making on the finding of facts in a trial, or on what sentence to pass, other than merely advising what the sentencing options were. In court he should be largely unobtrusive. He should go into the magistrates' retiring room after they have retired only at their invitation. John Tinn plainly contravened these rules and conventions on every count! Not only would he control the procedure in court, but he would subvert the rules of procedure. There was one regular example of this.

During the summer season, Skegness would be a holiday resort for thousands of people from the East Midlands. Cases of shoplifting would multiply at this time of year. Persons from Leicester and Nottingham charged with theft from local shops would be released on bail by the police to return to Skegness Court a few weeks later. As was not uncommon with persons charged with shoplifting, back in court they would enter a plea of 'guilty' but then would claim they had not acted dishonestly because they had forgotten they had the offending item or items in their possession when they came to pay. They would then be told by the clerk that the court could not accept their 'guilty' plea in those circumstances. In most, probably all, other courts they would be told that the case would have to be adjourned to another day so the witnesses could be called and a trial take place. Not John Tinn, however! His tack was to ask the defendant to go into the witness box, take the oath and tell his or her story. The unwary prosecutor would not cross-examine, as he or she simply believed this was simply a device for the court to establish whether the defendant really did have a defence. Mistake! Before you knew what was happening the bench, no doubt aided and abetted by Tinn, was dismissing the charge and sending the defendant on his or her way. Never mind all the evidence that could have been led against the defendant, such as his furtive behaviour in the shop, incriminating replies in police interview, etc. The court didn't want to hear this!

This was clearly an outrageous breach of the rules of procedure and natural justice, and we should have taken it on appeal. We never did, for whatever reason. When we broached it with Brian Coase he would just shrug his shoulders and say "Well, that's Tinn." It happened more than once and sometimes in the face of our objections. The court's (or to be accurate, Tinn's) attitude was that it was not worth the cost and inconvenience of a defendant travelling back from Nottingham or wherever for a trial on a small-value theft from a shop. I don't suppose the local shopkeepers would have seen it this way, but then their views were probably never taken into account, even if they knew this went on!!

It happened to me only once. On the next occasion I actually started to cross-examine the defendant and started to put to her observations as to her demeanour and conduct in the shop that had been witnessed by the store detective. At this point Tinn stopped me and stated that "there was no evidence" of these matters. My retort was "I haven't been allowed to call it." The court did then, eventually, grudgingly consent to an adjournment so the evidence could be called!

Generally speaking, however, standing up to Tinn was not a productive course of action. He was intractable and the magistrates would do as he told them, even if you tried to address them over his head, physically and metaphorically.

On one occasion at Louth I prosecuted a motorcyclist for exceeding the 30mph speed limit. Two police officers in a following police vehicle testified that, according to the speedometer in the police car, he was doing 53mph. The speedometer had been checked for its accuracy that day. The defendant, who was not represented, didn't want to cross-examine the officers or give any evidence himself, despite being encouraged and 'assisted' by Tinn. There was nothing suspicious or remotely untoward in the officers' evidence which, in effect, went unchallenged. Tinn retired with the bench and they came back and dismissed the charge, without giving any reasons for their decision (these days they would have to give reasons). The officers, who were still in court, were speechless - or at least until after court was over! On this occasion I did manage to persuade Brian Coase that we should ask Tinn to "state a case" for the opinion of the High Court, as we took the view that no reasonable bench could have come to this decision. This meant they would have had to set out their reasoning for the decision. Tinn, however, "declined" to state a case, on the basis that the matter was "trivial". We could have taken the issue further, but Brian felt it would have been disproportionate and we just wrote it off as another "Tinnism".

Some would have said that John Tinn was a 'character' and would have affectionately indulged his whims and caprices. To me, however, and to my fellow prosecutors, whatever other charms he might have, he was a menace, an arrogant and arbitrary little despot, and an obstacle to the interests of justice. The only redeeming feature was that, by the time I left Lincolnshire, he was nearing the end of his professional career as a clerk, and whatever came after must surely not have been worse!

* * *

In Lincolnshire I had, in effect, my first introduction to the mysteries of the Crown Court. The Court sat in the Castle in Lincoln and we used to go down there fairly regularly to deal with bail applications to a judge in his chambers. This meant being ushered into the judge's chambers along with the defence solicitor, where the judge, usually only partially "robed", would shortly adjudicate on the application. Unlike the magistrates' court, the judge would often not even want to hear from the prosecutor and would put the onus on the defence to make a case for bail. He would listen politely but, in most cases, would then give the application short shrift. Talking of "partially robed", I remember on one such occasion I found the judge was someone I had met in the showers at the police headquarters squash club a few days before. He greeted me with "Have we met before?" I only just resisted the temptation to reply "I think so, but I didn't recognise you with your clothes on!"

* * *

The police in Lincolnshire were essentially no different from the Derbyshire force. Many of the files produced by uniformed officers, and the quality of some of the uniformed officers themselves, left much to be desired, but there were some very good CID officers. I was particularly impressed, as indeed were some of my colleagues, by the quality of the officers in the Fraud Squad. I cannot remember there being an equivalent squad in Derbyshire. Early on I had a case conference with two detectives from the squad about a serious fraud, and found that their grasp of the intricacies of the case was quite awesome, not to mention their knowledge of the applicable law.

Unfortunately, I wasn't able to continue my association with the case as it turned out that the potential defendant was to be my next-door neighbour! Yet another bizarre coincidence.

The prosecutor I shared an office with, Richard (yes another!)Hare, was involved in a long-running case with the Fraud Squad. The evidence ran to many thousands of pages and had come about after a painstaking and extremely thorough investigation by officers on the squad. Prosecution Counsel was Igor Judge QC, who became, many years later, the Lord Chief Justice. He was enormously complimentary about the quality of the investigation.

The downside with fraud cases, as I later discovered on more than one occasion, was that they involved a great amount of work by both the police investigators and the prosecutor then responsible for preparing the case for trial. The amount of work was always totally disproportionate to the outcome as, even where conviction resulted, the sentence was invariably much less than what would be commonly imposed for many other categories of offences. The blow might be softened in more recent times by the advent of the Proceeds of Crime Act 2002, which enabled prosecutors to pursue convicted criminals for their assets and ill-gotten gains, but one was always left slightly disappointed by the level of sentencing.

Another police squad we had fairly regular contact with was the Regional Crime Squad, which had an office in Lincoln. I don't believe we ever knew where this office was situated, as the RCS tended to operate quite covertly and they would make contact with us when they wanted a conference and come to the office. Their remit tended to be the investigation of organised crime and "target criminals" and, as the name suggests, they operated over a wider area than just the county of Lincolnshire. They were a rather shadowy outfit and seemed to spend a lot of time in pubs, whether as part of an operation or not! Apart from the ubiquitous leather jackets they seemed to favour, they were usually fairly shabbily dressed and barely recognisable as police officers, which was probably the intention. For some reason and, it seemed, quite unfairly, they were known as the "Banana Bunch" – i.e. "bent, yellow and hang around in bunches." As far as I am aware, only the last part of the description was true!

Otherwise, we tended to have less contact with CID than I had known in Derbyshire, and our closest liaison was with the inspectors who ran the police prosecution departments or the commanders of the many local police stations we visited on our travels round the county. Before I left the county, however, I encouraged Brian Coase to let me initiate a regular weekly "surgery" in four of the principal police stations where CID officers, as well as others, could drop in for advice. This seemed to be working quite well by the time I left. Hardly a revolutionary idea but many years later something similar, albeit on a much grander scale, was adopted by the CPS as the basis for the "Charging" initiative, which is now an established part of the CPS operation.

There were some very able defence advocates throughout the county, although less numerous than they had been in Derbyshire. The ones that most spring to mind after more than thirty years are John Kendall at Grantham, Ray Ringrose at Boston and Peter Downing at Skegness. In Lincoln the most prominent were Ken Stanger and Terry Capp (inevitably known to everyone as "Andy"). There was a larger-than-life presence in Lincoln, in every sense of the word, in the form of Gilbert Blades. But Gilbert was not, in my view, a good advocate. He was full of bluster and flamboyance but not a great deal of substance and, to my mind, his knowledge of law and procedure was suspect. On one occasion I came up against him at Horncastle, where he was defending in a trial. He sidled up to me, all "hail fellow well met", before court and handed me a letter from a doctor which I saw related to his client's medical condition. "I'm putting this in evidence," said Gilbert. "You're not," says I; "It's complete hearsay and totally inadmissible!" Had I accepted that the letter was evidence and allowed it to go in unchallenged, it would have been handing the case to Gilbert on a plate.

I saw Gilbert again some twenty-five years later as an advocate at Carlisle Crown Court, where he was defending a soldier on a criminal charge. The case was adjourned, so I didn't have the opportunity to see if his skills had improved, but he had obviously done enough to qualify as a Higher Courts Advocate like myself. Looking him up recently on the internet, he is now described as an advocate with an international reputation in courts martial, where he regularly defends service personnel. I found another website where he is described as "the scourge of the UK MOD courts martial." You can interpret this in two different ways, of course, and looking at some of the comments from those who had witnessed him in action it rather looked as though he had been 'bull-shitting' his way through the military courts as well! He also attracted some brief notoriety in the 1980s, when he was chairman of Lincoln City Football Club and fell out in a big way with the supporters.

⋆ ⋆ ⋆

One of the small-time criminals in Lincoln was a man with an interesting past. We were told at some point that this man was, in fact, Bertie Smalls. To those who have never heard this name, Bertie Smalls was the original super-grass - an armed robber who, in return for immunity granted by the then DPP from prosecution for all crimes he had committed, gave evidence against dozens of his criminal associates in 1974-5, evidence which led to convictions of a number of serious criminals. Smalls had been given a new identity and was living in the area at this time. He continued to offend, however, albeit in a small way, and had no immunity from prosecution for these offences. One day he failed to answer bail at court and we didn't see him again. He did not end up in a 'concrete overcoat', however, and apparently returned to his old haunts in South London and died of natural causes in 2008.

⋆ ⋆ ⋆

The work of the prosecutor in Lincolnshire CPS was basically no different from that of the prosecutor in Derbyshire. The caseload was again mainly routine volume crime, and the tasks we carried out were identical to those I had performed in Derbyshire. No surprise, then, that after three years in Lincolnshire I felt I was in a rut once more. It was the same leisurely lifestyle, driving slowly back from distant courts with pleasant lunchtimes at country pubs, long lunch-times in the city when in the office, but with the same need to work after hours to prepare for court the following day. The office location was idyllic: a former large, country house, Riseholme Grange, with French doors opening on to lush green lawns, and situated at the end of a leafy lane (on which lived Sir Lawrence Byford, former Chief Constable of Lincolnshire and by then Chief of the Inspectorate of Constabulary, even then working on his report into the police handling of the investigation into the Yorkshire Ripper!). But it seemed as though nothing would ever change.

The CPS existed in most, but not all, the police authority areas in England and Wales, although others were at that time considering whether to go down this road - North Yorkshire, for example. There was, however, a much more radical upheaval looming. The Philips Commission handed down its report in 1981, in which it recommended the creation of an Independent Prosecution Service, severing the investigation of crime from the prosecution function. The government was already hinting that the report would be followed and a national Prosecution Service created.

This, however, was still a few years down the line, and I was looking now for more immediate and fresh challenges. Most of my lawyer colleagues were also restless (most of them were to leave the CPS shortly after my departure to Cumbria). In March 1982 I found an advertisement for a "Divisional Prosecuting Solicitor" for Cumbria Police Authority, to set up a new CPS office in Barrow-in-Furness. It would involve leading a small team of lawyers and admin staff.

I had only a vague idea of the whereabouts of Barrow-in-Furness, but the job appealed. I applied...

CHAPTER SEVEN

1982 to 1986: The Last Frontier

My application to Cumbria Police Authority resulted in an invitation to attend for interview in Barrow-in-Furness in April 1982. I drove across to Cumbria on the day on which the House of Commons sat on a Saturday for the first time in years, to debate the crisis generated by the Argentine invasion of the Falkland Islands.

I had discovered that Barrow lay at the southern end of a peninsula jutting out into the Irish Sea, and at the end of a road which ran for thirty-three miles off the M6 motorway. Both the indigenous population and its detractors referred to the town as being "at the end of the longest cul-de-sac in Europe". A fair description, being that there was nothing beyond Barrow except for Walney Island, which was attached to the mainland by a bridge across the Walney Channel.

The interview was to take place at Barrow Police Station on the Monday, but in Cumbria they adopted the very civilised procedure of the candidates meeting with the interviewers the night before in the pub. This was the format followed for all lawyer appointments. The idea was that both parties could get a more rounded impression of each other by meeting in more relaxed circumstances and outside the formal setting of the interview. It always seemed to me to be a very sound idea! So it was that on the Sunday night the four candidates met up with the County Prosecuting Solicitor and the police divisional commander in Barrow in the bar of the *White House Hotel*.

Chief Superintendent Max Ball left us after a couple of hours, but the rest of us sat drinking and talking until almost midnight (we were all resident at the hotel that night). Fortunately, the interviews did not begin until about 11.30 the following morning and mine didn't, in fact, take place until after lunch! As I recall, it wasn't a particularly challenging interview and I got the distinct impression that minds were already made up! One of the candidates was an 'internal' one - Greg Hoare was already one of the prosecutors in the Carlisle team and I picked up that he was also a personal friend of the boss, Duncan

Sharp. I was somewhat surprised then, not long after the end of the interviews, to be called back into the interview room and to be offered the job!

Having accepted the offer, I then discovered that I would have to be involved in the interviewing and appointment of the rest of the Barrow team forty-eight hours later. So we went through the same procedure again - Duncan and I meeting up with the eight candidates in the bar on the Tuesday night and then a whole day of interviewing in the police station on the Wednesday. I set off home on Wednesday evening having taken part in the recruitment of the two lawyers I would be managing. I was to return once more before I finally took up the reins of the job full-time, and that was in May to take part in the interviewing and appointment of a clerk/typist for the team.

I had no regrets about leaving Lincolnshire because I could see that Barrow was going to prove a new and different challenge. Furthermore, Cumbria was very much a second home for me for, although I knew little or nothing about the south of the county, I had been a regular weekend visitor to the fells and crags in the north for several years. There would come a time when I would be glad to move on again but, for the moment, I was really looking forward to what was immediately in store.

* * *

I started in Barrow at the beginning of July 1982. The team was to be housed temporarily in what had been the caretaker's lodge in the grounds of a residential care home on the main road into the town. (The care home has now long been the *Abbey House Hotel*). The lodge was a two-storey building in which, it soon became apparent, the previous occupant had kept rabbits! It was a warm summer and no matter for how long we kept the windows open, the smell was always there! We were there for a few months before we were moved into 'permanent' premises in Cavendish Street in the centre of the town. As it turned out this accommodation was no less temporary, as the building had structural defects and, when these were discovered, we had to be rapidly re-housed elsewhere. The building was demolished and a car park now stands in that location!

At first we were very limited in what we could do as a prosecution unit, as we had no facilities for copying documents. For the first couple of months or so all we did, in effect, was cover the courts, the police prosecutions inspector, Joe Moses, delivering us the original police files for court the next day. Eventually we did come into possession of a photocopier and were able to carry out the other usual functions of the CPS, advising on cases and preparing and serving case papers for matters destined for the Crown Court.

* * *

Cumbria was another essentially rural county, but very different from low-lying Lincolnshire. The large urban centres were at the respective edges of the county - Carlisle in the north, Kendal in the east, Barrow in the south, and the West Cumbrian towns of Whitehaven, Workington and Maryport. In the middle were mainly lakes and mountains. Although snow would fall on the fells and in the high mountain passes, we rarely had the sort of bad winters in Cumbria that were commonplace in both Derbyshire and Lincolnshire. The west side of the county especially, from Carlisle down to Barrow, didn't often see snow!

Cumbria had been 'created' in 1974 by piecing together the old counties of Cumberland and Westmoreland and adding a chunk of north Lancashire (including Barrow). Cumbria Police Authority had decided in 1979 to have a prosecuting solicitor's department and Duncan Sharp had been appointed as the first (and last) County Prosecuting Solicitor in the same year. Roger Exley from Derbyshire had also been invited for interview but, having broken his journey north at Buxton police station, had allowed Buxton CID to talk him out of going on! The interview process followed the same format as I have described above and rumour has it that, when it came to drinking whisky with the Chief Constable, Walter Cavey, into the small hours, Duncan was the last man standing. This is totally believable, although Exley would have given him a run for his money, no doubt, had he ever got there. Whether this was in any way instrumental in getting Duncan the job I cannot say, but it certainly wouldn't have done him any harm!

Having settled in, Duncan created a local prosecution team in Carlisle and one in West Cumbria (Kendal was to follow Barrow in late 1982). After that Duncan, or one of the other lawyers then in post, would occasionally venture down to Barrow to prosecute the odd case but, by and large, the prosecution functions would continue to be exercised there as they always had been, by the police themselves or by outsourcing to local firms of solicitors.

In July 1982, therefore, in Barrow a full-time prosecuting solicitor unit was something to which the police, and the court, were unaccustomed. Joe Moses and one of the local defence solicitors had done the advocacy and any advice or case preparation had been done largely by the local solicitor firms. I was a trifle apprehensive as to the sort of reception we were going to get. I needn't have worried on any count.

We never got less than a completely supportive attitude from Barrow police, from the Divisional Commander down, and we were welcomed as part of the team. It may have been different had we been coming in as an 'independent' prosecution service in 1986, but this was still in the future.

The Clerk to the Justices, Gary Tallentire, had campaigned since his own appointment, not that long before, for a CPS unit and he and his very friendly team were no less pleased to see us than the police.

Nor did we encounter the slightest animosity from the local solicitors, despite the fact that we had deprived them of some of their work and income! I got the distinct impression that they were quite glad to have off-loaded this work and that they felt it had been a distraction and had not done their 'street cred' with their criminal clients much good!

Within a few weeks we had our systems in place, we were up and running and we felt very much at home!

* * *

In our sector of Cumbria we had three courts to cover at that time - in Barrow itself, in Ulverston some eight miles further north, and in Millom on the other side of the Duddon valley. As in most areas, the 'culling' of small rural courts had been an ongoing process for some time, and both Millom and Ulverston had gone by the early nineties. In 1982, however, both were very much alive.

Gary Tallentire and his team ran all three courts from their office in Barrow. Gary was a year or two younger than me and was one of the young, or youngish, clerks who had trained at Nottingham Magistrates' Court under the tutelage of the celebrated George

Yandel, who had been the Clerk to the Justices there for many years. Many of that 'school' had gone on fairly quickly to senior posts and in Cumbria in 1982 three of the four full-time Clerks to the Justices were former pupils of George Yandel - Trevor Dearnley at Carlisle and Chris Armstrong at Workington being the other two. Gary himself, I believe, always had greater ambitions and it was no real surprise when he left in the mid-eighties to become a magistrate in Hong Kong.

All but one member of Gary's team were older than him, much older in fact. The Deputy, Norman Hobman, always gave the impression that he was winding down towards retirement - rumour had it that he kept a camp-bed in his office and took regular afternoon siestas. The most energetic of the clerks was Derek Archer, himself closer to retirement than Norman, and Gary largely delegated the running of the office to him. Derek found lasting fame one day when, clerking in number two court at Barrow, he called on the case of a defendant called Mycock. The court usher went out of court and returned to say that the said Mycock had been present but could not at that moment be found. An exasperated Derek then took it upon himself to go out into the waiting area, where he proceeded to shout to the gathering of defendants, witnesses and solicitors there: "Has anybody seen Mycock…?"

The courthouse at Barrow, long since demolished and now part of the new police station, had two separate courtrooms, one main one and a smaller one. There was a third courtroom across the road adjacent to the magistrates' clerk's office.

There was a dock in the main court where prisoners were produced from custody. Like most docks in those days, I suppose, it was reasonably easy for the agile defendant to evade his gaoler and vault over the side of the dock into the body of the court. This did happen once or twice, but no-one ever seemed to get very far. One Saturday morning I was in court when a defendant called Parker, having been remanded in custody after his bail application was refused, leapt over the dock and ran full pelt towards the doors of the court. These were swing doors and unfortunately no-one had told him that they opened inwards, not outwards and, charging the doors, he rebounded violently and was rendered unconscious.

Another feature of court number one was the special seat in the front advocate's bench - it was a single seat but partitioned off from the rest of the seats on the bench. I soon learnt that the prosecutor was expected to sit here. This was clearly an arrangement that had existed to keep the prosecuting police inspector apart from the civilian advocates. It was not to my taste at all, since it tended to identify us too closely with the police, and I managed to persuade Gary Tallentire fairly quickly that we should sit amongst the rest of the advocates rather than in splendid isolation. The other equally irritating hang-over from the past was the tendency of some of the bench chairmen to refer to us as "the prosecuting officer". I managed to secure the demise of this habit as well in due course!

These teething troubles in no way, I believe, affected our relationship with the magistrates. They seemed to soon warm to us as much as anyone else and, over the seven years I was appearing in that court, I felt that there was a good deal of mutual respect between the bench and the prosecutors.

Barrow was a most unusual place. The locals still regarded themselves as part of Lancashire rather than Cumbria and, perhaps because of its geographical situation, there was an attitude of insularity and parochialism about the place. People didn't tend to stray far from the town, and youngsters who went away to university often came back after graduation to find employment. The population at that time was probably just over sixty thousand, second only to Carlisle in size in the county, but as different from Carlisle as chalk from cheese.

By far the largest employer in the borough was *Vickers* shipyard and it remains so today, although the workforce is much diminished since the end of the Cold War. Another unusual feature I found was that it seemed most of the workforce went home for their lunch and cycled so, four times a day, the main street would be thronged with hordes of bicycles as the workers went to and from the shipyard.

The composition of the local bench seemed very much to reflect the profile of the community, with more than a few shipyard employees amongst the local traders and professional people.

The composition of the Ulverston bench was different again, to reflect the mainly rural catchment area. Its jurisdiction stretched to Grange-over-Sands in the east, to the Duddon in the west and to the southern end of Coniston Water in the north. There was a fine old courthouse (also now part of a police station, I believe) with a main courtroom and a smaller one downstairs. Again there was a link with the past which I felt it necessary to work to remove. The prosecuting inspector hadn't featured on the advocates' bench at all, but operated from a separate 'desk' affair immediately below the magistrates' bench and next to the clerk's table. Gary was more than happy to terminate this arrangement!

The main courtroom was only about seventy-five yards from the *Hartleys* brewery. *Hartleys* was brewed in Ulverston and was a wonderful beer but, sadly, has been no more for some time. On a Thursday morning in court number one, with the wind in the right direction, one could catch the delicious aroma from the brewery.

Millom court was different again. Millom was just across the Duddon from Barrow but involved a long, winding drive round the estuary to reach it. There was just one small courtroom next to the police station. It sat once a fortnight and there were only six magistrates on the bench.

The court's jurisdiction extended well up the west coast as far as Ravenglass and over the bleak fell country between Millom and Eskdale. It took a long time to get anywhere from Millom by road (and even longer by train!). Visiting CPS dignitaries would look at the map and think that they could get to Workington from Barrow in an hour by driving up the coast. They soon had cause to revise their estimate! There was a short cut across Corney Fell, but the fell road would often be closed in winter when snow would fall on the higher ground, and it was no place to get marooned, certainly before the mobile phone era!

Members of the Barrow prosecuting team would be required fairly regularly to travel to cover courts elsewhere in the county. This would often involve spending a long time on the road. The courts at Kendal, Windermere and Hawkshead could be reached in not much more than an hour, but Whitehaven and Workington took closer to two. Shap and Appleby were in much the same timescale, and Carlisle, ninety miles away up the motorway, was a 'day's march'.

Much like Lincolnshire, there were still a number of small rural courts and part-time clerks in the county at this time. Over the next twenty years or so, both were to disappear.

The full-time clerk at Workington, in addition to regular courts at the new courthouse in Workington and in Whitehaven, also had a weekly sitting in the tiny courthouse in Keswick (now closed and destined, it seems, to become part of a *Wetherspoons* pub!). The clerk at Carlisle had weekly court sittings at Wigton and Alston. The latter court was up in the hills and actually involved travelling through part of Northumberland to get there. Both courts now are long closed.

All of the part-timers and most of the long-lost courts were in the east. The full-time clerk at Kendal was a man called Neville Geary, very old-school. He was tall, distant and was in the habit of taking snuff in court! He had a large empire of little courts other than Kendal and Windermere - at places such as Hawkshead, Kirby Lonsdale and Sedbergh. Only Kendal survives to this day.

Then there was a weekly court sitting at Shap, a high-level, windblown village just off the M6, between Kendal and Penrith. The clerk to the justices was one Charlie Arnison, a solicitor in Penrith, whose family through four generations had been clerks of the same court. A hereditary clerk to the justices no less!!

There was always, I found, a distinct lack of formality with Charlie, both in his dress and in the novel way he would pick his way through the court procedure. Corners were cut and legal niceties overlooked, but there was never any danger of defendants failing to understand what was going on!

There were courts also sitting at Penrith and Appleby, both served by part-time clerks, Hugh Ellison and Bob Earnshaw respectively. Appleby closed a few years ago and Penrith in 2011. Even Whitehaven failed to 'make the cut' and today the only court centres are at the four points of the compass - Carlisle, Workington, Barrow and Kendal.

Personally I have always thought that the insidious process of closure of magistrates' courts is something to be regretted. Yes there is a case for it, both financial and otherwise. Keeping open buildings that housed courts that may sit only once a week, or even less often, is no doubt an expensive exercise, even without the cost of essential maintenance and repair. Having just one building that serves a large area brings economies of scale and enables the provision of better facilities for court users such as solicitors, victims and witnesses. But then Whitehaven and Penrith were relatively new, purpose-built courthouses and had excellent facilities for court users. The centralisation process also ignores the convenience of defendants and witnesses, who may have to travel significantly greater distances than hitherto. It also ignores the long-established principle of local justice, that persons should be tried by their peers, by men and women who lived and worked in the same community. And, more than that, it destroys an important part of our island tradition by consigning to history charming and quaint little courthouses that have been part of our rural fabric for generations. Courts like Keswick, Hawkshead, Ulverston, Wigton, Alston and Windermere all exuded and were steeped in history and tradition. Their loss is irreplaceable and very sad. Nowadays, however, cost will always win out against tradition!

★ ★ ★

What of Cumbria CPS itself? In 1982 it was a fairly new outfit, with an area office at Carlisle and a satellite office at Workington, and with Kendal and Barrow being added in that year. The County Prosecuting Solicitor was Duncan McSharp (although the "Mc" never seemed to be used by anyone!). He was a man who attracted a range of opinions as to his quality and his competence. There were those who dismissed him as a "legal lightweight" who had been promoted to a level way above his ability, and who got on only by luck and being in the right place at the right time. Others saw him as a skilled communicator, who built flourishing relationships with police and courts, and negotiated successfully for excellent facilities and resources for the local CPS.

In my book both sets of opinions were tenable. He was certainly not a great criminal lawyer on the face of it, and the tales I had heard of his advocacy hinted at preparation not being his strongest forte either. When I arrived in Barrow, Duncan had left a number of files on which he had tendered advice to the police and which cases were now the subject of prosecutions. Some of these took some unravelling! I have alluded before to the test we applied in those days as to whether there was sufficient evidence for a case to proceed - was there a 51% chance of conviction? The strong rumour abroad was that Duncan applied a 50% test - but that in his case this meant "always prosecute because there is always a 50% chance it will be the right choice!" True, or merely apocryphal, some of the cases I looked at that he had advised on did tend to suggest the application of the 50% rule!

One such case involved a neighbours' dispute between the owner of Rusland Hall in the Rusland Valley near Newby Bridge and persons living nearby. Duncan's only endorsement on the file was "Prosecute. I had often thought of visiting Rusland Hall but I have now thought better of it!" There was no obvious appraisal of the evidence and, indeed, neither I nor either of my colleagues in Barrow could find any cogent evidence to support the proposed charge. We didn't tell Duncan, but we agreed with the police that the matter could be quietly dropped!

A local solicitor in Barrow, and I had no reason to disbelieve him, told a tale of Duncan coming down to Barrow in 1981 to prosecute a trial of a man alleged to have been speeding on the A590 into Barrow. The first witness had been in the witness box for several minutes before it became evident that Duncan was asking him questions about a totally different speeding offence in a totally different location. Duncan had brought the wrong file to court with him and, despite the defendant and the alleged offence having been identified by the clerk before the trial began, he had failed to realise he had the wrong file until after the trial started!

On the other hand, Duncan was always completely supportive of his staff and seemed to be able to get us any equipment we wanted. He secured funding for us to attend conferences and the local Law Society dinner, including overnight accommodation if we wanted it. He persuaded the police authority that he should have a deputy. He was on intimate terms with most of the senior police officers in the county and a number of magistrates' clerks and solicitors. He was a skilled 'networker', no doubt about it!

Nor can it have been all luck, or being in the right place at the right time, when he became, in 1986, the first Chief Crown Prosecutor for North Yorkshire and Cleveland; when he secured for himself a palatial suite of offices in York to go with that job; when he became the Chief Crown Prosecutor for Yorkshire in 1993; and, before he retired in 1995, when he was awarded the CBE. He certainly had something, and whatever it was it was big enough and overwhelming enough to dwarf and mask his other shortcomings!

Duncan was also a very sociable animal. Unfortunately he also had, in common with many other senior prosecutors I have described in earlier chapters, a fondness for the drink. There were a couple of very embarrassing episodes. On one occasion, the members of the Workington team had to carry him out, feet first, from the West Cumberland Law Society dinner. Another event we attended every year was the National Probation Conference, which took place at the *Windermere Hydro* hotel. One year Duncan had over-imbibed even before dinner on the Friday night and, having covered his sirloin steak in about half an inch of mustard, he fell off his chair!

Some of the senior police officers in Barrow, who were perhaps less impressed by his general performance than others, apparently referred to him as "Drunken Duncan", although they were careful not to do so in the hearing of my colleagues and me! He was not a picture of health, being also overweight and a heavy smoker, but at least he managed to make it to retirement, which is more than some of his contemporaries did!

My opposite numbers as Divisional Prosecuting Solicitors were Ken Hay at Workington, Pat Dwyer at Carlisle and, by the end of 1982, Greg Hoare at Kendal.

Ken had come from Manchester CPS in 1979 or 1980 and then spent the rest of his career in Cumbria. He in fact became Duncan's deputy when the post was created and ultimately, in 1986, Branch Crown Prosecutor for the Cumbria Branch when the Crown Prosecution Service came into being. Ken was always a better lawyer and advocate than he was a manager and administrator. But this is perhaps a misleading and unfair comparison, because he was, quite simply, an outstanding prosecutor. He was an extremely knowledgeable and intuitive lawyer, and a clever and highly competent advocate, both in the magistrates' court and, in later years, in the Crown Court. He was highly rated by both police and his opponents. He was probably the best lawyer and solicitor advocate I came across in my career.

Pat Dwyer was as able a lawyer and advocate as most, if not of quite the same calibre as Ken in either respect. He secured the respect and admiration of the police, however, by his extreme diligence and thoroughness and his approachability. He worked long hours and led by example. He was not everyone's cup of tea as a manager - some found his intensity a bit too much - but he was successful in his career, becoming firstly, in 1985 or thereabouts, the Area Prosecuting Solicitor, and then the Branch Crown Prosecutor in Burnley.

He decided, temporarily at least, in 1997 that he had had enough of management, and he came back to Carlisle as a Senior Crown Prosecutor. He resumed in a management capacity a little later, however, taking over the running of the northern unit in the Cumbria branch/area and also qualifying as a Higher Courts Advocate, until serious illness brought about his premature retirement.

Greg Hoare had been on the shortlist for the Barrow job with me, but was successful a little after in securing the corresponding job at Kendal. I had never thought of Greg as an advocate, and it seemed that he felt himself that he had no such leanings because he left the CPS in 1986 and went into private practice with a firm in Penrith and Keswick, ostensibly with a view to doing Probate! It was much to my surprise then, when, seven or eight years later, I learned that he had "crossed the floor" and gone to the Bar. By 1994 he was appearing regularly at Carlisle Crown Court, mainly as a criminal defence advocate! Another Penrith solicitor, Malcolm Dutchman-Smith, took exactly the same route and, within a few years, he and Greg were doing a good 50% of the defence advocacy at Carlisle Crown Court. Greg is still doing this even as I write. He has obviously made a living at it, but how good a living I'm not sure. He was always complaining that he could never afford to retire and I believe that, from time to time, he did contemplate applying to return to the CPS, but he never actually went through with it.

Greg's departure to private practice coincided with the advent of the Crown Prosecution Service and to mark his departure he wrote a letter to *The Times*, which was published, detailing what he perceived to be all the faults of the old and the new CPS organisations and generally expressing his disillusionment with the prosecution process as it had developed. This prompted an edict from the newly appointed Deputy Director of Public Prosecutions, David Gandy, to the effect that Greg and any other "dissident" ex-prosecutors were never to be used henceforward as agent prosecutors for the CPS. Nonetheless, within eight or nine years Greg was being briefed occasionally as prosecution counsel at Carlisle Crown Court and still is, although he much prefers to defend!

The two lawyers I had helped to recruit to make up the Barrow team were both refugees from private practice - David Hartley and Charles Leyberg. David was also an ex-professional footballer with

Burnley, and the police pursued him eagerly and relentlessly to play for the South Division police team. David's heart was plainly still in Burnley and he left us to join Lancashire CPS in 1984 - the Burnley branch. I believe he is still there to this day. Charles was always going to progress and, when Greg left Kendal, Charles was promoted into his place. He managed the whole of the southern and eastern unit of the area at one time and was also, for a few months in 2005, acting Chief Crown Prosecutor. He ultimately, however, seemed to grow weary of, and disillusioned with, the CPS, or certainly Cumbria CPS, and resigned in 2007 some years short of retirement age.

The office team was completed by the clerk/typist, Eileen Eastham, who had a police background having previously worked in Whitehaven police station. She, too, was destined for greater things and eventually became a Crown Court caseworker before ill-health, brought on by years of carrying heavy bags of files, forced a medical retirement. I should mention that long before this she had become my wife! Early on in the job she answered the phone on one occasion and "Divisional Prosecutor's office" came out as "Divisional Prostitute's office". The caller was Gary Tallentire but, rather than being shocked, he was highly amused and apparently dined out on the story for some time thereafter!

By the end of 1982, then, there were four local prosecution units in Cumbria, all composed in the same way. In Barrow the size of the team was adequate in normal circumstances to deal with the workload and the court coverage although, if one of the lawyers was off, we had to receive assistance from one of the other teams. We reciprocated, of course, when necessary. A greater difficulty arose when the clerk/typist was away. Initially I would bring my typing skills out of retirement but, in due course, Duncan needed little persuading that the office did need a second admin person, and Judy Williams joined us in that capacity. She was to remain as part of the Barrow team for twenty-five years.

I find it very interesting to look back and compare the size of the Barrow office then with what it was to become in later years. The Barrow team survived as an integral unit until 2007, when it merged with the Kendal team. At its height it consisted of seven prosecutors, including an associate prosecutor, a Crown Court caseworker, and six admin staff. Almost three times the number of staff that existed in 1986, immediately before the start of the Crown Prosecution Service.

Whilst the nature and the amount of work did increase from 1986, we were still managing perfectly well with three lawyers and two admin staff when I left the area in 1989! It was after this that the size of the office grew like Topsy - in more senses than one, because the unit was moved to new accommodation in the early 1990s, accommodation that was about three times the size of the previous premises!

The other units, of course, increased at the same rate and the same explosion in staff numbers was replicated across the country. It was little wonder that the Chancellor of the Exchequer, when announcing his government service budget cuts in 2010, specifically referred to the "inflated" manpower resources of the CPS. It seems to me that there was a compelling argument for slashing the CPS budget by at least 25% by that time! Staffing levels, I believe, have dropped now to a point where they are closer to the 1989 numbers than they have been for many years, and I don't suppose this process has finished yet. Despite that, the prosecution of offenders has continued as before, without the process grinding to a halt because of lack of resources!

⋆ ⋆ ⋆

There was an interesting collection of defence solicitors that frequented the courts of south Cumbria in the 1980s. Some of them went on to greater things, others disappeared into other areas of the law, and some carried on as advocates.

In 1982 at least, the lion's share of the criminal defence work was being carried on by two firms of solicitors - Forresters, and Kendall & Fisher. I became very friendly with the three then partners of Forresters, and have maintained that friendship with two of them until this day. The third partner, Barbara Forrester became in time a Crown Court Recorder and then a Circuit Judge, and now sits full-time at Carlisle Crown Court, where I have many times appeared before her as an advocate. Barbara was not, to my mind, a great advocate, or even an outstanding lawyer, but she had some indefinable quality that attracted the loyalty of defendants, and the fact that she retained such a substantial number of criminal clients is a testament to her qualities and that clearly they believed that they were well-served.

Ken Fisher was, as far as I was concerned, the best solicitor advocate on the defence side that I have ever encountered. His eloquence and powers of persuasion would bear favourable comparison with any of the Queen's Counsel I have witnessed. He had a formidable reputation, and rightly so. He was not always easy to deal with, his correspondence could be acerbic and his wit and comments directed at the prosecution equally so, but he was a very worthy opponent and earned the enormous respect of both myself and my colleagues.

Another tenacious opponent who arrived on the local scene some years after us was Chris Barron. By the time I left Barrow he had forged a strong rapport with many of those who regularly appeared before the court and had become the 'go-to' solicitor for the core of local villains, many of whom abandoned their traditional loyalties, at least for a while. He seemed to have the common touch and to be able to win the confidence of even his most villainous clients by, no doubt, talking to them in a language and at a level with which they could identify.

The "man we loved to hate" was Graham Jackson from Ulverston. A physically diminutive figure, always wearing a bow-tie, he specialised in sarcastic and barbed wit and never missed an opportunity to make gratuitous attacks on the prosecutor in court, some of which bordered on the personal. In this respect he resembled a well-known advocate in Carlisle, Geoff Clapp. Both of them had the rather irksome habit of referring to the prosecutor by name, particularly when trying to denigrate some assertion he had made. The established protocol is that one refers to one's opponent as "my friend" or even "my learned friend" and if one disagrees with him, one prefaces one's remarks with either "with respect" or "with the greatest respect". Perhaps this sort of terminology is unnecessary and anachronistic, but it keeps the adversarial process on a civilised plane and I have always found it grating when advocates start to 'personalise' matters in this way, e.g. "Mr Binstead claims that…". It is fair to say that Ken Fisher, for example, always adhered very closely to the niceties of the protocol before he went on to try and demolish your arguments. For me this was always much more acceptable! For all this, however, Graham Jackson was no mean advocate.

A different kettle of fish altogether was Peter Murray, the eponymous partner in Brown and Murray in Barrow. Late fifties, silver-haired and as charming as Graham Jackson was obnoxious. He rarely appeared in Barrow or Ulverston but, as we found to our cost, often at Millom. The small bench at Millom appeared to be in thrall to Peter's advocacy and he seemed to be able to do no wrong! It became a standing joke with us that, in trials in which he was acting for the defendant, convictions rarely resulted. Whatever the strength of the evidence, Peter always seemed in his final address to minimise its importance or 'brush it under the carpet'. It was flatulent and charming waffle, worthy of the aforesaid Gilbert Blades, but it didn't often fail!

Another local solicitor I rated as an advocate but who, sadly, appeared only infrequently as such, was Gordon Nuttall. He was concise, articulate and had real presence in the courtroom. His interests, however, lay elsewhere and he went on to become a District Judge in the civil courts.

We already had one judge amongst the solicitors' fraternity in Barrow in 1982. Alan Dunn, from local firm Townsends, was an assistant recorder sitting mainly, I think, in Liverpool Crown Court. He did only a limited amount of criminal work locally, however, and his irregular forays into the magistrates' court did not demonstrate an enormous acquaintanceship with the criminal law. I have never been convinced, anyway, that being a good criminal lawyer is a requirement for becoming a judge in the criminal courts! Alan never, in fact, progressed beyond this first tier of the judiciary.

In 1987 or thereabouts Townsends merged with another local firm from Ulverston, Livingstons, to become Townsend Livingston. The merger was heralded by a big splash in the local paper under the banner heading "The Magnificent Seven" - a reference to the seven partners in the new firm. The partners, however, did not last as a unit much longer than their fictional counterparts in the film of the same name. I remember making the *faux pas* in court of referring to the firm as "Townsend Thoresen", a topical reference to the owners of the car ferry *Herald of Free Enterprise* that had capsized in 1987. An unfortunate allusion in the circumstances!

Townsends eventually remerged with yet another local firm, Pooles, to become this time Poole Townsend. Pooles had in the mid-eighties recruited a very good advocate in the form of Peter Yates. Peter had come up from Southampton but, again in one of those strange coincidences, I had first met him in Boston Magistrates' Court in Lincolnshire when he was employed by the local firm of Roythornes. Peter is now the managing partner of Poole Townsend and gave up his criminal advocacy many years ago, I believe.

I suppose it has always been the way of the world that, just as young CPS lawyers used to regard the CPS as a springboard for going into private practice after a decent interval, so young criminal advocates in private practice, as they rose in the ranks of their firm, gave up criminal legal aid work for the more profitable fields of personal injury litigation, probate or commercial law - a sad loss in my view. There are exceptions, however, Ken Fisher being an obvious one. And even in Cumbria, although exclusively in the north and west, there have been firms that 'major' in criminal law – K J Commons & Co in Workington and Carlisle, and a number of sole practitioners in Carlisle such as Geoff Clapp and Malcolm Dodds.

I cannot really leave the south Cumbrian solicitors' scene without mentioning Martin Tongue. Martin was no advocate and no great shakes as a criminal lawyer, or at least not in the early eighties, when he was in his sixties. He stands out, however, as a beacon of Christian and unselfish devotion to his small band of clients. Martin was a sole practitioner who had had, apparently, quite a thriving practice in the fifties and sixties, but by now he cut rather a sad figure who would turn up at court, whether he had any clients that day or not, just to see who was on the court list and to greet acquaintances in the defendants' waiting room. Martin knew an awful lot of people in Barrow. He spent probably one or two afternoons a week attending funerals of people he had known. His court mitigation for his clients would invariably be prefaced with "I know his mother and he's not a bad lad..." He would sometimes apparently forget to apply for legal aid, or simply not bother. One of his clients repaid his generosity by breaking into his office and stealing a chequebook and the petty cash tin. Not surprisingly, perhaps, his practice suffered. If you went into his office you would often find Martin himself at the reception desk, as he was unable to pay his office staff. He kept going, I believe, however, until he 'died in harness' in his eighties. Retirement would never have been an option for Martin.

* * *

Barrow police were as close-knit and insular a community as Barrow itself. Many of the officers at this time, and most of the senior officers, were ex-Lancashire Constabulary, or even ex-Barrow Borough police (Barrow, not so long ago, then had had its own chief constable!). Although Barrow police had become part of Cumbria Constabulary in 1974, there had not been a great deal of filtration from outside Barrow in that time and there was a local joke about Detective Sergeant David Dawes having been the first "escapee" from West Cumbria and to reach Barrow some years previously. Most of the rest of CID, however, were at this time still obstinately 'local'.

I had probably the closest relationship with the police I have ever had, before or since. Although we were in a separate building, my colleagues and I were always in the police station. We often dined in the senior officers' mess and we were often at functions in the Police Club. I hardly ever visited the police station without calling into the CID office, and I am quite certain this was to our mutual benefit. Although before 1986 it was still the police who decided whether persons should be charged or not, and they had no obligation to consult CPS before charging, I found that I was being constantly informed of the progress of investigations and often being involved in decisions to charge wherever CID were concerned. To my mind, the nature of this relationship made the transition to the changed relationship in October 1986 a much smoother one than it might otherwise have been.

The divisional commander, Chief Superintendent Max Ball, had been in Lancashire Police, mostly in CID I believe, most of his career. He regarded Barrow as the "jewel in the crown" of Cumbria Police and himself as the "king". He was certainly viewed with awe by his officers, and I felt that he had little time or regard for the hierarchy at police headquarters at Penrith. He was not always an easy man to deal with, but I think we rubbed along and it's fair to say that he was always very supportive of the CPS unit in Barrow. I believe he saw every case file that was generated by his officers in south Cumbria and wrote an endorsement on each in green ink. He always told us that we had complete discretion to do what we thought fit in court in terms of accepting pleas to lesser charges, etc., unless the file had been endorsed by him "no deals". He could be intractable, especially in sensitive cases. I recall the son of a police sergeant from Ulverston being charged with theft. The only evidence against him was that of an accomplice and I advised Max that, in these circumstances, without corroboration, the prospects of conviction were less than 50%. "No deals", however. The outcome of the case was as I had predicted.

Max, despite his support for us in CPS, was very old school in many ways, and the looming prospect of the Police and Criminal Evidence Act 1984 was not at all to his liking. He retired in late 1984, just before PACE came into force. He was succeeded by Chief Superintendent Harry Brown, another escapee from West Cumbria. Harry was just as supportive of CPS but a very different character from Max - down to earth and not one to stand on his dignity. He was also much more amenable to advice on cases from us.

Another great supporter of CPS was the head of CID, DCI Maurice Wilkinson. He was very hands-on, clearly revered by his officers, and a total workaholic. He had a lively and wide-ranging intellect and was always initiating discussions in the senior officers' mess on topics as diverse as the politics of Northern Ireland and the natural history of the Duddon Valley! Sadly, Maurice was in poor health, possibly exacerbated by his working patterns, and he died of a heart attack in 1984. He was succeeded by Ernie Garden, a Scot who had worked in West and East Cumbria previously. He was dour and not very popular, it seemed, with the CID officers, but he was very much to our taste in CPS.

The officer we routinely dealt with was Inspector Joe Moses, who ran the prosecutions department. Joe proved to be a very good friend to us and we rarely disagreed on casework issues. In fact, he was often engaged in heated confrontations with Max Ball about the disposal of cases, in situations where he completely agreed with our point of view and had thrown his weight behind our stance. Unfortunately, he had no more success with Max than we did! Joe, of course, had been the principal police prosecuting advocate before we arrived and so had a pretty sound idea of which cases would succeed and which would not. He was the ideal officer for us to work with and, after his retirement in 1986, we didn't share the same rapport with his various successors. Joe went on to be a "stringer" for Kendall & Fisher in the Crown Court but, like Maurice Wilkinson, had a heart condition and, sadly, only lived three years into his retirement from the police service.

Lower down the scale we dealt mainly with the CID men and we were able to develop a very good working relationship with the whole body of these officers. I suppose, by definition, the CID officers are going to be intellectually a cut above the uniformed officers. I hope I am not being patronising here, but I had always found that to be the case. Barrow CID proved no exception. There were three detective sergeants, the best of whom was Dave Dawes who, some years later, in 1995, became the county head of CID. His deputy then was Ian Douglas, who also was in Barrow CID from the mid-eighties. In about 1987 a very youthful, almost boyish, slim fellow with spiky hair joined the department. He was known, for some reason, as "cabbage patch". This was Ian Golding who, only sixteen or seventeen years later, was also to become head of CID in Cumbria. But, although he never rose above inspector rank, the stand-out man for me was DC Ian McBride. He could be a bit prickly sometimes, and I suspect he was not always flavour of the month with his superiors, but I was a tremendous admirer of his work, his work rate, his intelligence and his diligence.

This is not to say that there were not some very fine officers amongst the uniformed ranks. Two I remember in particular were Sergeant Eric Winfield, whose son was at school with, and has long been a good friend of, my son, and PC Dave Rogan. Both were, at one time or another, seconded to CID where, no doubt, their talents were exploited.

One officer whom I always admired, an unsung hero, was PC Frank Dearden. Frank was for years the village or community constable in Broughton-in-Furness. Frank was not a man to blow his own trumpet, but I heard many tales of how respected he was by everyone on his patch, and of how many people locally he had helped in one way or another. Frank is the subject of two of my endless catalogue of coincidences. I think it was in the late nineties I was on a fell-walking trip in the Cuillins of Skye. Descending from a fearsome blade of rock called *Am Basteir*, whom should I meet coming up but Frank, in the company of a probation officer from Barrow, John Cobb. Then, several years later, I was again on a walking holiday in the mountains of County Kerry. Reaching the summit of *Carrauntoohil* in the McGillycuddy Reeks, we found there to be six people on top. Two of them were Frank and his wife!

The drinking culture was as prevalent with Barrow CID as it was elsewhere. Barrow Police had their own licensed club in the police station (police clubs, in Cumbria anyway, have long since gone, victims of the 'cuts'). This was heavily patronised most nights of the week, and my colleagues and I went to many of the frequent events there - quiz nights, retirement dos, etc. Rumour had it that Barrow CID also had unfettered use of a back room of a pub in the town, which was known as the "Winchester Club". This was a reference to premises of the same name that featured in the TV series *Minder*, premises where there were no recognised licensing hours! I can confirm at least the existence of the "Winchester Club", as CID invited me there for a night when I was about to leave Barrow in 1989!

* * *

In many ways our work and our working pattern between 1982 and 1986 were no different from what they had been in my two previous counties. We reviewed evidence, advised and prepared cases for the Crown Court, and prosecuted cases of volume crime in the magistrates' court. It was the routine as before. There were, however, some differences. As far as Crown Court case work was concerned, as ever we put the papers together, arranged service on court and defence, and then packed the file up to the Crown Court section in Carlisle and probably never got to hear the result unless we specifically asked for it, and certainly never had any dialogue with prosecuting counsel. Most of the Crown Court cases were heard at Lancaster or Preston. However, there was then, as there is still, a Crown Court sitting at Barrow - then three days a month, now four I believe. There had been, and have been, attempts to shut the court down in Barrow, but I think there have always been strong interests opposed to this and it has survived, much against the odds!

The advantage for us in Barrow was that we could sometimes make time to actually go and watch the proceedings and see the results of some of our work. Most of what went on, of course, were 'guilty' plea hearings and sentencing, since three days did not really allow for many trials to take place. Furthermore, it seemed to me that a lot of the time the court was not actually sitting for one reason or another, and there was a lot of sitting around and waiting. The days were short anyway - 10.30 start and the judge did not like sitting beyond 4.00 pm. Many years later I came to realise that this was hardly uncommon in the Crown Court and that there was often a lot of 'empty time'. We also covered most of the bail application hearings before the judge in his chambers. This was about the most we were exposed to contact with counsel, albeit defence counsel!

Another difference was that, because of my working relationship with CID, I was often involved with decisions about charging in the more serious cases, albeit in an advisory rather than a decision-making capacity. This hadn't happened in Derbyshire and Lincolnshire.

There was also a far more common tendency with the defence to have what we called an "old-style" committal. With cases destined for the Crown Court, and after they had received the evidence, the defence in those days could opt to ask the prosecution to call their evidence in the magistrates' court for the magistrates to determine whether there was a prima facie case to go to a judge and jury. "Old-style" because, prior to 1968, all such cases were conducted in this way. The prosecution only had to call such evidence as it felt was sufficient to found a prima facie case, but the procedure gave us a taste of sometimes handling in court the sorts of cases which otherwise would only just 'pass through' the magistrates' court. During my seven years in Barrow I conducted several "old-style" committals, including cases of Robbery and Causing Grievous Bodily Harm with Intent. The high point for me was the Pennington Robbery, where three men had attacked a middle-aged couple in a lane in a village near Ulverston. The couple were on their way to an antique fair in Charnock Richard and were robbed of the substantial amount of cash they were carrying. The investigation was largely carried out by DC (by now DS) McBride and three professional criminals from Manchester were arrested and charged with robbery.

The evidence against the three - Hayes, Shearer and Milbank - was not overwhelming and, not surprisingly, they opted for an "old-style" committal. The proceedings took place at Ulverston Magistrates' Court and the defendants were represented by solicitors from three well-known criminal practices in Manchester. As was often the case with these sorts of advocates, they made it fairly plain that they had little regard for the magistrates or me and that appearing in a rural court was rather beneath their dignity. The proceedings lasted two days and the witnesses were shaky. I feared the worst but the magistrates, somewhat to the consternation of the defence, found that there was a prima facie case and all three defendants were committed to the Crown Court. To my great satisfaction, they were later convicted after a trial and sentenced to substantial terms of custody. Two of the three defendants used to write letters to me for some years afterwards, complaining that they should never have been committed for trial, as if this were my fault!!

It was comparatively rare, however, at this time for criminals to travel to Barrow and South Cumbria to commit crime and the overwhelming volume of local crime was committed by local men and women. There was a good deal of house burglary, car crime, some serious violence offences, the occasional robbery and the usual diet of shoplifting and public order offences. I don't know what the comparative figures were, but it always seemed to me that the level and type of crime in Barrow were no less than in the city of Lincoln or Chesterfield.

There were a number of local criminals who could be described as serial or prolific offenders. Three in particular stood out, and two of them to my certain knowledge are still offending to this day, thirty years later. Jeffrey Richard Trengove was only ever not appearing in court when he was serving a sentence. So frequent were his arrests that the defence solicitors in Barrow joked that the police had created the offence of "being Jeffrey Richard Trengove". He must have served dozens of prison sentences over the years, but the fact that he was often in court is an indication that most of these sentences were of short duration and that most of his offending rarely rose above the mundane - theft and relatively low-level violence on the whole.

Trengove had no obvious, attractive features - he was a foul-mouthed, obnoxious lout. Gary Jones, on the other hand, had some redeeming features. Known universally as "Garibaldi" Jones because of his shaven head, he stole, committed burglaries and took cars at will; that is, when he was not in custody. However, he was always ready to admit his offending, was unfailingly polite in the dock and never complained about his sentence. I used to see him in the street quite often, when he was at liberty, and he never failed to acknowledge me politely. He was apparently a gifted mechanic and for a while he held down a job in a local garage, and the feedback was that he was the best fitter and mechanic they had ever had. If only he could have channelled his energies into legitimate enterprise! I have to say that I was saddened to hear some years after I had left Barrow that he had taken his own life by driving a car into the dock.

No-one could have entertained any sympathy for "Tarka" Robinson. As a teenager and a young adult he established himself as a one-man crime wave in Millom. He was committing so many burglaries and so much car crime that the local police eventually invoked what became known as "Operation Tarka". This, I believe, involved keeping him under almost constant surveillance. Eventually he went away for fifteen or eighteen months' custody and the community had a rest from his activities. When I came back to Cumbria in 1995 I found that he had resurfaced in Carlisle and was as prolific as ever. Most of his offending was of the same type as before - burglary and theft, but in more recent times he has branched out into Class A drug trafficking. Offending appeared to be an all-consuming obsession with Robinson and when he wasn't actually committing crime he was thinking about it. I was involved in one case in about 2002 when, after a police operation, he was charged and convicted of Conspiracy to steal. Part of the operation had involved the evidence from a listening device that the police had planted in his car. I can remember listening to part of the recording that had been picked up on a journey from Hexham to Carlisle. The whole of the conversation between Robinson and his passenger was about stealing and other criminal activity. He must now be in his late forties, but still a relentless and unreconstructed offender!

One of the strangest affairs in Barrow, and one that later gave rise to another of my "coincidences", was that involving one Thomas John Painter. Painter had been employed by Barrow Borough Council and one of his functions was to take large sums of cash to the bank in an attaché case. It sounds astonishing now but, in those days apparently, that did actually happen! According to what he later told the police, Painter was set upon by three men in a back street behind the bank, knocked to the ground and his case seized. He claimed to be able to identify his assailants as "Scousers". Road-blocks were set up on the exit roads from the town, but no-one matching this description was stopped. I was told that there was "not a detective in Barrow" who believed Painter's story, but no money was ever recovered and no evidence to confound his account ever emerged. Shortly afterwards, Painter's wife opened a photographic studio in the town, an enterprise which seemed at odds with the Painters' known financial circumstances, but the police were unable to find any evidence that the provenance of the funding for the studio was suspicious.

That was not the end of the story. Not that long after, £20000 disappeared from a safe in the town hall and suspicion fell on Painter, who was still employed by the Council. There was again, however, no evidence worthy of the name that he was the culprit. Nonetheless, for whatever reason, he was dismissed from his employment. The law caught up with him a year or two later. First of all he was successfully prosecuted for Obtaining or attempting to obtain money by deception after making a number of false claims against his holiday insurance policy - it appeared that, every time he went on holiday, he lost property or had it stolen! Then I successfully prosecuted him for Driving with excess alcohol and Failing to Stop after a road accident. He denied the charges, claiming that he was not the driver at the time of the collision and that someone must have taken his car without his consent from outside his house and without his knowledge - he had been in the attic and had not heard the car being driven off. Nor, apparently, had he been aware of it being returned, the considerate person who had unlawfully removed the car actually returning it to exactly the same spot from whence he or she had taken it!!

I believe Painter left the area after this. This was, however, not the last I saw of him. In 1993 I walked through the doors of Newham West Magistrates' Court in east London one afternoon and saw a figure I recognised amongst the defendants gathered in the waiting area. Yes - it was Thomas John Painter! When I got back to the office I checked the court list and discovered that Painter was being prosecuted for several offences of theft from Newham Borough Council. I looked at the file later and, to my astonishment, found that he had been employed by the council as a rent-collector (presumably having declared his employment history??) and had allegedly been appropriating some of the money he had collected!! I never found out the result of the case, as I moved on not long after and before the matter came to trial.

* * *

By September 1986 our little team in Barrow was in a good place. It was a comfortable, unstressful existence. We had excellent working relationships with the court, police and other local criminal justice agencies. We had little interference from the area headquarters at Carlisle, and had been free to develop and use our own systems and the working practices which suited us. As far as I am aware we were, as a unit, well-thought-of and well-respected. We were on the verge, however, of dramatic change and things would never be quite the same again.

CHAPTER EIGHT
1986 and all that

On 1st October 1986 the Crown Prosecution Service came into being. It had been heralded by the passage of the Prosecution of Offences Act 1985, which implemented the main recommendations of the Philips Commission.

The Act created an independent prosecution service, which was to take over the conduct of the prosecution of all criminal offences once the police had instituted proceedings. The Service was a national one. There had been debate as to whether a national service or a locally-based one was to be preferred, but there never appeared to be much doubt that the national option would prevail.

The arguments in favour of a national CPS were strong ones: principally, that only a national service would ensure consistency in decision-making and working practices. In my view, however, this was the wrong decision and I believe history has shown this to be the case. Decision-making has always been a subjective process anyway. The CPS nationally can publish Codes for Crown Prosecutors, Charging Standards and all the guidance under the sun about deciding whether to prosecute or not and for which charges but, at the end of the day, in most instances it is one person's individual decision. I know from the many discussions we prosecutors used to have about individual cases that, on many occasions, there were different views about the right course of action. In more recent times in particular, I know that office-based prosecutors who inherited cases from CPS Direct lawyers, who had made the charging decisions after telephone conversations with police officers, often used to disagree fundamentally with the decisions made by their colleagues. How can you possibly acquire consistency in decision-making?!

As far as working practices are concerned, over the twenty-five plus years since 1986, CPS management has many times prescribed different working practices that should be followed by every CPS area, branch and unit in the country. The 'one size fits all' approach, however, takes no account of local differences in terms of the number of personnel, the size of units and their geographical disposition, criminal profile of the area, etc. What might be a good working practice for London or Manchester might not work in Derbyshire or Cumbria.

A national service also inevitably meant the creation of a national headquarters and enormous bureaucracy. Over the years the size of national headquarters burgeoned and the number of posts grew and grew. There were headquarters "divisions" created for all manner of activities - Proceeds of Crime, Forfeiture, International crime, Serious Crime, etc., etc. Reams and reams of directives streamed out of HQ to tell local areas what they could and could not do, where to refer certain cases to, what reports had to be written and who to copy them to, etc., etc. The tentacles of the central bureaucracy would then stretch out to the local areas, and area offices would develop their own administrative bureaucracy – area administrators, business managers, estate managers, training officers, human resource managers, etc. They too would issue their own paper streams. It was, of course, what was bound to happen once we were part of the Civil Service. How on earth did we manage without this bureaucratic edifice prior to 1986??

Being part of the Civil Service also meant that there were targets to be met, performances to be measured, statistics to be kept, monitoring schemes to be run and, of course, forms to be completed. All this would be passed down to the local areas and, of course, to local staff. It meant that there would have to be meetings locally, both with other agencies and internally, to discuss why we weren't meeting this or that target, how we were to implement this or that scheme, and to discuss the results of agencies monitoring each other's performance.

I doubt whether anyone can point to any single benefit that ever accrued, to the CPS in particular or the criminal justice system in general, as the result of these meetings and schemes and statistic-gathering. I make the same observation about most of the catalogue of systems and working practices that were imposed on us in the CPS by the centre. Many of these simply withered on the vine, their passing unmourned and unlamented.

The payroll costs and the costs of running the Service of course escalated and, indeed, escalated out of all proportion and, in 2010, when the Chancellor of the Exchequer was looking to substantially reduce departmental budgets, the CPS presented as an easy target for the 'axe'. I can still hear his words as he reached the subject of the CPS in his Spending Review speech - "the inflated budget costs" of the CPS would have to be much reduced.

With the benefit of hindsight, but in the view of many at the start, the locally-based CPS arrangement would have been better. The structure was already in place in most areas by 1986 and was working well. With a minimum of tweaking, the local system could have rolled happily on, avoiding the massive bureaucratisation whilst not compromising the virtues of competent and independent decision-making and effective prosecution of offenders. It was not to be!!

For the avoidance of doubt, I make it clear that I do not regret the creation of the Crown Prosecution Service. I have always been a whole-hearted champion of there being an independent prosecutor who should have complete control over the prosecution, as opposed to the investigative, process. Nor do I believe that every initiative introduced into the CPS since 1986 has been unworthy or unworkable. There have been some notable exceptions, the "Charging" initiative and the Higher Court Advocate scheme amongst them. I still believe the job is worth doing, warts and all!

* * *

There was no overnight transformation to the way we worked in South Cumbria on 1st October 1986. There was, however, an immediate change to the nature of our employment and to the local structure of our organisation. From that date we were no longer employed by the police authority - we became civil servants employed in the non-ministerial government department, the Crown Prosecution Service, a Service headed by the Director of Public Prosecutions under the "superintendence" of the Attorney General (whatever this meant!). I ceased to be Divisional Prosecuting Solicitor and became a Senior Crown Prosecutor. We were now part of the CPS Area of Cumbria/Lancashire. The Chief Crown Prosecutor was John Bates, based in Preston; Ken Hay, who had been Deputy County Prosecuting Solicitor, became the Branch Crown Prosecutor for the Cumbria Branch.

For a week or two there were no obvious changes to our working practices. But shortly we had to start creating copies of each police file, as we became obliged in our new role to review the evidence in every case and make a decision as to whether the prosecution continued or not and, if so, on what charges. We had racking installed to house the copy files (the police continued to keep the originals). In time the CPS centre designed and issued special file-jackets to keep our files in; these jackets had boxes on for us to record review decisions and other entries, including hearing details. Within a couple of years, technology and the IT revolution had reached us - we had a fax machine installed and then a primitive, computerised case-tracking system known as CATS.

We kept the same staff profile for the next three years, however, and the same office premises. By now we were housed in the far end of a single-storey building, most of which was occupied by the Benefits Office. John Bates insisted we did not "hide in the attic" and we had a sign prominently fixed to the outside of the building announcing that we were the "Crown Prosecution Service". Next door to us was a local nightclub. We had substances regularly deposited on the outside of the windows by passers-by but, in my time, I think only one broken window. It could have been a lot worse, I suppose! Perhaps this was a mark of the esteem in which we were held by the local villainy, or recognition that we were independent of the police and worth keeping onside!!

We remained fairly isolated, receiving few visits from Ken Hay and even less from John Bates and, initially at least, there was little interference from anyone with our decision-making process or any edicts from HQ nationally or locally. We did, however, have to start using "agents" to prosecute when we were short-handed. There were a couple of local solicitors who were only too pleased to mix their routine work with the occasional session prosecuting in Barrow Magistrates' Court, and we found that their performance was very satisfactory.

For a while in 1986/7 we were, indeed, short-handed for quite a period of time. Charles Leyberg had gone to Kendal to replace Greg Hoare, and Glynn Mitchell, who had replaced David Hartley, had departed to private practice (Forresters). Phil Bates, who had been a lawyer on the Workington team, had joined us, but it proved impossible for a while to recruit a third lawyer. This meant regular use of our agents and it also meant that I spent most Saturdays in the office trying to catch up with the backlog of review work and preparation of papers in cases destined for the Crown Court. Eventually John Bates decided that my efforts in keeping the casework afloat should be recognised in some way, and he petitioned national headquarters to pay me a one-off "premium payment". This gave rise to my receiving a stream of minutes from London demanding to know whether my overtime was "authorised" and whether it was being "supervised" by my line manager, and if not, why not. It took some time for them to appreciate that my line manager was ninety miles away and he couldn't just hop on the tube or a bus or get a cab to come and "supervise" my work on a Saturday. Eventually HQ agreed grudgingly that my unsolicited and voluntary efforts had "no doubt benefited" the Area and the Service, and a one-off premium payment of £500 would be awarded but, in future, if such a need arose again, would I ensure that there was "more formality, with proper authorisation and supervision"! The £500, needless to say, was taxable.

This wasn't our only brush in Lancs/Cumbria with HQ in those early days. They showed a general lack of understanding as to how we needed to incur so much by way of travelling expenses to courts. Wasn't there public transport, rather than using cars? They took some convincing that, for example, it could take half a day to get to Carlisle from Barrow on the train and that rural bus services didn't operate like they did in London. It took a visit to Cumbria for anyone at HQ to realise how far places were apart and how difficult it was to get from one to another!

We did get a visit from the Director of Public Prosecutions - in 1988 I think it was. Sir Alan Green had succeeded Tony Hetherington as Director in 1987. He was a man I much admired. From the first he took on the media, who seemed intent on disparaging and undermining the infant CPS with constant publicity about files going missing and the police criticising what they perceived as poor decision-making. Sir Alan appeared to be on the national news every night, endlessly pointing out that the press stories were just "anecdotal evidence" and they should consider the thousands of cases that were being prosecuted successfully every day. He led from the front and was entirely supportive of the Service and its staff. Unfortunately he fell foul of the "lawyers' curse" in 1992 and had to resign when he was caught kerb-crawling outside Kings Cross railway station, an offence for which he accepted a caution. I don't believe the DPPs since have measured up to Sir Alan's standards, and his passing ushered in the "reign of terror" (see later).

In any event, Sir Alan came to see us in Barrow in 1988. It was an indication of the bureaucratic hierarchy that had developed that he came accompanied by no less than three other levels of 'manager' - the Regional Director, John Bates and Ken Hay. They all trooped into our humble office, no doubt trying to ignore the obvious remains of last night's Chinese meal that had been deposited on the outside of my office window. It was, however, I think, a successful visit. The press also attended to interview Sir Alan. As he headed off towards an empty office with the journalist, John Bates made as if to follow the pair - "I'll come with you, Director," he said. "Thanks, but I can manage, John," was the Director's response. I always found John Bates to be a likeable fellow and a first-rate lawyer but, on occasions, he could be somewhat pompous and self-important. To the quiet amusement of the rest of us he was clearly quite deflated by his 'rejection'!

We received one further visit in Barrow from the hierarchy before I left the Area. In 1989 the Deputy DPP and Chief Executive, as he was styled, and the Regional Director, Brian Crebbin, came to see us. The former, one David Gandy, had been previously the Chief Prosecuting Solicitor in Greater Manchester, and I believe he had entertained some hope and expectation of becoming DPP himself in the fullness of time. It was not to be, as successive Attorney Generals had, until recently, been set upon filling the post from the senior Bar. So David Gandy had to settle for second best! He and his senior lawyers had become known to many of us in the wider pre-1986 CPS as the "Manchester mafia". This was largely because they had the reputation of being a close-knit, mutually supportive "brotherhood" and, as individuals, they seemed always to progress to senior positions elsewhere in the CPS when they left Manchester. Two of the four Regional Directors had been members of the "mafia", and several others filled Chief Crown Prosecutor posts in the new order after October 1986.

As it was, the Regional Directors as a group all 'bit the dust' before 1990. Sir Alan apparently decided he did not require this intervening level of management and the posts were all abolished. The post-holders were made redundant but, of course, were well compensated for their loss!

* * *

How did our relationship with the police fare after 1st October 1986? I like to think that in South Cumbria the transition was fairly seamless and that we worked together as well as we had before. For such a major change it is perhaps surprising that neither we nor the police were prepared, or given any real training or guidance, before the change as to how our respective roles were to alter. It must have been a real culture shock for the police in areas where there had been no CPS department previously. We, at least, had the advantage of being in a position where before the change we had been accustomed to giving advice on casework issues and, more often than not, having that advice accepted. Nonetheless, it must still have been a fairly big pill for the police to swallow, to realise that they no longer were to have the last word when we couldn't agree. Not exactly a reversal of the master/servant scenario, but a major shift in roles, nonetheless.

I don't believe it dawned on the police for quite a while as to exactly how things had changed. The situation was blurred anyway by a number of factors, starting with the closeness and effectiveness of our working relationship. Then the police still had control over the charging process. And finally, we always treated the situation sensitively and, otherwise than when in court, we never stopped prosecutions or downgraded charges without consulting with the police.

There were occasions, of course, when we couldn't agree, and we had to 'flex our muscles', but I am quite convinced that this never became a bone of contention between us. I was never aware of any lingering animosity or resentment, and we remained welcome visitors in the senior officers' mess and the police club! When I moved to London in late 1989, however, I soon found that things were rather different there!

* * *

As we moved away from 1986, gradually the way we worked and the way we conducted our business did change. Before long we were handed down the Code for Crown Prosecutors. This was a document that, under the Prosecution of Offences Act, had to be drawn up and issued to all Crown Prosecutors. It set out the tests that we had to apply when reviewing criminal cases. The old 51% test of evidential sufficiency was no more. Instead we had to be satisfied that the evidence in the case provided a "realistic prospect of conviction". This was later further defined to mean that "conviction was more likely than not". Yes, sounds suspiciously like the 51% rule!!

Where there was real change, however, was in the second test we had to apply. We also had to be satisfied that it was in the public interest for the prosecution to continue, something we had largely steered clear of in the past. Now we had to look at things like the age of the offender, his or her character, the seriousness or otherwise of the alleged offence, whether the likely sentence was only going to be nominal, etc., etc.. Did the public interest factors in favour of a prosecution outweigh those against? I suspect it took most of us quite a while to get to grips with this part of the test and, in the early days, the tendency would be to err in favour of prosecution, assuming the evidence was considered sufficient.

I recall that at some point before 1989 we were also made responsible for the drafting of "indictments". This is the document on which defendants in the Crown Court are "arraigned" - an official charge sheet, in other words. Previously this had been drafted, we were led to believe, by the Crown Court staff, although I rather suspect that they farmed the task out to prosecuting counsel more often than not. This was a very important and potentially challenging new responsibility for CPS lawyers. Indictment drafting is an art in itself. There are all sorts of things that have to be considered: not just the wording of the "counts" (charges) on the indictment, but in what order to list the defendants, how many counts to have, in what order to put them, etc. There were also rules about "joinder" – i.e. whether a particular count could be "joined" in the same indictment as other counts. In those days we did get some decent training on the skills needed to draft indictments, and we had a good manual from which to work. Nowadays, when drafting the indictment is a routine part of Crown Court case preparation for lawyers in the CPS, there is no such training and nor has there been for some time. Lawyers are expected, it seems, to learn 'on the job' or do the 'book-learning'. I was operating as a Crown Court advocate regularly from 2001, and it was my experience over that period that the standard of indictment drafting was poor in at least 50% of cases; I routinely had to amend or redraft the documents before defendants could be arraigned at Court. Indeed, the standard of Crown Court case preparation generally left much to be desired. The CPS centre had never put much of a premium on training its lawyers in case preparation for, and procedure in, the Crown Court and, by the turn of the century, it had abandoned any pretence at all of education in this area.

I have alluded to this topic before and I will do so again. "Crown Court awareness" was, and is, something that was, and is, sadly lacking in CPS lawyers, in my experience. The culture remains what it was in 1986 - that the lawyer did enough to see the case through the magistrates' court and then effectively forgot about it. The law clerks, or "case workers" as they were to become, then took up the mantle - they took over the file, instructed counsel, dealt with issues arising on the case and went to court with it. Apart from the odd occasions when prosecuting counsel wanted a case conference, the lawyer would have no contact with the barrister instructed to prosecute. The only times lawyers, other than those who were to become Crown advocates, went to the Crown Court was to deal with bail applications and later "preliminary hearings", and even this level of attendance has dried up in the last ten years, in Cumbria at least.

When I became a Crown Court advocate I came to realise how different things were in that court from in the magistrates' court. I came to realise that I had little or no "Crown Court awareness" - that my lawyer colleagues and I simply weren't 'streetwise' about the Crown Court. One of the most important skills you have to learn as a Crown Court advocate is "How do I present this case to the jury?" Consequently, the question you have to ask yourself when preparing a bundle of evidence for the Crown Court is "Can I present this case to the jury as it stands?" Lawyers who aren't exposed to the Crown Court situation do not have this awareness. They have to work in a vacuum. It is scarcely surprising, then, that the standard of their Crown Court case preparation may be lower than it should be.

Despite the differences from the magistrates' court, my other recurring theme is that there is no mystique about the Crown Court. Once he or she learns the ropes and has been exposed to the experience for any length of time, then any advocate worth his salt can pass muster and compete with the mix of counsel who regularly attend.

Still on the subject of Crown Court matters, one other development for us lawyers in Cumbria, within a few months of October 1986, was the drafting of the "brief" to counsel. Until then, this had been done by the law clerks in the Crown Court section at Carlisle. Now John Bates insisted, and rightly so in my opinion, that the lawyer who had put the case papers together should also prepare a full brief for the barrister who was to be prosecuting in the Crown Court. This, he said, was our opportunity to at least initiate a "dialogue" with counsel, particularly as there was unlikely to be any other communication or contact between us. As I saw it, "doing a full brief" meant not only setting out the facts of the case and the nature of the allegations, but also giving counsel the benefit (or otherwise!) of my thought processes on a number of issues - why I had drafted the indictment as I had, why I thought there was a realistic prospect of conviction, why I had asked the police to consider obtaining some further evidence and, importantly, whether pleas to lesser or alternative charges or part of the indictment would be acceptable to me.

I continued to draft briefs in this way until the day I finished with the CPS. I seriously doubt, however, whether many instructed counsel actually read them, and I know for a fact that in some instances they did not. There were some fairly rare occasions when counsel would, in those days, ring me up from court and ask: "Have you thought of this…?" "Yes," I might reply, "It's in your brief!" It seemed fundamental to me that a brief of this nature should be an integral part of instructions to prosecuting counsel. The CPS, however, never encouraged such an approach - indeed, in its growing fondness for proformas, templates and 'prosecuting by numbers', it later produced a computerised template of a brief that we were instructed to use, which contained a number of standard paragraphs and totally militated against the sort of comprehensive, freestyle brief that I used. I rebelled against this tendency by routinely deleting most of the standard paragraphs and drafting my own version! Many lawyers, however, and this was symptomatic again of the culture I have already referred to above, fell into the lazy approach that this template encouraged and would confine themselves to such entries as "Counsel should read the case summary and the witness statements", when the 'model' asked for the "facts of the case". No wonder the barristers didn't bother to read the briefs!!

* * *

As time went on, and the central and local bureaucracies gradually stirred themselves into action, we began to receive various minutes and documents detailing how we should conduct our business, prescribing what we should do in certain situations and how we should approach certain categories of offences, and generally restricting our movements and circumscribing our activities. By 1989, each member of staff had been issued with two large manuals - a "Policy Manual" and a "Practice and Procedure Manual" with which we were expected to familiarise ourselves, or at least consult at every twist and turn! John Bates sent out a direction that certain categories of cases were not to be reviewed but to be forwarded to him for his consideration - Attempts to Pervert the Course of Justice and certain types of sex cases, for example. I don't believe John did actually consider these cases personally as, by 1988, at least he had a "serious casework lawyer" who reported to him. Shades of "Fred" in Lincolnshire - but at least he was a qualified lawyer! This was also a sign of things to come.

There were also moves afoot to start the insidious process of converting lawyers into managers, courtroom advocates into desk-bound administrators. By 1987 the "performance appraisal" system began with a vengeance. We had managed perfectly well without this before, but this was now the Civil Service, and the Civil Service seems to demand that everyone's performance is appraised and that there is a formal reporting system to accomplish this! So, every year, I was expected to write a report on the two lawyers in my 'command' and appraise every aspect of their performance, hold a formal interview, and award a performance marking. My line manager would have to come down and do the same to me, even though he would have had little idea as to my performance as he seldom saw me or my work!. The 'senior' administrative officer had also to travel down from Carlisle to 'appraise' the two admin staff in the Barrow office, about whom she would know even less than Ken Hay knew about me! Furthermore, each report had to be countersigned by the line manager's line manager, who would add his own uninformed observations to the report and confirm the content of the report and the performance marking. A completely worthless exercise, in my view! The report also had to contain a number of "objectives" for the person reported on to achieve by the time of the next report - this led to all sorts of totally fanciful or artificial requirements. Funnily enough, no-one ever failed to meet their objectives!!

Then I had to attend an intensive management course. I had actually gone on one prior to 1986. This was a week away at Cumbria County Council's country house, Higham Hall, near Bassenthwaite, where we ate and drank excessively, listened to lectures and indulged in role-play exercises. Then we came back to the office and promptly forgot everything we had been told! The CPS week at a hotel in Scarborough was not much different - excessive eating and drinking, lectures and role-play exercises. And then I came back and promptly forgot all I had learnt and been told! Such courses would proliferate in the years to come and of course, in those days, the CPS had a very generous training budget and could afford to put up fifteen or twenty lawyers for a week in a good hotel and employ outside trainers. Not nowadays!!

To me, management and management style were not things that could be taught. I don't believe there was a right or a wrong way of doing it. It was something one developed by instinct, trial and error and experience - very much an empirical exercise. I don't think I was ever a great manager, but I always felt that I won respect and got people to do what was required of them, and no-one ever complained! My belief was also that the manager of a CPS unit, or certainly the size of unit that I ever 'managed', should lead from the front. I could never understand how a manager could know what was going on, or how his members of staff were performing, unless he or she did what they were doing. I always made a point, even as a Branch manager in Cumbria with many lawyers to manage, of going to court at least once, if not twice, a week and of carrying a caseload like them. I felt and believed that this earned respect from staff, that I was sharing their 'pain' and difficulties. It also meant that I was a visible presence to other court users with whom we worked - court staff, police, probation officers, magistrates, and not some anonymous person sitting in an office day after day. In a small, busy unit such as Barrow it would have been totally impractical anyway to have become totally desk-bound, and it was never really an option when I managed a larger unit in London.

I cannot say that this was the right way to manage, but it was my way, and whatever those above me thought about it, as I say, no-one on my teams complained!

Another indicator of burgeoning bureaucracy and of one's developing status as a 'manager' was the ever-increasing number of meetings one had to attend. The CPS was always a great believer in the value of meetings. I have never found, however, that very many of them had any value or that any lasting benefit accrued to the criminal justice system or the core business of the CPS. Nonetheless, we had meetings of senior crown prosecutors in Cumbria, meetings of senior staff in Preston, meetings of court users, meetings of all staff in Cumbria. And this was only the beginning. By 1996 I could have gone to a meeting almost every day of the week!

⋆ ⋆ ⋆

By 1989 the criminal profile in South Cumbria, in Cumbria generally, and no doubt elsewhere, was changing. The incidence of drug trafficking, and of Class A controlled drug trafficking in particular, was growing steadily. There were also an increasing number of cases of child abuse. There appeared, for the first time in my experience, the odd case of 'historic' child abuse. I can recall the first case we received, where there was a complaint made by a woman, who was now in her late thirties, of sexual abuse some thirty years previously by a male relative. The police were not anxious to charge and it came to us for pre-charge advice. This was one of the categories of cases that had to go to John Bates for decision-making, but I had a look at it and recommended to him that we didn't advise charging. My view at that time was that there was never going to be a realistic prospect of conviction where we were relying on unsupported evidence of events that occurred that long ago. Was it, anyway, in the public interest to dredge up cases where the alleged offences were of such antiquity? John Bates did not agree and he felt the Code tests for starting a prosecution were met in this case. The defendant was charged with a number of offences of indecent assault that had taken place in the late 1950s and early 1960s.

John Bates was right and I was wrong. Time proved that it was possible to secure convictions for historic sex offences committed against children. This particular case failed, as I recall, because the judge "stayed" the proceedings on the ground that the defendant could not have had a fair trial and the proceedings amounted therefore to an "abuse of process". Initially in such cases, the "abuse of process" argument often won the day. How could a defendant have a fair trial if he were, for example, deprived of the opportunity to locate and call witnesses who were available 30 years ago but were not now, and would have helped him to assert his innocence? A fairly compelling argument, one might have thought?

Be that as it may, as time went on, judges seemed to become less willing to accede to such arguments. The trial process itself, it was said, could more than adequately deal with the difficulties thrown up by evidence from that long ago. Provided the jury was given appropriate directions by the judge about acting with caution before relying on such evidence and recognising the difficulties a defendant may face, then the case could be left to the jury.

So the number of such prosecutions multiplied. Convictions, however, were hard to come by. I don't know what the statistics show, but I suspect more cases failed than succeeded. The failure of such prosecutions in high-profile cases against 'celebrities', in recent times, is nothing new. The prosecution is nearly always going to be on the back foot. The standard approach taken by prosecutors in court is: "Why should the complainant make up such an allegation and put himself/herself through the ordeal of giving evidence and being cross-examined on such painful and embarrassing recollections?" Against that, however, are ranged a number of strong counter-arguments. By the very nature of this type of alleged offence, there are unlikely to be any eyewitnesses as the incidents will have occurred in private. Although there may often be a number of separate complaints of similar conduct at different times against the same defendant made by other children, there is rarely going to be any direct corroboration of the individual offences. Then there is the point that "Why didn't the complainant make a complaint at the time - why now?" There are often very good reasons why it takes people thirty or forty years to pluck up the courage to bring the matters to light, but juries may not understand or accept those reasons. Finally, of course, the evidence of events that occurred so long ago from people who were young children then may well be seen as unreliable, and it is fair to say that defence advocates can often draw out inconsistencies and errors in the evidence of such witnesses.

It is scarcely surprising, then, that so many such cases result in acquittal. It has to be questionable whether, in many such cases, there ever was a "realistic prospect of conviction". It has always seemed to me that such is the pressure and imperative to prosecute cases of abuse of children that the Code for Crown Prosecutors is thrown out of the window, although no-one is ever going to admit that, of course! The CPS response to acquittal is always: “It was considered the evidence provided a realistic prospect of conviction,” and comfort seems to be taken from the fact that the case actually got to the jury without being halted by the judge!

* * *

Despite the increase in drugs offences and child abuse, most of the cases we were dealing with were the mixture as before - violence, public order, theft, burglary, car crime. Certainly the type of case I was prosecuting in court was no different from that which I had been prosecuting in 1976 and 1979. It was frustrating never to have more than passing involvement in more serious crime, even where one might have been involved in the charging decision, or at least the decision to continue with the prosecution.

By 1989 I was again becoming restless. Indeed, well before this, I had come to the conclusion that Barrow was, work-wise, as much a cul-de-sac and a backwater as it was geographically. I simply couldn’t envisage staying another twenty-five years in the town, however magnetic the attractions of the Lake District and however comfortable the various working relationships. I had attended two interviews in 1986 in London for more senior posts, the later one for jobs on Tyneside and Wearside. I had not been successful - indeed, the Wearside job was filled by Paul Grieveson, whom I was later to work with over many years and who became a firm friend.

In 1988 or 1989 I went to the Carlisle office on the occasion of a visit by the Solicitor General, Sir Nicholas Lyell. There I fell into conversation with Dick Williamson, who was then one of the ill-starred Regional Directors, soon to become extinct. Dick, of course, had before that been County Prosecuting Solicitor in Lincolnshire, so we had some common acquaintances to discuss. He also strongly hinted that I should continue to apply for senior jobs and that I shouldn’t be “languishing” in Barrow, as he put it. I took the hint and applied for some jobs at the next grade up for me in North London. I was called for interview in late summer 1989. The chairman of the interviewing panel was Colin Hoad, another of the dying breed of Regional Directors. The interview was notably unchallenging and, rightly or wrongly, I was flattered to believe that I might have been 'earmarked' for one of the jobs. A few days later I was offered the post of Assistant Branch Crown Prosecutor in the Stratford Branch of Outer London North. With only momentary hesitation, I accepted the offer....

CHAPTER NINE

1989 To 1993: Into the Maelstrom….

The Area headquarters of Outer London North CPS were in Solar House on Romford Road, Stratford, London E15. The Stratford Branch of the Area was in the same building. My team, the Newham team, was one of the three teams on the Stratford Branch.

When I arrived in 1989, Stratford was in many ways a very different place from Stratford in 2014. Since the Millennium, the area has undergone drastic regeneration and is now a substantial commercial and cultural centre. Much of the change was connected with Stratford's pivotal position in the summer Olympic Games of 2012. In 1989, however, all this was some way in the future and Stratford then was a drab, unprepossessing, depressing sort of place.

Stratford was in the London Borough of Newham, and the rest of the borough was made up of the districts of West Ham, East Ham, Plaistow and Forest Gate. The borough then had a population of about 225,000 (more than three times that of South Cumbria), contained in a very small geographical area. It was one of the most ethnically diverse places in the UK, and one of the most deprived.

My team, which I ran as the Assistant Branch Crown Prosecutor, was responsible for the portfolio of criminal cases that arose in that borough. It was very different from those places to which I had hitherto been accustomed. Serious crime was rife. Cases of rape, grievous bodily harm with intent, Class A drug trafficking, serious fraud and child abuse abounded. There was rarely a time when we were not dealing with a murder and, at one time, there were six or seven cases involving charges of murder or conspiracy to commit murder on the team's books, at various stages of preparation.

The four years that I was at Stratford were undoubtedly the most challenging and stressful period of my career. Things were not helped by the fact that there was always a daily commute to work of at least an hour and a half's duration and, in the first year, also a weekend commute back to Cumbria.

* * *

The Chief Crown Prosecutor for Outer London North, Bob Chronnell, had been Chief Crown Prosecutor in Hertfordshire previously, and before that a senior lawyer with the "Manchester mafia". He had, prior to 1986, run a busy team in Stockport. Needless to say, his days of attending court were well behind him and he would not get involved in any casework matters other than in the most exceptional circumstances. He inhabited an office on the floor above us, with his personal assistant in close proximity, and was rarely seen by any of the teams.

My immediate boss was John Ringguth, the Branch Crown Prosecutor. Up to earlier in 1989 he, too, had been a busy courtroom prosecutor and casework lawyer in his previous job. Now he was never seen in a court of any description and his forays into casework were confined to looking at the odd *cause célèbre*. There were times when we could very much have used his former skills by doing the odd court for us, or taking on some case review, but the offer was never made even though he must have been very aware of the pressures we were under. The demands of management, it seemed, were all-consuming for both John and Bob. There appeared to be an endless round of meetings they attended. One monthly meeting was that of the "Area Management Team", which was reputed often to last for two days!

I once stood in for John Ringguth for a fortnight when he was away on holiday. Granted I was spared attendance at any meetings but, after a day or two, I was looking around for work to do and actually ended up helping the teams with their casework!

Two of the biggest challenges that confronted me from the outset were the size and composition of my team itself. When I arrived, there were eight lawyers on the team other than myself. Over the next four years, despite an apparently endless recruitment campaign, I cannot remember there ever being more than nine. Given the volume of routine and particularly serious casework we were required to deal with, even had all the lawyers had any sort of modest experience, we would still have struggled to keep on top of the work. As it was, we never had the luxury of an experienced team.

In November 1989, of the eight lawyers on the team only one, as I recall, had more than two years' experience. There was also a constant turnover of prosecutors and, as individuals gained experience, I found that they either left or were moved to another team, so I always had a core of new recruits and 'rookie' lawyers! This meant that the review, processing and preparation of serious and complex casework were almost always in the hands of two or three members of the team. One of those, inevitably, was me. Had I ever had any illusions that I could be just a "manager", then these were soon dispelled. I remember ringing Roger Furness just before I came to Stratford. Roger was now one of my opposite numbers on the Wood Green Branch of Outer London North and had once been a prosecutor with Derbyshire CPS; indeed, when I was there. I had inquired of Roger what the job entailed. His response was that it was supposed to be mainly a management role, but the level and volume of casework and courts were such, and the numbers and experience of those on the teams were such, that "there was no time for management". This turned out to be a very accurate description!

The Crown Prosecution Service in London had been up and running (if that is the correct description!) for three years by November 1989. It was very apparent, however, that inadequate consideration had been given to the numbers and quality of staff that were required to deliver the core business of the organisation in the Metropolis - that is if Stratford was anything to go by! One of the results of this was that a totally disproportionate burden was laid upon those charged with the operational management of the teams created. My two immediate predecessors had been temporary only, simply occupying the seat after the departure of the last permanent post-holder and pending my own arrival. I was aware that the permanent post-holder before me had been one Noel Williams, who had done the job between 1986 and early 1989. I did not know at first, however, how and why he had come to cease doing the job, and no-one told me. Then, after I had been at Stratford a couple of weeks, I came across a letter in a correspondence file. The letter was addressed to one of my temporary predecessors from a previous Chief Crown Prosecutor, Stephen Wooller, dated sometime in early 1989. The gist of the letter was to impart that Noel Williams was terminally ill, suffering from liver failure, and would not be returning to work. I learnt soon afterwards that Noel had had a significant drink problem during his time in the job, whether or not he had such a condition prior to his appointment. I did not take this as a good omen!

I had always managed to avoid falling into the heavy-drinking culture that I had encountered in Derbyshire and, to a lesser extent, in Lincolnshire and, although there were times when I could cheerfully have taken to drink over the next four years, I did succeed in resisting that particular temptation. There was a drinking culture amongst some of the lawyers on the team, and on the other teams, and I became a part of this, but it was kept well within bounds. The pressures of work, the need often to prepare for court the next day after a full day that day in court, the relentless pile of files to review and papers to prepare for service in cases destined for the Crown Court, all meant that there were invariably a number of lawyers on my team (and the other teams) still at their desks well into the evening. Particularly in the first twelve months, I was with them more often than not. At seven o'clock, or thereabouts, we would adjourn to the pub. I was living then on the other side of London and often wouldn't get home before 10 pm. When I moved into Essex in late 1990, I would tend to 'burn the candle' at the other end of the day and get into work early, but there were still plenty of occasions when I would join the after-work drinking sessions. These sessions were very 'therapeutic' after the trials and tribulations of the day. As most people used public transport to get to and from work, there were also no concerns about drink-driving to put a damper on proceedings!

* * *

The lawyers on the team were keen and well-motivated, but their collective lack of experience was alarming, and this remained the case for most of the next four years. Only one had more than two years' experience of advocacy or prosecuting. Three had less than six months' relevant experience. No-one, it seemed, had received any real training in how to review cases, how to prepare "committal papers" (i.e. the set of papers for service in cases going to the Crown Court), criminal advocacy, how to prepare for trials, etc. I found that one of the "more experienced" lawyers was dealing with a case of Conspiracy to supply Class A controlled drugs involving some sixteen defendants. He was clearly out of his depth and was struggling to make progress with the case. Nevertheless, he was keen to retain ownership of the case and I didn't want to undermine his confidence, so I confined my involvement to 'helping him' prepare the committal papers and draft the indictment.

Training was largely a process of trial and error, as the CPS wasn't providing any formal instruction and I didn't have the time to provide training sessions even if I could have freed up time for the lawyers to take part. All I could do was to snatch moments to watch their advocacy, or monitor a selection of files that had been reviewed or committal papers that had been prepared, and then provide feedback to the individual lawyers. This was hardly satisfactory, and the standard of committal preparation, in particular, was to remain poor. Matters were not helped by lawyers being moved off the team when other teams became short-handed, and being replaced by a succession of new recruits. It was a case of one step forward, two steps back, and this remained the pattern of events until I left!

Another difficulty that they and I faced was that there was precious little 'office time' for most of the lawyers. They were trapped in an unremitting cycle of preparing for court, going to court, preparing for court, going to court, and so on. We covered two different magistrates' court centres, Newham West and Newham East. I never really discovered how cases were distributed between the two, but both centres were sitting full time every day and all day. There were, as I recall, six courts that would sit all day, although possibly half of them would have a morning session and an afternoon session rather than one all-day session. Bearing in mind that there were always prosecutors who were on holiday or off sick at any given time, the reality was that, even with careful planning, lawyers were having to attend court four days out of five; that they never got more than one full day and two half days in the office; and that probably more than half that time would have to be spent in preparing for the next court appearance!

We did have the use of a couple of agents to prosecute - solicitors from private practice who would cover a court for a fixed fee - but these were thin on the ground and not always available. As it was, I found that there was a need for me to go to court on two days a week and, on occasion, even three. This was necessary to allow the other lawyers to have the sort of minimum office time I have referred to above. Even then it was quite common for a lawyer to be in court all day, come back to the office at 4.30 pm, and then spend at least a couple of hours preparing for a court appearance next day. However much I juggled with the rota and tried to ensure, as far as possible, that lawyers had at least a half-day in the office between court appearances, it was constantly the case that prosecutors had to spend a good deal of their own time in making sure they were adequately prepared to discharge their professional duties in court. A later DPP, Dame Barbara Mills, often proclaimed that "There was never any need for lawyers in the CPS to work overtime." How little she knew! It has always been the case, and still is today to my knowledge and in my experience, that "working overtime" is unavoidable for advocates in the CPS if they are to prepare properly for court as they have a professional obligation to do, not to mention dealing diligently and in timely fashion with their personal caseload.

Senior management in the CPS, often far from the 'coalface', and even if in the recent or distant past they have been through the same process themselves, tend not to recognise that the rank-and-file prosecutors have this sort of working pattern, or at least choose to shut their eyes to the obvious. Hence the sort of uninformed, glib remarks such as I have highlighted above!

The demands of the court/preparation for court cycle on the body of the lawyers inevitably meant that I, and perhaps one or two of the more experienced lawyers that I could spare from having to go to court on four days every week, at least took on the bulk of the serious casework - reviewing the evidence, preparing committal papers and indictments - as well as a not insubstantial volume of the more routine casework.

In my case there was an even greater burden, because my job had another dimension as well. As a "manager" I was obliged and expected to write annual appraisal reports on all the lawyers on the team, keep their performance under constant review, monitor their advocacy and their casework and decision-making, provide feedback and mentor, analyse court outcomes, casework and performance trends and report thereon and suggest solutions to problems, attend meetings with senior police officers and court staff, and branch management meetings, rota lawyers for court, and allocate casework to lawyers. One redeeming feature was that I didn't have to manage caseworkers or admin staff, or run the admin support side of the operation, as this was in the hands of other junior managers.

I found the task of discharging the management role, combined with attending court and carrying a heavy caseload, at best very demanding and at times almost intolerable. My line managers clearly felt that the "management" part of the job was the most important part and that my caseload should have been minimal, and my court appearances infrequent. I could have conformed with those expectations: left the casework to the rest of the team and appeared in court once every three weeks; and spent my time simply discharging the management responsibilities I have referred to above. I would never have had to have worked outside normal office hours! Had I done so, however, what would the results have been? Less burdened, less stressed - yes! A better manager? No, not in my view! I would have lost much of the respect of the team if I had withdrawn from court and casework and increased their burdens as a consequence. I have always firmly believed that if one leads from the front and gets involved in the same activities as the team members, then one earns their trust and respect and it is far more likely that they will perform well and do what they are required to do. Furthermore, I would have found it considerably more difficult to make meaningful contributions in meetings with the court and senior police officers if I had not had that close involvement in casework and attending court regularly. I would have felt that, in a meeting of court users, for example, where most of those in attendance were routinely in court, I would have been at a distinct disadvantage, with no personal experience of matters under discussion and where I would have been relying on second-hand information. And there again, in those meetings I am quite sure that, by having been a regular and visible presence in court, I was a more credible and respected figure in the eyes of the magistrates' clerk, and the magistrates and defence practitioners who attended the meeting, than I would have been had I been simply someone who only appeared at meetings. John Ringguth also attended court-user meetings, and I always felt that his contributions there were not accorded much heed or respect, for the very reason that he was perceived as a remote figure with no awareness or first-hand experience of the matters under discussion.

As far as the serious casework was concerned, apart from any other considerations, much of it was complex or sensitive both in terms of decision-making and subsequent case preparation. It would have been completely unfair and inappropriate to have expected most of the lawyers on the team, at their stage of development, to have contended with this sort of casework. Yes, of course they would have to learn to deal with it in the fullness of time, but this would have to be a process conducted under supervision and not by dropping them in the deep end.

The demands and expectations of me as a manager escalated as time went on. As well as monitoring and appraising lawyers' performance, from the outset I was required to monitor "outcomes" and produce regular reports on failed and discontinued cases and "cracked" and ineffective trials. Much of this was fair enough - a manager should be monitoring performance and checking why cases are discontinued or lost. But constantly analysing and discussing why trials didn't go ahead has always seemed to me an exercise in futility. CPS and courts have been doing this for ever and it has never made an iota of difference. Trials continue to "crack" or be ineffective at the same rates as they ever have. It should be recognised that it is always going to happen and not agonise over it! Many defendants are always going to change their plea to 'guilty' on the day of trial, and there are always going to be witnesses who won't turn up at court. These are facts of life!

I felt much the same way about writing staff appraisal reports. This was a very time-consuming exercise and I don't believe it served any useful purpose. We had managed perfectly well without such a formal, bureaucratic system before 1986. No-one performed any better by having a written staff appraisal report and having objectives set. If someone was not performing, then we dealt with this before 1986 and it was just as possible to get rid of constant poor performers prior to 1986 as after.

Then the number of meetings I had to attend increased as time went by. I have said before that I have never been a great fan of meetings. In my experience most of them are 'talking shops' and achieve little or nothing. There is a meetings culture in the Crown Prosecution Service, however. I had to attend court-user meetings, meetings with senior police officers, meetings with the police Criminal Justice Unit, meetings with British Transport Police, and branch management meetings, to name but a few.

The court-user meeting was more useful than most, as it at least gave me the opportunity to explain to the magistrates' representatives who attended, why the shortcomings that they perceived existed with the CPS were not necessarily entirely our fault and, generally, how we worked. Whether this convinced them or not, I don't know, but at least I felt better for it!

The meetings with senior police officers, which were attended by and chaired by John Ringguth, really were a waste of time in my view. We talked around general topics, as the officers were not interested in the minutiae of day-to-day casework and court issues, and it was clear to me that they no more wanted to be there than I did! Meetings with the Criminal Justice Unit were at least about operational matters, but they achieved little in the way of improving the service we got from the police, which was really the object of the exercise as far as I was concerned.

The Branch Management team meetings took place monthly and involved all three of us team leaders, John Ringguth, and the Branch Admin Manager. They generally took the whole day and 75% of the business discussed, it seemed to me, was of little or no value or relevance.

Then it was decided by Area Management that we needed an "Area plan" to guide our future activities, and that there would need to be "Branch plans" to deal with the local implementation of the "Area plan". This involved meetings of all the senior staff in the Area and trooping off to a series of "conferences" at City Airport, where we broke up into our individual Branch Management Teams to discuss and compile the plans. This was done after many hours of deliberation. We were then told by the Chief Crown Prosecutor that these were not for 'cascading' down to the rest of the staff - they were for local managers' use only! The plans went into a drawer in my desk and never saw the light of day again. An exercise in fantasy and futility!

Then I was taken away from the office, court and casework to attend "management courses". These underlined the importance, amongst other things, of managers "thinking strategically" and managing our time so that we were able to spend quality time in considering the "wider picture" and doing some 'blue-sky thinking', whatever that was! One suggestion was that we should make ourselves unavailable and inaccessible to staff before 11.00 every morning so we could indulge in "strategic thinking" without being interrupted. If only! One of my counterparts at one of the other branches apparently tried this, and ended up having a breakdown and resigning the job after her lawyers mounted a campaign against her when she could never be consulted about casework and court problems until after 11.00 am!

The upshot for me, of balancing the demands of being a "manager" with those of being an advocate and of carrying a significant caseload of serious offences, was a need to work long hours. Routinely I found that I was spending ten hours a day in the office, often taking work home, and working at home most Sundays; a sixty-hour week, more often than not. This was clearly not how it should have been. I was responsible for the local delivery of our core business - effective review, preparation and prosecution of criminal cases. No argument with that - I could do that and had no objection to putting the hours in for that purpose. To my mind, management should have been incidental to that central purpose, at my level, and not a troublesome and largely unnecessary burden.

* * *

Up until I moved to London I had been accustomed to working with lawyers who were, by and large, both able and experienced. This was now not the case. There were exceptions, but for four years I was running a team composed largely of raw inexperience and less-than-average ability. Lawyers came and went and, as soon as anyone showed signs of becoming useful, they seemed to be transferred to another team or left the Service, and then there was another influx of 'rookies'. Over the four years, however, there were certainly some interesting characters on the team.

Diarmuid Doorly was on the team when I joined it, although he was whisked away to the Barking team after a few months. He was the one man on the team with any substantial experience of criminal law and advocacy. He had been at the Irish Bar and clearly knew what he was doing, although most of his work had been on the defence side and his heart was never entirely in prosecuting. He was an intuitive lawyer and advocate and an amusing man. He was also extremely laid back and very much a free spirit. He was a prodigious drinker and often seemed to be out all night on the town; nonetheless, he was always there at court when it was required, and ready and able to deal with anything thrown at him. I suspect he didn't go in much for preparation for court, but this never seemed to affect his performance. He left in 1992 to join the office of the Attorney General of the

Bahamas, but it wasn't compatible with his lifestyle and he came back to join the English Bar less than a year later, I believe.

Linda Dudley, who was also on the team when I arrived, was one of those who benefited from joining the CPS at the right time. She was in her forties, an ex-dancer on the cruise ships, and had been a court clerk at Waltham Forest Magistrates' Court after qualifying as a barrister. She had joined the CPS, in 1988 I think, and because of the rapid turnover of lawyers on the Branch and her relevant experience and maturity, had been rapidly promoted to the level of Principal Crown Prosecutor, the grade below me. She was diligent and industrious, but her lack of prosecuting experience was obvious, and no more than most of the junior members of the team. Despite her seniority she was out of her depth, certainly to begin with, when it came to serious or complex casework, and I think she never really felt at home in the job. It came as not a great surprise when she left in 1992 to get married and run a pub in Norfolk!

Another lawyer who joined us in 1990 as a Principal Crown Prosecutor was Charles Saunders. He did have probably as much experience as I did in prosecuting, joining the CPS after service in the Royal Navy. He had various eccentricities, one of which was never wearing any shoelaces in his shoes. He was also a complete workaholic, and would have gone through the year without taking a single day of his holiday allowance. In the end I had to bully him into taking time off but, even then, it was only a fortnight and he came back before the end of the two weeks! He was a good lawyer, but rather 'gung-ho' in his prosecuting decisions: he was very pro-police (his wife was a police inspector) and he dismissed all defendants as "oicks"!

One Cecil Cheng passed through very briefly. He had been head of CID in Hong Kong, then qualified as a solicitor in the UK, and had worked both in private practice and, latterly, in the CPS. He had also had a parallel career as an actor. He had appeared in at least one *James Bond* film in a small role, and his most recent TV appearance at that time was as a Chinaman alongside Paul Hogan in a *Fosters Lager* advert. On an underground station platform he is seen asking Paul Hogan: "Can you tell me the way to Cockfosters?" The response is "Stick it in boiling water." Cecil was, in fact, sixty-seven years of age when he came to Stratford from Hertfordshire CPS. In those days you had to retire at sixty-five unless you could persuade the CPS to extend your employment. Cecil had managed this twice, but then the organisation, rather short-sightedly I thought, given the ongoing recruitment campaign and the level of inexperience in the CPS, refused his next application and Cecil left us to take up a role in an American TV series!

It would be remiss of me not to mention in passing the notorious John Abbott. John came to us in 1990 or 1991. He had been with a number of CPS Areas apparently, lastly Lancashire/Cumbria, and had been marked up in his staff appraisal reports as an unsatisfactory performer. Instead of being dismissed from the Service, however, he had simply been passed on to another Area. Getting rid of someone was a convoluted process, and it would appear that other Areas had shrunk from it and passed the buck onwards! Charles Saunders was to be his line manager and he and I came to the conclusion that we were half-expected to complete the job of getting him thrown out of the CPS. Instead we entered into a conspiracy to do all we could to save him!

This was an unenviable task. John was an intelligent man - in fact I rather think he was an Oxbridge graduate. He was, however, 'not of this world'. He was physically unprepossessing, resembling a rotund Ken Dodd. And he was an accident waiting to happen. On one occasion he managed to get himself locked in a lavatory cubicle in Newham East courthouse and kept the court waiting for some time; on another, he stood up in court and got his trousers snagged on a nail or large splinter projecting from the bench, with a 'ripping' result! When he left the CPS building he would attract a crowd of onlookers from the office window - he would set off across the road seemingly totally oblivious to the traffic and cause complete mayhem, with blaring horns and torrents of abuse from motorists who had had to jam on their brakes. And then there was the occasion he told the magistrates that "this defendant had no previous convictions which, as he is black, your worships might find quite surprising." His work in the office was totally disorganised - he would lose files and miss deadlines.

Having said all that, there was nothing much wrong with his judgment and decision-making. He would write full and sensible review endorsements on files, often using olde-worlde terms like "felons". Nor was there much wrong with his advocacy, the aberration above notwithstanding. Aided and abetted by me, Charles set him some short-term objectives about timeliness of his case review and committal preparation. After some initial failure he began to meet these and, within twelve months, he was getting a satisfactory staff appraisal report. He remained as eccentric as ever, but we had saved him. I do believe John is still in the CPS, having gone back at some point to Lancashire.

⋆ ⋆ ⋆

Probably the biggest challenge the CPS in London faced was the working relationship with the police, although the quality and inexperience of its lawyer workforce must have run it close. In 1986 the edifice of the CPS was imposed on the Metropolitan Police, and it must have come as a great shock, or at least an unwelcome surprise, to them. There had been the DPP's office and Scotland Yard solicitors' office in existence previously, but the great bulk of serving police officers in London would have had no experience of dealing with an organisation like this, one that was taking over conduct of prosecutions and making all sorts of demands for delivery of files in a timely and trial-ready condition. Certainly by 1989 it was apparent that the police were still a long way short of providing anything like a satisfactory service to the CPS. Nothing had much improved by the time I left. One would hope that things are better by now, although I suspect they are still far from perfect, particularly in the light of fairly savage cuts in the police budget.

The infant CPS had agreed systems with the Metropolitan Police for supply of files and notifying details of witnesses required for trials. The systems, however, were failing on both fronts. Copies of files to be supplied initially for first hearing in court didn't always arrive on time and, in some cases, lawyers were going to court without any information. This situation was compounded by the fact that the CPS would, routinely at this time, lose or misplace files, and admin staff would be scrabbling around just before the start of court looking for files that either we hadn't received or had gone missing.

Then, if a defendant pleaded 'not guilty' at court, or the case was directed to go to the Crown Court, we sent another notice to the police for the file to be "upgraded" so that it contained all the evidence necessary for the case to be prepared for trial or for committal to the Crown Court (the initial file would normally have been an abridged file). Agreed deadlines would exist for delivery of these files so that the necessary work could be done by us before the next hearing. The police failed lamentably in this regard. The worst situation of all was that they routinely failed to deliver files for committal at all in many instances or, at best, we got them the day before the hearing. We were constantly having to ask at court for cases to be adjourned as no committal papers had been prepared for service on the defence or the court, and several times I had to go down to court to explain why half a dozen cases on the list could not proceed.

The situation regarding delivery of files for committal cases improved hardly at all over the four years to 1993. It was a permanent issue between us and the police but, although they recognised the need to get files to us in a timely fashion, they seemed quite incapable of complying. This has not been a phenomenon unique to London. More than twenty years later, Cumbria Police are still routinely failing to deliver full files of evidence to the CPS for Crown Court cases in any sort of acceptable way. Bearing in mind that these are the most important cases that we deal with, it is really quite remarkable that this situation has never been resolved.

The responsibility for putting these files together and arranging delivery to the CPS lies with the police Criminal Justice Units. These are, and were in 1989, units composed of police civilian staff, sometimes headed by a serving police officer of at least sergeant rank, but not in London and probably not anywhere now. Someone in the unit would be responsible for an individual case, gathering all the witness statements and documentary exhibits together, arranging typing of handwritten evidence and, theoretically at least, determining if there was any further evidence that was required to complete the case and seeking that evidence. The last function was not often satisfactorily discharged, as the civilian staff were not lawyers and were not really qualified to assess if the case was complete or not so, in reality, the unit operated largely as a 'post-box', assembling what they had got and sending it on to us. In my experience, the task of calling for additional evidence to make the case complete and trial-ready would nearly always fall to the CPS lawyer responsible for preparing the case prior to service on defence and court.

Because these units were police units rather than CPS units, we had no control over their composition or organisation and could not bring any real pressure to bear upon them to do our bidding. We had no input into their training. It always seemed quite apparent to me that there was no imperative on them to meet deadlines - there was no sense of urgency. Because they were detached from us and not part of the courtroom process, they were never subjected to any pressure to meet the deadlines they were set and to which they had agreed. Had it been the case that, every time the Criminal Justice Unit failed to deliver files on time their manager had to appear in court to explain why, I am quite sure deadlines would have been met with far more frequency.

As it was, the CPS advocates were on the front line and took the brunt of the criticism for, and the embarrassment of, constantly being not ready to proceed at hearings when committal papers should have been previously served on the court and the defence. One tack that I tried was not to apply for an adjournment when we were not ready and, in effect, to invite the magistrates to discharge the defendant. This meant that, if the case were to be revived, which it could be in these circumstances, the police would have to arrange to have the defendant re-charged and we would go through the court process again. This would involve the police in extra work and inconvenience, and I thought it might bring it home to them that it would be better if they got it right first time. I can't say that this was a great success, however, and, in any event, the magistrates seemed strangely reluctant to discharge defendants rather than adjourn the case! In the end we simply gritted our teeth and just hoped for the improvement which never came!

The other unacceptable face of police performance at this time was the failure of police officers to attend the magistrates' court when they had been warned to attend to give evidence in trials. Once a defendant pleaded 'not guilty' and the case had been adjourned to a trial date, our file would go back to the lawyer who had reviewed the case initially, to identify the witnesses who needed to attend the trial. A notice to this effect would then be sent to the Criminal Justice Unit. It is fair to say that we didn't always perform this function as expeditiously as we might, but there was usually quite an interval between the hearing when the plea was entered and the trial date, and the police, nineteen times out of twenty, got more than sufficient notice of the witnesses required. Often we would both send a notice via the usual courier service and fax it direct to the CJU. Be that as it may, hardly a week went by when a case wasn't adjourned or dismissed because the police officer witnesses had failed to attend. I don't know what the percentage of these cases was, but suffice it to say that the incidence was too high and completely unacceptable.

One of my responsibilities was to monitor such cases and take them up with the senior officers as, apart from anything else, it was a "disciplinary offence" for an officer, without good reason, not to attend court when required to do so. I was doing this on a regular basis. Sometimes the response I got was that the CJU had never received the notice from us - this was simply not plausible; sometimes we were told that the officer had been unavailable for some reason, but it was accepted that we hadn't been told of this prior to the trial date, or even on the trial date! Sometimes we got no response at all; occasionally, I was informed that an officer was, or officers were, being disciplined. I entertained the hope that bombarding senior officers with complaint after complaint, week in, week out, would produce a significant improvement. There was, however, no noticeable improvement! Strangely, or perhaps not, we did not experience the same phenomenon in the Crown Court where police officers did normally attend for trials!

I experienced rather a mixed relationship with the Metropolitan Police. The lawyers and I found that police constables we met at court, when they attended, were often sullen and hostile. I also found that the very senior officers, i.e. those at chief superintendent rank with whom John Ringguth and I met, showed only grudging acceptance of the existence of the CPS, and their support for us was never very enthusiastic. On the other hand, I dealt personally at an operational level with a number of middle-ranking officers from West Ham, Plaistow and Forest Gate - mainly detective sergeants, inspectors and DCIs – and, almost without exception, found them to be extremely helpful, amenable and friendly. The same applied to the senior officers from the specialist squads I came into contact with in serious casework, notably Detective Superintendent Albert Patrick, formerly of the Flying Squad and then heading up a team investigating murders. Not only was he a very diligent and clearly very able detective, but he understood and believed in the CPS and was anxious to involve us in consultation at every turn. He was also very quick to inform our superiors of how he had benefited from our assistance and advice, where that was the case.

As ever, the quality of files we received from the police varied quite substantially. Many of those submitted in connection with serious crime were fine; in many cases of volume crime, however, we were constantly having to ask for additional evidence to make the cases ready for trial or, in many instances, the evidence simply wasn't there and we had to discontinue the proceedings. There was a high incidence of "discontinuance" at this time.

⋆ ⋆ ⋆

The Clerk to the Justices at Newham and his court clerks were very supportive of CPS. This was in stark contrast to some of the magistrates, who were constantly critical of our performance, whether or not this was justified. These seemed to be, in fact, the same magistrates who attended the court-user meetings, where they would maintain their barrage of criticism. These particular magistrates seemed to be forever unimpressed and unconvinced by our explanation that shortcomings weren't necessarily our fault! It was just inherent hostility to the CPS as an organisation.

In 1991 or 1992 we learnt that a stipendiary magistrate was to be appointed for Newham. Stipendiary Magistrates are now known as "District Judges" - they are professionally qualified and sit alone as a permanent magistrate in the criminal courts. There had long been "Stipes" in some courts in central London and in other cities in the country. The Stipendiary in Newham would not replace the lay magistrates, but would occupy one court each day whilst the lay benches would continue to sit in the other courtrooms. The Stipendiary, of course, would work much faster than his lay counterparts, as he or she would have no need to consult with colleagues and would consequently get through a much greater volume of work in the same amount of time.

There were half a dozen short-listed candidates for the post, and part of the final selection process that was adopted was the rather novel device of each candidate having to sit as a "temporary" Stipendiary for a week in court, so that his or her qualities could be assessed - a sort of judicial 'beauty contest'. We were actually invited to contribute our feedback on the individual 'contestants', although I'm sure that wouldn't have had much influence on the final outcome.

So this process took place and ultimately a 'winner' was announced. He was, I believe, an existing Clerk to the Justices from somewhere just outside London and, in my opinion, was the pick of the bunch! He began to sit permanently not long after his appointment.

I have appeared before several Stipendiaries/District Judges since 1993 and I appeared a number of times before this one. Although I became accustomed to the experience, it took some little time to adjust to the different approach that was required from appearing before a lay bench. Like Crown Court judges, they prefer conciseness and are unlikely to be impressed by flamboyance and verbosity. They will also be far more ready to cut one off if they have heard enough, or upbraid the advocate who has not adequately prepared. You can't 'wing it' before a "Stipe" because he is likely to tell you if you are, and you need to know your subject matter well because there is always a chance of probing questions from the bench. He will also, of course, be familiar with, for example, the Bail Act and will probably need only a few headline points from the prosecutor on a bail application.

One or two of the CPS prosecutors found this "Stipe" quite intimidating at first, and one totally fell to pieces in the face of his critical interventions in her presentation of the facts in a 'guilty' plea hearing. As we got to know his ways, however, so it became easier. The key was good preparation and confidence. He was equally robust with the defence and, like most "Stipes" in my experience, was a tougher sentencer than the lay magistrates and far more likely to refuse bail.

⋆ ⋆ ⋆

There were some excellent defence advocates that plied their trade in the Newham Magistrates' Courts. Many were from criminal practices or did nothing but criminal advocacy, and these solicitors appeared in court day in, day out. There was a local firm called Duthies who had a whole raft of impressive advocates, but the most impressive of all, in my view, was from another local firm. David Forbes was an excellent advocate, but he was also a very canny practitioner. It was almost the norm for the local defence lawyers to advise their clients to have an "old-fashioned" committal rather than let the case proceed to the Crown Court 'on the nod'. They knew only too well that things might go wrong - in particular, that the witnesses might not turn up at the hearing, that the defendant would then be discharged and the CPS might take the view that the case was a lost cause. This did happen. In David Forbes' case, he often opted for an "old-fashioned" committal but without the witnesses having to attend - this meant that the witness statements would simply be read out in open court. The defence would then submit that the evidence read did not disclose a case to answer against their client. It was obvious to me that, when David took this course, he had spotted a defect in the evidence which he could exploit. I soon discovered that our lawyers often didn't pick this up and, when they got to court at the committal hearing, they found that David was making a successful application for the defendant to be discharged on the ground that there was no prima facie case against him. I warned the lawyers that they needed to be vigilant where David Forbes asked for such a committal - it was almost certain that he had identified a hole in the evidence and that hole needed to be filled before the hearing! Gradually, they got the message!

Although he was a clever lawyer, David Forbes was no shyster and, indeed, he was in many ways a good friend to CPS in those early days. He used to attend the court-user meetings, where he often supported the CPS position. I recall that after one meeting he was generous enough to tell me that he admired and appreciated the way I countered adverse comments made by the magistrate or police members at the meeting.

Another affable individual was John Pilling. He was, I suppose, in his late fifties and an assistant solicitor in a local firm. He had had, I believe, a somewhat chequered past and it soon became apparent that he had a drink problem. In the mornings at court he was a lucid and very able advocate and served his clients well; in the afternoon, however, on some occasions he became a liability. I never experienced it, but some of the lawyers came back with tales of how he had been palpably 'under the influence' during a trial and had effectively wrecked his client's chances of an acquittal by his performance. The lawyers' curse again! I thought seriously of bringing such events to the notice of his employers and, no doubt wrongly, I decided against it. I took the view that, on balance, it was up to his client, or even the court, to do this. I assume no such complaint was made because John continued to practice in those courts and was still doing so when I left the area.

Counsel used to appear quite regularly in the Newham courts. They varied from reasonably competent young hopefuls to not-so-young no-hopers. None of them, in my view, compared with the regular solicitor advocates that appeared for defendants in those courts.

* * *

One of the reasons I had opted to move from Cumbria to east London was to become far more involved in the prosecution of serious crime. This hope was, indeed, realised. There was a very high incidence of serious crime in the London Borough of Newham. We were constantly involved in the prosecution of offences of Rape, child abuse, Grievous Bodily Harm with Intent, Class A Drug Trafficking and, indeed, Murder. Because of the inexperience on our team and the need to cover a large number of courts, I soon found that I needed to review and prepare a significant number of these cases myself. Not that I was objecting to this - my wishes and necessity coincided!

Probably most of the Murder cases were uncomplicated. A lot of such offences are perpetrated by spouses or by persons known to the victim, and the identity of the offender is not an issue. Those cases, however, may well throw up defences of provocation or diminished responsibility. Not many defendants are inclined to plead 'guilty' to a charge of Murder, and will seek to be convicted only of Manslaughter.

Of the more complex Murder cases I dealt with, three stand out. One was an 'acid bath' murder. The victim was the wife of the defendant. She had been tied up, dumped in a container of highly corrosive acid and locked in a garage. Her cries were heard and police officers forced entry to the garage, in time to catch her last and dying words which identified the defendant as the culprit. The defendant, when arrested, denied responsibility for the offence. Initially the evidence against him was tenuous or circumstantial - the "dying declaration" of the victim, and evidence that he had taken out a large insurance policy on her life shortly before her death. But then a diligent police investigation also revealed evidence of an identical vat being purchased previously by a man who could be identified as the defendant. He denied the purchase, but this strengthened the evidence against him. The defendant parted company with two sets of solicitors and, by the time of committal proceedings, he was unrepresented. This meant that there had to be an "old-fashioned" committal. All the evidence had to be read out or summarised to the court, and the court had to decide whether there was sufficient evidence to put the defendant on trial by jury. This was my first and last involvement in advocacy in a murder case, when I conducted the committal proceedings. The defendant was duly committed to the Crown Court (the *Old Bailey*) and was later convicted after a trial.

Another case in which I was involved was the so-called "Memory Lane" murder. This was a killing in a pub which bore that name. Unfortunately, the case was similar to many other cases which arose in our area, in that most of the eye-witnesses or potential eye-witnesses knew the offender and either declined to make a statement or maintained that they had seen nothing! There was a likely suspect and he had been charged by the police, but the evidence against him, as far as I was concerned, was inconclusive and certainly not enough to afford a realistic prospect of conviction. I had a very fraught conference with the investigating officers, who were not prepared to agree with my advice and they demanded a second opinion! I asked John Ringguth to read the file, and he agreed with and supported the advice I had given and we duly offered no evidence against the defendant when he appeared in court. I have to say that, over more than thirty-five years, it has been fairly rare that the police and I have disagreed over a course of action in a case of any substance, and this was certainly the fiercest resistance I ever encountered.

The most complex case of murder I dealt with was the petrol-bombing of a house by six defendants, resulting in four deaths amongst the occupants of the building. This was in fact a 'turf war' between two rival groups involved in drug trafficking. The case against the defendants was complicated, involving identification evidence, circumstantial evidence and evidence of dubious reliability from survivors of the group who had been attacked. The senior investigating officer was Detective Superintendent Albert Patrick, and he and I and the other investigating officers were involved in a number of conferences immediately before and after the defendants were charged. I took the decision to involve prosecuting counsel early in the case, and we had a number of conferences with Nigel Heslop QC of Treasury Counsel and his junior, Jonathan Laidlaw (now Jonathan Laidlaw QC, currently defending Rebekah Brooks in the phone-hacking trial). The investigation, the assistance rendered throughout by counsel, and the subsequent prosecution in the trial in a very difficult case were all first-rate, and convictions were secured all round.

I was also involved in a number of Class A drug trafficking cases in which arrests had been made following operations by specialist police squads. These operations were usually based on surveillance of targeted defendants. One or two of them included the use of "participating informants" – i.e. a police informant who had infiltrated or was part of the gang and was allowed to actually take part in the crime. Such cases raise difficult issues, such as balancing the need to protect the identity or the status of the informant against the need not to mislead the jury. And is the informant to be called to give evidence, or is there enough evidence without calling him? Inevitably there would be a number of conferences with the investigators in such cases at an early stage in the proceedings. Such issues were new to me and I had no experience of dealing with such cases prior to 1989, so I was on quite a steep learning curve myself.

One of these cases resulted in a charge of Conspiracy to supply Heroin against three defendants and led to a two-day hearing in "old-fashioned" committal proceedings, with several of the officers being called to give evidence at the hearing. As I had been involved in the case personally up to that point, I decided to conduct the proceedings myself. John Ringguth was not too pleased with this decision - he thought I should have been sat in the office poring over one set of statistics or another! For me, however, it proved a rewarding and successful experience.

The three defendants were separately represented by counsel. These were a cut above the sort of barrister we regularly saw in the magistrates' court, but no more than what we would now refer to as Level 3 counsel – i.e. barristers who would deal with 'guilty' pleas and fairly low-level trials in the Crown Court. The two male barristers were personable men and we got on well; the female counsel, however, was an example of the worst kind of barrister in my book - arrogant, disdainful and making little attempt to disguise the fact that the court staff, the magistrates, and particularly me, were inferior beings and that she was 'slumming it'. Her attitude brought her into conflict with the court more than once and attracted several rebukes from the chairman of the bench. The most serious incident, however, occurred right at the end of the proceedings. In proceedings of this kind, which do not amount to a trial because the defendant is not in jeopardy of being found guilty, it is perfectly legitimate and acceptable for the prosecutor to call only such evidence as he feels necessary to establish that the defendant has a case to answer. In her final address to the court, however, this female counsel accused me of "dishonesty" because there was clearly material evidence I had not brought before the court. Naturally I replied to this accusation. Not only, I said, did I resent the accusation of dishonesty, but it was wrong anyway, and I was able to quote the legal authority for not having to call all the material evidence. Presumably this woman had not heard of the authority in question or hadn't bothered to research the law before making this accusation, as she didn't or wasn't able to reply to my point. She earned a further strong rebuke from the chairman for the accusation she had made.

It is unprofessional in the extreme and it just isn't done to accuse one's opponent in court of dishonesty. There are devices for conveying that the other advocate is wrong, or misleading the court, or misrepresenting the facts - usually by prefacing one's remarks with the phrase "with respect" or, more strongly, "with the greatest respect" and then restrained language to follow! In this instance the clerk and I, after the hearing, discussed briefly whether the barrister should be reported to her professional body, the Bar Council, for her language, but I felt it would be more trouble than it was worth and we let it ride.

I can recall only one instance of a barrister being so reported and that was after an incident in Alfreton Magistrates' Court in Derbyshire, in 1978 or thereabouts. Following the bench finding his client guilty after a trial, the idiot had been unable to restrain himself from announcing, still within earshot of the magistrates, that he had always believed that a "bench" was "something hard, wooden and unbending," and that "nothing I have seen or heard today has caused me to change my mind."!! I don't believe he was disbarred, but I think there was a severe financial penalty from the Bar Council and he also got hauled over the coals by his head of chambers.

I don't know whether this woman appeared for her client in the Crown Court, but she did him no favours in the magistrates' court hearing. Having been committed for trial by the magistrates, all three defendants were convicted after a trial at Snaresbrook Crown Court.

There was one other case in which I became involved which 'changed the course of history' - at least in the CPS!

Charles Saunders had discontinued a charge of burglary against a defendant, whose name escapes me now, on the ground of insufficient evidence. Unfortunately, Charles also included in the notice a charge of Assaulting a Police Officer against the same defendant. The evidence on this charge was perfectly sound, and the intention had been to continue with this part of the case. I first heard of the matter when I received a visit from a local senior police officer who wanted to know why we had dropped the Assault charge. I soon realised that this charge had been discontinued in error, and I had no hesitation in agreeing that the police could recharge the defendant with the Assault. This happened, but then his solicitors asked for the proceedings to be halted while they sought "judicial review" of our decision to resurrect the Assault charge. Judicial review is a procedure in the High Court whereby a judge can be asked to determine whether a decision such as this is unlawful. In this instance, the defence were saying that it was unlawful as the prosecution had determined there was insufficient evidence to support the charge and had discontinued it, and it couldn't now be brought back, not, in any event, without more material evidence coming to light. Our position was that the decision was simply a mistake, and mistakes could be rectified.

At this stage we took advice from counsel with experience in such matters and he was quite adamant that we were in our rights to revive the charge and judicial review would support this position. However, the matter had blown up out of proportion by now and the DPP, by now Barbara Mills QC, had got to hear about it! She sent for the file and, after a short while, we were instructed to drop the revived charge and notify the defence that they needn't pursue their judicial review application. The feedback we got from CPS HQ was that the DPP thought we would be strongly criticised in the High Court for not having adequately documented our reasons in the file for dropping the charge in the first place and then resurrecting it. She didn't want the adverse publicity, whether or not our decision was the correct one.

Whatever views I had about Barbara Mills (and see later!) I had no argument about her decision in this instance. At this time lawyers in the CPS generally, I think, were not good about recording our thought processes behind decisions, or even recording the fact of the decision itself. I have to confess this case was no exception and neither Charles nor I had adequately endorsed the file when decisions were made. I have always totally agreed that openness, transparency and detailed documentation of decision-making are essential in an organisation like the CPS. It has not always been the case, however, as we shall see later, that the CPS has practised what it preached when it came to dealing with its own staff....

There were two national developments in the CPS that followed from this case:

a) All managers were asked to ensure that endorsements on case files properly recorded decision-making and gave detailed reasons for all decisions.

b) A written direction was issued about the circumstances in which discontinued cases and charges could be resurrected and proceedings reinstituted (this could include where the decision to discontinue was palpably wrong).

* * *

Whilst I was at Stratford there were some very significant changes in the law and criminal procedure.

The tape-recording of police interviews with prisoners had been introduced in PACE, but had become the norm only in the late 1980s. It safeguarded defendants in that it provided an accurate record of the content of the interview and put an end to any possibility of their being 'verballed' by the interviewing officers. On the other hand, it reduced the number of occasions that the admissibility of confessions was challenged, and these days this is quite a rarity. It could also provide evidence of a defendant's demeanour in interview - perhaps surprisingly, however, tapes of interview are very rarely played in evidence in trials. The contents of the tape are summarised by the police in a written "record of interview". There are rules about the content of these "ROTIs" as they are called, such as when conversation must be recorded verbatim - in particular, where a confession is made or a defendant is putting forward a defence or an explanation for his conduct. In practice, therefore, "ROTIs" are quite detailed and long and, in my experience, it is not often that the defence take issue with their accuracy - they then become part of the evidence. By 1989 the tape-recording of interviews was routine.

Another statutory change was the implementation of the provisions first introduced in the Prosecution of Offences Act 1985 to impose limits on the time a person could spend in custody. There were limits, for example, of ten weeks up to committal proceedings taking place and 112 days from committal to the Crown Court to the start of the trial. Once it had expired, the defendant would be released on bail unless the prosecution successfully applied for the limit to be extended. This meant the devising and implementation of various systems to enable custody time limits to be monitored. Inevitably, across the country there were failures of monitoring and a few persons did get bail as a result. In my experience these failures have always been few in number and it has never happened in any case in which I have been involved. It never seemed to me, anyway, that it was the end of the world if someone was released on bail as a result of a custody time limit being allowed to expire. However, as the years have gone by, the CPS top management have become quite obsessed with the subject and nowadays, if there is a failure of custody time-limit monitoring, then there is a major inquest, detailed reports are required and someone has to have an interview with the Director! It has become a 'hanging' offence!

The most important and far-reaching of the changes, in my view, however, was that concerning the Disclosure of Unused Material. Up until the early 1990s, the word "disclosure" meant, to a CPS lawyer, disclosure of the evidence. No-one ever gave any serious thought to the issue of whether we should be disclosing the material gathered in the investigation which we were not using in evidence. If we tendered a witness to the defence, we probably didn't even think about providing a copy of his or her witness statement to them unless they specifically asked for it. There was really nothing new about "disclosure of unused material". It's quite clear that we should always have considered it and disclosed anything to the defence which might assist them or detract from the strength of the prosecution case. But it didn't happen. Either we just didn't do it or, more likely, the police never made us aware of such material anyway.

The issue came bursting on to the scene with the "miscarriage of justice" cases that hit the headlines at this time - the "Birmingham Six", the "Guildford Four", and the Judith Ward case. Suddenly it became very apparent that the prosecution was not always complying with its common-law duty to disclose to the defence material which was relevant to its case, material which in some cases greatly assisted the defence case, or possibly fatally undermined the Crown's case, material which would otherwise never have seen the light of day.

I rather suspect that the existence of such a duty on the prosecution came as a complete surprise to most CPS lawyers and, certainly, I was only dimly aware of the responsibility and had never taken it really seriously. Nor, to the best of my knowledge, had most counsel who had been instructed to prosecute criminal cases. Now, suddenly, it became very much flavour of the month and systems were hastily devised to create arrangements for the police to identify unused material and reveal or copy it to the CPS. There was a burst of training for lawyers on the subject, and standard letters were drafted to cover service of such material on the defence or to tell them there was nothing "relevant" to disclose.

"Relevance", indeed, was the test. If the unused material was considered relevant to the defence case then it had to be copied to them or they had to be given the opportunity to inspect it. The exception was that material which it was considered should not be disclosed in the public interest was not disclosed.

The whole exercise was fairly rough-and-ready and hit-and-miss in the first year or so. It would be some time before the police would get to grips with it and understand their responsibilities, and the same applied to lawyers. It is my view and experience that it wasn't until the system was put on a statutory basis in 1996/7 that we really started to deal with "disclosure" routinely and appropriately and, even today, the situation is not perfect.

* * *

There were also changes in the way we operated as a Service in these years, and there were also profound structural changes looming on the horizon.

The CPS top management was always looking for ways to change the way we operated. No matter how well we felt our systems were working, and how comfortable we were with them, this was not good enough and someone at the centre would come up with some new system which we must implement. I have said this already, but it's worth repeating. Over the years we would have one new system after another imposed upon us. They were always hailed by the top brass as the 'best thing since sliced bread'. More often than not they would be quietly shelved or forgotten about in a few years, or overtaken by some exciting new way of working!

In 1992 or thereabouts we were suddenly handed down "National Operational Practice", or NOP for short! To be quite honest I can't remember what it was all about, and no-one remembers what it was all about now! It was the brainchild of Graham Duff, an ex-Chief Crown Prosecutor in Lancashire and now a sort of joint Chief Executive of the CPS (these days back at the Bar in Newcastle). He went round the country proclaiming the joys of NOP and angrily shouting down any detractors or any negative responses. It was all something to do with the way we worked in preparing Crown Court cases but, for the life of me, I can't recall what benefits it brought in this regard and, in any event, a couple of years later it was superseded by another half-baked scheme! One of the few positive developments I can remember was for senior lawyers such as me to be required now to attend Snaresbrook Crown Court to make decisions about accepting 'guilty' pleas, etc., after direct consultation and discussion with prosecuting counsel. I did this quite often and it was quite an eye-opener. We included one or other of the senior caseworkers in the discussions and they were always wise to the sometimes devious ways of counsel - wanting to avoid trials so they could go and do something more lucrative elsewhere, for example, or they had tickets for the Oval or Lord's, always, of course, trying to retain as much of their brief fee as possible! It never ceased to amaze me that counsel might have had the brief for weeks, but suddenly decided on the morning of the trial that there wasn't a realistic prospect of conviction and the case should be dropped or compromised in some way. The cynical, of course, would say that they probably hadn't read the brief until that morning! Although there were sometimes good reasons why we should agree with counsel, I suspect I must have irritated many of them by insisting they got on with the trial!

In 1992 the DPP, Sir Alan Green, resigned. He had been caught kerb-crawling outside Kings Cross Station and had accepted a caution from the police for the offence. It was a sad moment. For me, Sir Alan was the best of the holders of that position in my time in the CPS. He was always a staunch defender of the organisation and its lawyers and staff when we were pilloried in the media and, on the one occasion that I had met him, I found him to be warm and approachable, a very good listener and interested in people. A notable contrast to his successor!

In his place we got Barbara Mills QC. She had been a criminal barrister and an experienced prosecutor. Not, I believe, in the first rank of QCs, but then these were never going to be attracted to the post of DPP. Why would anyone want to take a substantial drop in income to take on a 'poisoned chalice' such as was the job of heading up the CPS!? Barbara Mills eventually became a Dame of the British Empire - this gave rise to the standing joke within the Service that "every pantomime needs a Dame," a phrase that was coined within the CPS rather than by anyone outside the Service! She never, however, became a High Court Judge, which most holders of the office probably believed would be their reward for doing five years' penance in the role of DPP. The "Dame" was DPP for six years, but stood down after widespread criticism of what was perceived as her failure to prosecute police officers after deaths of prisoners whilst in police custody. There is no doubt, either, that under her stewardship morale in the CPS amongst the staff reached rock bottom.

For me and for many others in my experience, Barbara Mills was everything Sir Alan Green was not. She came across as arrogant, not interested in listening, unapproachable, bloodless and autocratic. After her appointment, and over the next two years, she went round all the CPS areas in England and Wales in what might be described as a sort of "royal progress". She put a damper on all office parties by proclaiming that there was to be no alcohol on CPS premises. I managed to avoid meeting her on all but one occasion, and then it was unavoidable. I was interviewed in 1998 by a panel at HQ which she chaired. Throughout the interview she spent the whole half-hour fidgeting in her chair and looking everywhere except at me. To me and many of my colleagues, she was "that bloody woman" and worse!

Many of the senior managers, initially at least, tried to whip up some enthusiasm for her amongst the staff. She came to visit the Stratford office in 1993. I missed the visit because I was away on holiday, although some of the senior management couldn't understand, apparently, why I wouldn't break my holiday and come back early so I could be present. As I was on a walking trip on the Isle of Rhum, coming back early to meet Barbara Mills was the last thing on my mind!!

Early in her tenure the new DPP decided that there needed to be a major structural shake-up of the CPS. This was something that was to happen again and again over the next twenty years. A new DPP would come in and wouldn't like the set-up, and we were all reshuffled once more. We went from 'small is beautiful' to 'big is beautiful' and back again, and back again once more!!

This DPP decided that she didn't want to be dealing with twenty-odd Chief Crown Prosecutors and that their number could be reduced to a manageable handful by creating about twelve or thirteen much larger CPS Areas. In 1993, therefore, London became one Area and, amongst other changes, Cumbria, Cleveland, Durham and Northumbria were lumped together as "CPS North".

One parallel change at this time was one that I applauded, and which was to have an impact on the rest of my career. This was the recognition that dealing with serious and complex casework could be more effectively carried out by a specialist Special Casework Lawyer on each Area. We got our first "SCL" in 1991 in Outer London North and, by 1993, he or she was taking on some of the cases which we had struggled with as a team - large drug-trafficking conspiracies, large-scale frauds, large-scale public order, etc. Whilst the SCL was a 'one-man band', however, there was a limit to the number of cases he or she could take on but, from 1993, there was a move to increasing the size of the resource to more than just the one lawyer per Area. When I moved to the CPS North Area in 1993 the SCL unit consisted of three lawyers.

* * *

As the new CPS structure was being implemented in 1993 senior lawyers were asked by CPS HQ for their preferences as to their role in the new set-up. This was an opportunity for someone at my level to change direction.

After four years as an Assistant Branch Crown Prosecutor I was ready for a change. There were a number of positives I was able to take out of my time in Stratford. I had managed a fairly large team of prosecutors; I had been actively involved in the decision-making and case preparation in a lot of very serious criminal cases; I had been responsible for conducting advocacy in some complex cases in their preliminary stages in the magistrates' court; I had become more engaged with the Crown Court side of things by a goodly number of case conferences with counsel and interaction with prosecution counsel at the Crown Court.

On the other hand, there had been much that I had not welcomed: the constant demands of being a "manager" and trying to balance this with being, out of necessity as well as desire, a front-line operational prosecutor; the relentless pressure of managing and supervising a team of lawyers whose composition was invariably at least 50% raw inexperience; on occasions, the very long hours and the out-of-kilter work/life balance; the long commutes to work and back. And still I had not managed to penetrate the Crown Court beyond the CPS office at Snaresbrook Crown Court!! Above all, I often resented the intrusions of what I regarded as pointless and unnecessary management functions into the pursuit of the core business of prosecuting criminals, and what I perceived as attempts by senior management to marginalise my involvement in casework and advocacy. The whole Stratford experience I had found rarely unstressful and at times oppressive. It was certainly time for a change.

With this in mind I indicated to HQ that I would be interested in moving into a Special Casework Lawyer role. In August 1993 I was informed there was such a job for me in CPS North, based in Newcastle, and that there was also a job for my wife there (she was by now a caseworker with CPS Essex). I gratefully accepted the job offer (as did my wife!)...

CHAPTER TEN

1993 to 1995: North Eastern Interlude

CPS North in 1993 was a vast geographical area consisting of the counties of Cumbria, Northumbria, Durham and Cleveland, and stretching from Barrow to Berwick and from Middlesbrough to Carlisle. It was divided into six branches, each headed by a Branch Crown Prosecutor, and had a Special Casework Unit consisting of three full-time lawyers supported by two (later three) admin staff.

The senior management team of the Area comprised a Chief Crown Prosecutor, two Assistant Chief Crown Prosecutors and an Area Administrator.

The CCP was "Dickie" Dickinson, who had spent most of his career in Lancashire. Dickie could talk for England but was an affable, easy-going fellow who seemed happy to let his two subordinates do the day-to-day running of the Area.

Of the two ACCPs, one was responsible for the 'operational' side - this was David Farmer, who had also spent most of his career in Lancashire but had been the Chief Crown Prosecutor of the Northumbria/Durham Area for a year or two until its merger into CPS North. The other ACCP was responsible for casework issues in the Area and also headed up the Special Casework Unit. He was my boss - Michael Graham. Mike was probably not more than thirty-five or thirty-six in 1993 and had spent his entire career in Northumbria, rising up the ranks of the local CPS. He was extremely well-thought-of at both local and national level, and was a very personable, supportive and understanding boss to boot!

I was pleased to leave the trials and tribulations of management behind me, for the time being at least, and enjoy the pure casework role. There was one slight fly in the ointment in that, on the day of my arrival, I discovered that I was to have an articled clerk, whose development and mentoring I would be responsible for over the next twelve months. I had had, successively, three articled clerks in London and this had been another burden I had been asked to carry.

From the first I was never given any choice in the matter - I was just told that I would have one!

My issue with this was that the relationship between a solicitor and his articled clerk is a personal one. It wasn't a requirement of the job and I should have been consulted beforehand and my consent sought before an articled clerk was assigned to me or, indeed, before any other solicitor on the team was 'given' one. The relationship is formalised by a set of "articles", a document that is drafted by the parties and formally executed by them. I often wondered what the consequences would have been if I had declined to sign the articles in any of these instances. I cannot see that I would have been in breach of my contract of employment, or that I could have been dismissed. I did complain about the situation and expressed my views, but no-one listened and, in the end, I 'rolled over' and took the articled clerks on. This was, in my view, inconsiderate and blinkered management by CPS HQ. They decided they wanted "trainees" to be recruited and developed, but gave no thought to the unreasonable demands that would be placed upon those deputed to train them.

So it was I got my fourth articled clerk. For the next twelve months I would have to find "Adrian" work to do, act as his mentor and exercise some sort of supervision over him. I could have done without this, particularly when I was starting in a new job and was on something of a learning curve myself. Adrian was a pleasant lad with a good sense of humour and we got on well, but he had a thick anti-establishment streak running through him and I couldn't see him making a career in the CPS! After his twelve months he went off to do a similar term in private practice and I lost touch with him, but he never returned as a CPS prosecutor!

The Special Casework Unit and other Area Management staff were housed on the top floor of Benton House in Jesmond in Newcastle. CPS had just moved into this building and refurbishment work was still going on around us at this time. Adrian and I initially were sharing an open-plan office with two other members of the management staff. Ian Groundwell and Ian Edmondson were ex-Chief Clerks from Crown Court sections in CPS Areas that had been merged into one of the new, larger areas and had been effectively displaced as a result. Instead of making them redundant the CPS had offered them posts in CPS North, but clearly had given little or no thought to what their roles might be in the new Area. They were at this time, then, just a couple of 'spare parts'. The former Chief Clerk from the previous Northumbria/Durham Area, Bob Dodds, was also on our floor as a 'displaced person' and was at a similar loose end. Within a few months Bob had decided that there was no meaningful role for him in the new Area and resigned, and Ian Edmondson transferred to another Area. Eventually some sort of role in the management hierarchy was found for Ian Groundwell, but he must have found it quite alien to the work he had been doing for many years previously.

After a few weeks the building work was completed and I moved into a separate office down the corridor, and working conditions improved substantially.

* * *

The other two prosecutors in the Special Casework Unit were interesting characters and also vastly experienced lawyers.

Kingsley Hyland, who was on the same grade as me, had spent his entire CPS working life in Northumbria and, indeed, was to remain there until he finally left the organisation in 2013. At first acquaintance he came across as unfriendly and almost hostile, but this was a front and later I found him to be good company and the possessor of a wicked sense of humour. He worked very long hours and was held in very high esteem by the police in Northumbria, particularly by the specialist squads from whom most of his work seemed to come. He also had a high profile nationally in the CPS and was involved in projects that took him away from the Area. He became the CPS national lead on undercover policing and surveillance, and delivered training countrywide on the Regulation of Investigatory Powers Act 2000 (RIPA) when it came into force. His efforts and industry led to him being ultimately awarded an OBE.

Initially I was responsible in the Area for delivery of training in, and advising Area lawyers on, any issues arising from the subject of Disclosure of Unused Material. After I left the unit in 1995, however, Kingsley took on this mantle and made himself a considerable expert in this ever-expanding and complex field. It is somewhat ironic therefore, that it was a failure to disclose such material to the defence that brought Kingsley into severe disfavour with the judiciary and into what was for him, no doubt, the worst moments of his career.

In December 2010 Kingsley, as head of the Complex Casework Unit in CPS Northumbria, was responsible for the conduct of a case of Conspiracy to Pervert the Course of Justice and Witness Intimidation that was being tried at Woolwich Crown Court in London. Two of the three defendants were members of a notorious Newcastle family, the Sayers. The Sayers were a prominent criminal gang and Kingsley would have been involved in a number of prosecutions against them over many years. John Henry Sayers had, indeed, been acquitted of murder in 2002 and now he was accused of being involved in 'jury nobbling' in that case. Unfortunately, the prosecution in the trial at Woolwich Crown Court failed to disclose material to the defence which would have shown that a principal prosecution witness was lying, which evidence may well have led to an acquittal of the defendants.

This failure came to light during the trial and the trial judge decided the failure was so serious that it amounted to an abuse of process, and he halted the proceedings. However, the judge, Mr Justice Cooke, did not stop there but launched into a torrent of criticism of the prosecution - and not just the prosecution but Kingsley, whom he singled out apparently as the person solely to blame for the failure to disclose this important undermining material to the defence. Kingsley, the judge said, was responsible for a "deliberate conscious decision to flout the rules of disclosure." He was to blame for "a gross failure which has undoubtedly prejudiced the defendants and has resulted in an unfair trial."

I do not think I have ever heard a judge criticise a CPS lawyer in such severe terms - not far short, in fact, of accusing Kingsley himself of Attempting to Pervert the Course of Justice! Was the criticism justified? Of the Crown, the prosecution as an entity, undoubtedly. But from information I was later given by another person on the prosecution team, Kingsley was wrongly singled out as the culprit.

As the CPS lawyer responsible for the conduct of the case, Kingsley would have had the job of identifying and sifting the unused material in the case (there is, apparently, no suggestion that the police had not revealed the existence of this particular material to the CPS). It would have been his decision in the first instance to determine which material to disclose to the defence. But there was a QC and a junior counsel involved in prosecuting the case at trial. They both would have had copies of all the unused material in the possession of the prosecution and would have been aware of which material had been disclosed and which hadn't. Ultimately, the decision whether to confirm or reverse the decision made by Kingsley would have been theirs; and the ultimate responsibility for decisions about disclosure would have been theirs. They cannot hide behind a decision made by a CPS lawyer, not when they have the conduct of the trial in court!

My information, from a reliable source, is that both prosecuting counsel were indeed aware of the existence of this material and that Kingsley had sought their advice about whether it should be disclosed or not. Even if he hadn't, it seems inconceivable to me that they wouldn't have known about it and considered its significance in terms of disclosure.

I do not know why Kingsley did not disclose the material in the first place, or why counsel did not advise or arrange disclosure later in the piece. But with the benefit of hindsight, the decision not to disclose was wrong and proved fatal to the outcome of the trial. But the point is that the judge should not have put the blame on Kingsley, and counsel should not have allowed this to happen!! What were the prosecution counsel doing whilst the judge was laying into Kingsley? Sitting on their hands?! Did leading counsel offer a word in his defence, let alone accept responsibility for the error? Kingsley was a salaried employee of the CPS; leading counsel would be on at least £300 an hour and his junior on at least half that. They are paid to know about such material, to make such decisions and to accept responsibility for errors that are made in the conduct of the prosecution!! They clearly failed in their duties!

The line taken by the judge does not, I am afraid, surprise me. I have seen this happen on other occasions. Judges may sometimes lay into or criticise young junior counsel for ineptitude or lack of proper preparation. But they will never criticise a QC! They will probably know each other well; they may even have been in the same set of chambers! They are in the same 'club'. The Bar is the biggest 'closed shop' of all and doesn't encourage outsiders to penetrate its mystical world. It is far easier for a judge to pillory someone not of the 'wigged' brethren, someone, moreover, not in a position to defend himself or herself from a verbal attack!

I gather that Kingsley was devastated by the criticism and contemplated resignation from the CPS. This is hardly surprising and, whilst he did not resign, no doubt these events played a part in his decision a couple of years later to accept a voluntary redundancy package at a time when he would still have much to offer the CPS. I do not know what, if any, steps were taken by the Chief Crown Prosecutor on Kingsley's behalf after the case was over. It isn't 'done' to publicly criticise anything done or said by a judge, particularly a High Court Judge. One would hope, however, that explanations were demanded from counsel. I wouldn't have been instructing them again in a hurry!

⋆ ⋆ ⋆

The other lawyer in our unit, Geoff Mason, was another immensely experienced and very talented prosecutor. Although he was, in theory, junior to me, I had no hesitation and felt no shame in seeking his advice on many occasions. He had an intuitive grasp of the right way to proceed in cases and, like Kingsley, he was held in high esteem by the police he dealt with and, indeed, by the local Bar. What I could never understand was why he didn't progress further in the CPS. I recall him attending a job interview at CPS headquarters, but with an unsuccessful outcome. You could get feedback on your performance in interview at this time and Geoff's came back as "prolix and discursive", referring to his responses in interview. I could not imagine anyone less prolix and discursive! Well their loss was our gain!

Before this time, and particularly before 1986, I had conducted or taken part in quite a few recruitment or promotion interviews. You were looking for someone who you felt could do the job in question, would fit in with others on the team; someone you could work with. It was often an intuitive decision, a gut feeling. Not everyone performs well in interview and you make allowances for this and try to look beyond how someone does in a twenty-minute slot. I cannot recall ever regretting a decision I made or with which I was associated. Gut feelings, however, by now had no place in the process of assessing the suitability of someone for a job. The candidate had to be able to demonstrate he had the "competencies" that the interviewing panel considered were necessary for the post, and to provide evidence of these. In fact, an applicant had to demonstrate this on the application form itself and if you didn't, or filled the form in incorrectly, you didn't even get an interview, let alone the job!

I have known people in the CPS who would have been ideal for a job for which they were applying, but who were not considered for interview because they didn't, or couldn't, show evidence of having all the competencies when they completed the application form. This could produce absurd results. On one occasion I recall, some years later, there was an admin assistant-cum-typist who applied for a permanent job with CPS Cumbria - the job she was applying for was, in effect, the same one she had been doing most successfully as a temp for about eighteen months. Everybody knew she could do the job standing on her head. However, those responsible for drawing up the short-list, in their wisdom (and they knew this lady), decided she had failed to demonstrate evidence in her application that she had all the necessary competencies and she was not called for interview! Fortunately, none of those who were interviewed was considered suitable for the job and it was re-advertised. This time, some of her colleagues helped our lady to complete the application form in an acceptable fashion and she eventually got the job, to the relief and satisfaction of all of us!!

There is also more than one example of the interview process I have described producing disastrous appointments. We had the appointment of a barrister from the independent Bar to a Crown Prosecutor job in Cumbria. He no doubt completed the application form with great skill and passed the interview with flying colours. The interview panel, incidentally, included one non-lawyer. It was not unknown for such panels to be actually chaired by an administrator, or at least by someone who was well-removed from the day-to-day activity of prosecuting, so I suppose it should be no surprise that they sometimes got it wrong! In this instance, the candidate no doubt seemed an obvious choice for recruitment as a Crown Prosecutor. No-one thought to inquire, however, why it was that after several years at the Bar he was still doing the overwhelming part of his advocacy in the magistrates' court. If he had any real advocacy skills, a barrister of that experience should have been a regular Crown Court Advocate. As it was, it was soon discovered that he was not up to the job. In particular, his review and case preparation was lamentable; he was also fast-tracked as an advocate in the Crown Court but, after being lambasted more than once by the resident judge for one reason or another, he was withdrawn from the ranks of our Crown Court prosecutors. In the end he decided to leave the CPS - he 'jumped', in fact, 'before he was pushed'!

I sat on one interview panel in the late nineties, chaired by a Chief Crown Prosecutor. We were seeking to fill two vacancies for Crown Prosecutors in Cumbria. The only two candidates being interviewed were two lawyers who had been doing that job on a 'casual' basis for more than a year and, as far as I was concerned, had been doing an excellent job and should have been 'shoo-ins' for the vacancies. One of the two, however, had a bad day and didn't interview well, for whatever reason. We had to award points in various 'boxes', and insufficient points meant failure! My two colleagues marked him down and he was in danger of not making 'the cut'. This would have been a ludicrous result. I knew his capabilities and knew he'd been a first-rate prosecutor to date, but had I agreed with the other two he would have been out of the door with no job. I chose therefore to inflate my markings sufficiently to ensure he passed the interview! Needless to say he proved to be a great asset to the CPS in Cumbria, and is now a Crown Advocate in Dorset!

The interview process we were obliged to adhere to was no doubt a direct result of becoming part of the Civil Service and all that entailed in terms of ticking boxes and bureaucratic 'straitjackets'. I am all in favour of open and transparent procedures when it comes to recruitment and promotion interviewing but, in my view, this needs to be tempered with common sense and less slavish subservience to the rules. It also makes sense, I believe, if those doing the interviewing have some comparatively recent experience of either doing the job in question or at least directly and closely managing those who do it! Much less chance then of making a duff appointment!

In the Special Casework Unit, for the first time in my prosecuting life, I was intensively involved in handling very serious casework, and involved from the beginning to almost the end of the process. I was in at the beginning of cases, with advising on sufficiency of evidence, charges and issues of bail or custody. I was responsible for piloting the case through the magistrates' court, the preparation for Crown Court, correspondence with defence and police, and handling the disclosure or non-disclosure of unused material. Invariably, given the type of cases I was dealing with, there were several conferences with prosecuting counsel and I attended the Crown Court for at least any preliminary hearings of the case. It was never less than challenging work, but a blessed relief from the burdens of managing a team.

Initially, I was assigned to handling casework that arose in Cleveland and County Durham. Kingsley covered Northumbria and Cumbria and Geoff also picked up work from Northumbria, as most of the cases tended to arise in the Tyneside area. Kingsley, however, was a non-driver and it soon became apparent that he would struggle to get to conferences with police or to court in the north-west and, before long, I took over the Cumbrian side and he relieved me of Durham.

The first thing that struck me about the type of work we were dealing with was the number of cases involving solicitors who had allegedly 'had their hands in the till' - stealing from their firm's Client Account, in other words. I have mentioned before the "lawyers' curse", the tendency to get involved in crime, drunkenness or sexual impropriety. In the north-east, the propensity to dishonesty seemed to have reached epidemic proportions. I think there were half-a-dozen such cases on our books at this time, and these from Newcastle alone and, before long, I picked up another one involving a solicitor from Stockton-on-Tees.

Often, these cases related to sole practitioners and this was the case with Llewellyn from Stockton. He had appropriated many thousands of pounds of his clients' money and, as they always do, had resorted to various devices to cover up his activities and delay the process of detection. The case involved many documentary exhibits and reams and reams of unused material which required sifting. I had no great experience at this time of dealing with fraud cases, and I took a little time to determine the type and number of counts to go on the indictment. The defendant actually took the matter to trial, I recall, and was imprisoned after conviction. Needless to say, his career as a solicitor was over.

Fraud of one sort or another was probably the most common variety of case that came into the unit. This was not surprising, as most rank-and-file CPS lawyers do not like fraud, for some reason, and needed little encouragement to seek to persuade their managers that these were cases for the Special Casework Unit. I suppose a lot of fraud cases are not clear-cut and they tend to involve a lot of headaches in drafting charges; they also tend to require a great deal of work and an awful lot of paper and the end result, even where there is a conviction, is often disappointing. Custodial sentences for convicted fraudsters tend not to compare in severity with those imposed on violent offenders and Class A drug traffickers, for example.

Another common type of case was Attempted Murder. This is one of the most difficult cases in the criminal calendar to prove, as it requires proof of an intention to kill. Ironically, if the victim actually dies then the task is easier, since the prosecution can then rely on an intention merely to cause grievous bodily harm! Convictions for Attempted Murder tend, therefore, to be comparatively rare. The defendant charged with such an offence will, if he has done the act, nearly always offer to plead 'guilty' to Inflicting Grievous Bodily Harm with Intent but not Attempted Murder and, more often than not, the temptation will be to accept the offer!

Other cases that would find their way to us included sex cases involving more than one defendant, and multi-handed public-order cases; also road traffic cases involving fatalities (something I was to become only too familiar with over the next fifteen years); Conspiracies to supply Class A drugs; and cases involving high-profile defendants, or which were otherwise sensitive in one way or another.

It might be expected that cases of Murder would fall to our unit, but this was not necessarily the case, since many such cases were of a domestic nature (man kills wife or vice-versa) and not particularly complicated. There were, however, two notorious murder cases that arose in 1994 that we did deal with.

Hassan Shatanawi was convicted at Newcastle Crown Court in 1994 of the murder of his wife. The unusual feature of the case, although it is not as uncommon a feature as one might think, was that Mrs Shatanawi's body has never been found to this day. We spent long hours discussing the case in the unit before we made a joint decision to advise the police that there was a realistic prospect of conviction.

Without the body the evidence, of course, was always going to be limited and there was always a residual danger that she might turn up after the trial!! The circumstantial evidence on which we relied, however, was considered sufficiently compelling to justify prosecution and, subsequently, conviction. Mrs Shatanawi had been reported missing and, for no good reason, seemed to have disappeared without trace. At this time, the defendant had paid a workman to demolish a shed he owned on an allotment at Seaton Carew, near

Hartlepool. The workman, however, had sold the shed, and it was tracked down to a location in Middlesbrough. There were traces of blood that could have been the wife's, on shavings that had slipped though gaps in the floor which appeared to have been created by a chisel. The defendant had a lover, and there was evidence that he had told her days after the wife's disappearance that they could go away together. The defendant said that his wife had gone abroad, but no trace was found of her leaving the country or being elsewhere. It was quite a gamble to proceed with this case in the absence of the body but, ultimately, a successful one.

I would be involved in other high-risk prosecutions in 1997 and 2004.

Stephen Wilkinson was convicted at Leeds Crown Court in 1995 of manslaughter, after killing 12-year-old Nikki Conroy in March 1994. He had been charged with her murder, but was convicted of manslaughter on the grounds of diminished responsibility. The case attracted national headlines at the time and led to widespread debate about security in schools. Wilkinson had burst into Hall Garth School in Middlesbrough and stabbed two girls with a knife, one fatally. He never denied the act, but maintained that it was not he but his dark *alter ego*, Wilson Jinks, who was actually carrying it out, whilst he watched from nearby. He was unable to control what happened. "Wilson Jinks" was an anagram of "S J Wilkinson". Arguably, it was a better result for the public for Wilkinson to have been convicted of manslaughter rather than murder, for he will be detained in a secure unit for the rest of his life. We established quite a close relationship with Nikki's parents during the life of the case, and they were very appreciative of the sensitive way we had handled it and how we and the family liaison officer had kept them in the loop from the beginning of the proceedings to the end. For all its faults, I have always thought that dealing with families in this type of case is something that the CPS has done sensitively and well.

Another case that I dealt with at this time and which also attracted national attention, albeit ultimately for the wrong reasons, was the Bishop Auckland child abuse case. The case began with an eleven-year-old boy and a six-year-old girl making allegations of sexual abuse against a husband and wife. They were charged, and then other young children came out of the woodwork and, along with the original two children, made allegations of ritual satanic abuse against the same defendants and three other couples living in the same street. The offences were said to have occurred over a period of time in attic bedrooms and involved rats, "devil clothes", whips and drugs. All eight defendants were, on the face of it, respectable people. It would have been easy to dismiss the allegations as preposterous and, with the benefit of hindsight, they almost certainly were. However, there was then, as there is now, a strong imperative for prosecutors to take such allegations very seriously. I spent many hours watching video interviews that the police had conducted with the children and their accounts were by no means unbelievable. There were inconsistencies between their respective versions of events, but there was also a degree of support offered by each of them for allegations made by another. Rightly or wrongly, I advised the police at this time that we had a sustainable case for indecent assaults against all the eight defendants.

The case went through various hearings in the magistrates' court and several in the Crown Court before we arrived at a trial date (all defendants had entered 'not guilty' pleas to all charges on the indictment). We had engaged David Robson QC to prosecute and a very experienced junior in John Evans, both counsel from the same chambers in Newcastle. There were innumerable conferences with counsel prior to the trial date and, although we all agreed it would be a difficult case to prosecute, neither counsel expressed the view that it should not be prosecuted or, indeed, that there was not a realistic prospect of conviction - at least, not until we engaged the services of an eminent child psychologist. The lady in question was North American or Canadian and relatively young, but had a lot of experience in being involved in this sort of case. She proceeded to look at the evidence, watch the video interviews with the children and, ultimately, interview the children in person. I suppose her conclusion was not an enormous surprise, but she advised us that in her opinion, and from her experience, all the children were fabricating their accounts.

Having sought an expert opinion on the truthfulness of the children, we really had no option now but to accept her opinion and drop the case. We were very close now to the scheduled trial date at Newcastle Crown Court and an exit strategy had to be quickly planned. This was going to be difficult, as the case had generated very high emotions, not only amongst the children's families but also in the immediate locality of the defendants' homes. There was some potential for eruption of violence once the decision not to proceed became known. It was decided to delay informing the children's families until the morning of the trial and for a police presence to be introduced in the vicinity of the defendants' homes, for that day and the following day at least.

What followed was, for me, one of the most stressful experiences of my life! The prosecution team - both counsel, me and the senior investigating police officer- gathered in a meeting room at the court. The families were brought in and seated, clearly quite oblivious as to what was about to take place. David Robson imparted the information to them in a quietly-spoken and sensitive way, including a full explanation for our decision. It was alarming, however, to observe the reactions of the parents as it slowly dawned on them that there was to be no trial - at first bewildered, then incredulous, and finally angry and strident. Fortunately they did not become abusive or violent, although I was concerned this might happen. Their venom was largely directed at the child psychologist, whom they had met, and for whom they clearly had no time, but who was fortunately absent on this occasion!

After the parents had trooped angrily from the room, we left to go into court. Counsel had already alerted the judge earlier that morning as to what was to happen, and defence counsel were told just before the hearing commenced, so that the defendants did not become aware before the families of the 'victims'. The hearing took the rest of the morning - David Robson carefully and thoroughly explaining the rationale for the decision not to proceed, and defence counsel all having their 'four-penn'orth'. I was expecting the CPS, and particularly myself, to come in for some strong criticism. I needn't have worried. David Robson went out of his way to assert that I had "no option" but to advise charges and let the case proceed as far as it had; and neither the defence nor the judge was critical of the prosecution in any way. The prospect of violence in Bishop Auckland also proved to be a 'damp squib'.

Such were the highlights of my twenty-two-month stay in the Special Casework Unit. There was one last piece of excitement, however, before I departed. One of the Sayers gang was shot at with a pistol on the quayside in Newcastle and I found myself prosecuting the alleged culprit for Attempted Murder and firearms offences.

Kingsley had to back off from the case because of his enduring campaign against the Sayers. There were "old-fashioned" committal proceedings in Newcastle Magistrates' Court, which I conducted, my opponent being Chris Prince, then a junior counsel, now the Recorder of Durham (i.e. the senior judge in Durham Crown Court). The defendant was sent for trial to the Crown Court and one of my last acts was to draft the brief to prosecuting counsel, Paul Batty QC (now the resident judge in Carlisle Crown Court and the Honorary Recorder of Carlisle).

* * *

As well as my casework responsibilities, I was also the "lead" in CPS North for issues of Disclosure of Unused Material. This meant that I had to fairly swiftly make myself an "expert" on the subject, which was fast becoming a very important topic in the criminal justice process. It was also a growth industry, with cases and learned articles being generated left, right and centre. I found that it was to take up a lot of my time, constantly fielding questions from our lawyers all over the Area, liaising with the police and delivering training to police and prosecutors. Despite this, by the time of my departure my experience was that many of our prosecutors hadn't really grasped the essentials of how to handle unused material, and defence practitioners either didn't grasp them either or didn't want to grasp them - they were keen to demand disclosure of all sorts of material, but without considering whether those demands could be justified. Most police officers were even less aware of what it was all about! But even twenty years later it is a subject that is still not clearly understood by many in the criminal justice system, and cases are still being lost because of failure to disclose material that should have been disclosed!

* * *

By the summer of 1995 there had been a number of changes of personnel in the upper echelons of CPS North and there was a need to 'shuffle the pack'. Dicky Dickinson had moved on to head up CPS Yorkshire, where our old friend Duncan Sharp had been the Chief Crown Prosecutor and, having been awarded his CBE, had decided to call it a day and take early retirement! I do not know what Duncan had done to earn himself this honour, any more than any other person in the CPS of his status or experience that is! But then a number of people in the organisation are singled out every year for the same or similar award and it never seems apparent to me how they are any more deserving than anyone else in the CPS! You could perhaps make a case for Kingsley Hyland, just, but it is beyond me how one of my contemporaries in Derbyshire, Anna Zimand, came to earn her 'gong': she joined the CPS at much the same time as myself and reached the same grade as myself but, beyond that, she was just another employee doing a job for which she was paid, like the rest of us. I do not think for a moment that I ever deserved to be honoured in this way and I never coveted any such honour, but it has always seemed to me that it very much diminishes the value and significance of the honours system if awards are handed out, apparently, on the basis of 'Buggins' turn' rather than for achieving any notable distinction at work or outside work, or for doing something above and beyond the call of duty!

I digress, however! With Dicky gone my boss, Mike Graham, was elevated to the position of Chief Crown Prosecutor, CPS North. As far as I was concerned this was richly deserved and he was the best man for the job, despite his inexperience at senior management level. Mike, in fact, was not replaced in his previous role but nonetheless continued to keep a guiding hand on the tiller of the Special Casework Unit.

Paul Grieveson, who had been the head of the Tyneside Branch, had left the CPS, temporarily at least, and set up as a sole practitioner in Wallsend, and his opposite number in the Wearside Branch was about to retire. At this point, Mike persuaded me that my management experience ought to be brought to bear in a Branch Crown Prosecutor role and, somewhat reluctantly, I agreed to head-up the Northumbria and North Tyneside Branch in place of George Morley, who was transferred to the Wearside Branch.

* * *

I had found my stay in the Special Casework Unit a very fulfilling experience and I was determined not to become a desk-bound administrator, as my predecessor had clearly been. The branch office was at Cramlington, seven or eight miles north of the city and the Tyne Tunnel, and I found that George had organised for himself a large office with an expensive and attractive suite of furniture. Within a few days of my being at Cramlington I received a telephone call from Mike Graham. "Dick," he said, very plaintively, "Would you mind swapping your office furniture with George?" I decided to play 'hardball'. "Oh," I said, "I didn't realise that George actually owned this furniture!" "He doesn't," said Mike, "But he can't live with the furniture in his new office and he's complaining." It would "get him off my back," he said. I thought this was really pathetic, and I'm sure a less easygoing fellow than Mike would have told George exactly that. However, in the interests of management team harmony, I agreed to the exchange and told Mike he "owed me one!" (The 'debt' was to be repaid in the not-too-distant future!). The distinctly down-market furniture from Wearside arrived a day or two later, and my superior chair, desk and conference table were whisked away. I suppose, as he spent so much time in his office, George needed something more comfortable and ornate!

There were about forty or forty-five staff at Cramlington, lawyers, Crown Court caseworkers and admin. They were, to a man and woman, an extremely friendly and likeable bunch. Not a bad egg amongst them. I was only there for four months, but it was a most agreeable experience. There was, however, a definite laxity amongst the systems and working practices and, to my horror, I discovered that there were between eighty and a hundred pieces of post that had not been matched up to case files, some of the correspondence being weeks old and never dealt with. I have always regarded a failure to reply to letters within, say, five working days at the outside as very unprofessional and totally unacceptable, and here we were sitting on an enormous pile of unanswered correspondence. I discovered that George Morley had been aware of this, but had left it to the staff to deal with and had never apparently checked to see if they had done so! I immediately set about getting people to do holding replies to the letters and then organised two Saturday-morning working parties to tie up post to files and allocate to lawyers to do substantive replies to letters. I made sure I was involved in both overtime sessions and did my fair share of responses also. Within four weeks we had reduced the backlog to acceptable proportions, but dealing expeditiously with correspondence was still a problem when I left. It was also a problem I found later in Cumbria and there has always been, it seems to me, a lack of urgency in dealing with incoming letters, whether they come from police, defence or private citizens. Not a failing confined to the CPS but, nonetheless, unacceptable.

Whilst I was at Cramlington I made sure I got to court at least once a week and that I had a personal caseload. I was also still partially involved in cases that I had left behind in the Special Casework Unit. The level of my involvement in the core business was obviously a novelty to the staff in the branch but, from the feedback I was getting, one that they welcomed and admired!

All too soon, however, my sojourn at Cramlington was over, albeit in an acceptable way for me. My opposite number in the Cumbria branch, Ken Hay, had decided that, after many years, he had had his fill of being a manager and had persuaded Mike Graham to let him transfer to the vacancy that had now cropped up in the Special Casework Unit. I had always hankered after returning to the lakes and mountains, and I now saw the opportunity. The ever-amenable Mike Graham, no doubt recalling my co-operation over the office furniture issue four months before, was happy to accommodate me and, in November 1995, I was on my way back to Cumbria as Branch Crown Prosecutor, working out of the Carlisle office. It was "management" again, but I convinced myself that I would be able to do the job in my own way and it was sufficiently far away from Area HQ not to have senior management breathing down my neck...

CHAPTER ELEVEN

1995 to 1999: Back to Cumbria

My second term in Cumbria began in November 1995 - as Branch Crown Prosecutor, managing about fifty to fifty-five staff spread over four offices across the county. The Branch office was to be found on the first floor of a building opposite the cathedral in Carlisle. At this time the office was a warren of separate offices, but that was soon to change. The 'sub-offices' were located at the other three extreme points of the county, at Workington, Barrow and Kendal, just as they had been when I was last in the area in 1989, although not necessarily in the same buildings. As they did then, the office locations coincided with the location of the four police divisional headquarters, but no longer by this time with the magistrates' court areas as there were now just three magistrates' clerks, one in the west, one at Carlisle and one covering the east and south of the county.

We had twenty-one or twenty-two lawyers, divided amongst the four offices, and each team led by a Principal Crown Prosecutor; there were half a dozen Crown Court caseworkers, a Branch Office manager, and the remainder of the staff were admin officers of various grades.

Within days of starting, I hit the road and met or renewed acquaintance with, as the case may be, all the CPS staff, magistrates' clerks and police divisional commanders across the county.

As far as our people were concerned, I knew most of them from before and some I had known many years. There was a fairly experienced team of lawyers at Carlisle, the team leader, David Hansford, having been in the CPS probably as long as I had. There was a husband and wife team as well in Peter and Julia Bailey, and here I inherited a problem with which I was never able to deal successfully. They were totally symbiotic, and had been permitted to share an office since they had been together in the Branch. Later on it became necessary to billet a caseworker in their 'space'; this did not go down well and the 'intruder' was made to feel just that! Several times I tried to contrive to split them up under the guise of "restructuring" the office, but I failed to do this on any permanent basis; and several times I tried to encourage Area management to move one to another branch when the occasion presented itself (they lived in Northumbria, in fact, so were closer to Cramlington or Newcastle than to Carlisle). All of us agreed that the situation was unhealthy, but Area seemed no more able than I was to take the decisive step! So they carried on working together, quite literally, as it seemed highly likely Peter did much of Julia's review work and committal preparation so Julia could get on with domestic tasks!

The other not entirely dissimilar local problem I inherited involved David Hansford and his opposite number at Workington, Linda Vance. Although they did not, apparently, live together, or not on a full-time basis in any event, they were an 'item' (and are, I believe, to this day!). Again this presented an unhealthy situation. At branch management team meetings, for example, they would always have a united front, they would always 'come from the same place', and this would often make things difficult in such meetings. They would, of course, always want holidays at the same time and they always managed to claim their respective times off so far ahead that it was impossible to refuse their leave applications. They were always on the phone to each other, giving the impression of hatching one plot or another! Ultimately, their 'togetherness' would create a far more serious difficulty for me and Area Management.

The lawyers at the other three offices were no less experienced than those at Carlisle - indeed it seemed that no-one ever left Cumbria! There was, in fact, significant continuity amongst all the staff members across the Branch and, at this time anyway, there were rarely any vacancies on the teams.

Yet another problem I inherited, however, was that of an imbalance between the four teams, largely in terms of lawyers. The Kendal team had one more lawyer than the Workington team in 1995, despite Workington having a much greater caseload. This disparity was the source of much friction between the two teams. It stemmed from the visit previously of a team from headquarters which had been tasked to visit Cumbria and carry out some sort of needs analysis in terms of lawyer resources. I learnt that, as ever, they had completely underestimated travelling times and distances in the county and had arrived at Workington very late one winter's afternoon and had scrimped the exercise in their urgency to get away, resulting in a miscalculation of the Workington office caseload! Hence they advised Area that the western office didn't warrant as many lawyers as the eastern one. They had apparently got the eastern calculation wrong as well!

The imbalance was very obvious to me, but how to cure it was not as obvious. All the Kendal lawyers lived close to Kendal, so simply to transfer one to Workington would have been oppressive, not to mention expensive, as we would have had to pay out a lot of excess travelling expenses. Eventually I managed to persuade Area that we should recruit another lawyer to Workington, which at least mitigated the problem. In the short term I did most of my personal court attendance in the west and drew most of my personal caseload from there in order to alleviate the situation!

We also had a pretty experienced hand of Crown Court caseworkers at this time. Three worked from the Carlisle office and there was one at each of the sub-offices. The Workington-based caseworker had an interesting pedigree. His name was John Churchill. Facially and physically he closely resembled Winston of that ilk and was, indeed, related to the Duke of Marlborough! He always gave the impression that he felt himself cut out for better things, and he was often quite dismissive of less experienced caseworkers. We had one, Jane Mackrill, who had graduated from being a clerk/typist and, by her own efforts, to becoming a caseworker. John, behind her back, referred to her as a "jufty". We discovered this meant "a jumped-up fucking typist". Jane found out about this but, with typical good humour, never made any sort of issue out of it! She had the last laugh in any event, because she graduated in due course to become one of Cumbria's first "associate prosecutors", something to which I am sure John could not have aspired. As it was, he eventually gave up hope of ever progressing further in the CPS and left to teach English in Dubai, or some such place!

* * *

When I moved back to Cumbria in November 1995, I was tasked by Area Management to oversee and implement two major initiatives. The first was yet another CPS centrally-driven and inspired scheme known as "Team Working" and, like many other national initiatives, it came in with fanfares and a blaze of publicity and then quietly died a year or two later, mourned by very few!

"Team-working" had been the brainchild of some outsider who had been appointed to the hierarchy of CPS national HQ and whose name I have long since forgotten. He was not a lawyer, but either someone recruited from the business world or a career civil servant from another department. He clearly had no idea how the CPS worked on the ground, but nonetheless came up with this wonderful way of working which he managed to sell to the DPP and her deputies. I cannot now remember all the details of the scheme but, basically, I believe it worked on the basis that local CPS units were too compartmentalised and that things would be much more efficient if admin, caseworkers and lawyers worked together as a "team" when dealing with casework. The most obvious feature of the scheme was that when committal papers were being prepared for cases that were going to the Crown Court, the lawyer and the caseworker should prepare them in tandem or, more frequently, the caseworker should prepare them and then the lawyer would vet them afterwards. The obvious drawbacks to this were twofold: firstly, because of the demands of court attendance, lawyers and caseworkers would rarely be in the office at the same time in order to allow them to collude; secondly, the caseworkers were not lawyers and did not have the training, the aptitude or the inclination to put committal papers together, draft indictments, make decisions about evidence, deal with unused material, etc.

The scheme had been piloted in the Tyneside Branch of our Area and, as a prelude to its implementation, many thousands of pounds had been spent in knocking down walls and partitions to create an open-plan environment so that "team-working" could flourish, as clearly it wouldn't work if lawyers were shut away in separate and secluded offices!! The tearing-down of walls in Cumbria, however, had to be delayed for a little while, as Area Management were preoccupied at this time in the search for new office premises for themselves after some ne'er-do-well threw a fire-bomb through the windows of Benton House, leaving the building gutted by fire. Fortunately, the attack occurred during the night when the building was unoccupied. As far as I am aware, no one was ever brought to book for the offence.

Eventually, at some time in 1996, the moment arrived and the builders came into the Carlisle office and destroyed the rabbit warren of offices, leaving us with an office for me and a small conference room, the rest of the floor space being open-plan. There was, however, no other building work required at the offices in the rest of Cumbria. Workington office was already open-plan. The Barrow office was also open-plan, having moved from the antediluvian quarters next to the Unemployment Office and the nightclub some years previously. The Kendal team was situated in Kendal courthouse, and I don't think alterations to the internal structure of the building were feasible at this time.

The alterations at Carlisle pleased no one there and no one could see any benefits of the scheme itself. The author of "Team-working" did make one visit to the office and waxed lyrical, if unconvincingly, about "Team-working" and then hurriedly departed without meeting most of the lawyers and the staff.

I cannot say the scheme was a success. But then I cannot say it was unsuccessful either. The plain truth is that we never actually implemented it and no one ever came to see if we were working it. I was never really asked by Area HQ how it was progressing. Within a year the word "team-working" had disappeared from the lexicon of CPS terminology and we continued on our merry way as if it had never been!

It's not that our way of working was perfect - it wasn't. For me the obvious defect was the continuing way the lawyers did not become involved in Crown Court cases after they left the magistrates' court. "Team-working", however, was a misconceived and half-baked initiative. It was not to be the last!

* * *

The second initiative was a locally-driven one. Area Management had been unhappy from the outset with the structure of the Cumbria Branch. I agreed with their views. Having four separate teams in four separate offices was an expensive and inefficient state of affairs. Every week we were reminded of how inefficient the arrangement was. Basically, the teams were not self-sufficient. The demands of holidays, sickness, training, etc. meant that a team never had a full complement at any time and, a good deal of the time, were two lawyers short or two admin staff light. Other teams then had to supply one or more of their number in order to make up the shortfall so that courts could be covered and the work done. It was a constant fight to keep the operation afloat.

At first glance this might seem surprising when you consider that we were running the Barrow office, for example, only six years before with three lawyers and two back-up staff. Now the Barrow team had five lawyers, a caseworker and five admin staff! There were certainly several differences from 1989: there were more courts to cover; although the caseload was no greater, the requirements of detailed and recorded review of cases, and the demands of indictment drafting and particularly that of dealing with unused material, meant that lawyers had to spend far more time in the office than hitherto; and the increasing need for training and the number of training courses constantly took lawyers, and other staff, away from the office far more often than previously. The net result was that although on paper, and certainly across the Branch as a whole, we did have sufficient resources to do the job, the individual teams were, in reality, too small to be entirely viable.

It was apparent to anyone, therefore, that the structure was wrong for 1995 and that the obvious answer was to have two teams, or even only one, in the Branch. This would give economies of scale and would also lead to significant savings in terms of accommodation and accommodation running costs. There would be increased costs in travelling expenses and, in the short term, the costs also of transferring staff from one centre to another, but these costs would be far outweighed in a year or two by the overall savings to be made.

I was therefore tasked by Mike Graham with producing a blueprint for "restructuring". Ken Hay had already done a good deal of the preparatory work, presenting the alternatives and costing them up. He had, however, shrunk from identifying what he thought was the best option and was even tentatively suggesting that the *status quo* was to be preferred. The *status quo*, however, was not an option for Area Management. I made use of Ken's figures and drew up a paper putting forward the option of a two-team branch as the best way forward. This, in fact, seemed to me to be the only sensible option, as to have only one team would present great difficulties in terms of locating an office and travelling in a large geographical area, where getting about was difficult at the best of times.

I did my work covertly, as I did not want to panic staff unnecessarily into believing that change was imminent, as such changes were inevitably going to be very unpopular with many of them. What I was proposing was a team in the north and a team in the south, in effect combining the Carlisle and Workington teams and the Barrow and Kendal teams respectively. It would be necessary, however, to find new accommodation or secure expansion in existing buildings to house the new teams. It seemed to me that the arrangements would permit some reduction in the number of lawyers and admin staff, such reduction to be obtained by natural wastage.

Area Management professed great enthusiasm for the proposals, and I was asked to draw up another paper selling the proposals to staff and inviting comments. This I did. That, however, was the last I heard of the plans! I don't know whether Area Management got cold feet or whether national HQ had vetoed the idea, but I never did find out why it didn't happen. To my mind, however, it was inevitable that such a plan would come into being one day and so it did, albeit fourteen years down the line!

⋆ ⋆ ⋆

As the Branch Crown Prosecutor, I soon found that my time was not my own to do with as I wished! There were meetings and more meetings to attend, and the number of meetings escalated as time went on.

As a member of the Area Management Team, I was required to attend the monthly meetings of this team in Newcastle. These would last all day. Whilst the meetings were necessary, some of the topics on the agenda were not, in my opinion. As I had found in London, national HQ required each Area to devise and implement an Area "Business Plan", which was to set out how it was to operate as an Area, set targets and objectives, etc., etc.. I had to contribute to this and also devise a Branch Business Plan to dovetail in with the Area plan. The plans had to be regularly updated. All this took a great deal of time and it was clearly not for the benefit of the Area or the Branch because, once the plans or their updates had been delivered to the national HQ, we forgot about them! The Branch Business Plan lay in my desk drawer gathering dust, and I never ever made any reference to it other than to carry out the periodic updates - a complete waste of time.

I also had to attend monthly meetings in Newcastle with the Area Administrator to discuss the Branch budget, which I was responsible, in theory at least, for administering. These meetings never took more than twenty minutes and often less, and could quite easily have taken place on the phone!

In the Branch we had monthly Branch team meetings, attended by myself with the four team leaders, the Branch office manager and the caseworker manager. These, again, were necessary meetings, but I tried as much as possible to keep their duration down to a morning.

As in London, there were court-user meetings. However, I soon decided that I did not need to attend these regularly as the matters for discussion were really between the local managers. I did, however, attend occasional meetings with the three magistrates' clerks when there were matters for discussion that affected all the courts in the county.

Similarly, I left the matter of liaison with local police commanders largely to the local team leaders, unless they specifically wanted me to be with them.

One meeting I was more or less obliged to attend was the Carlisle Crown Court User meeting, as this was chaired by the resident judge. Prior to 1999 my knowledge of how the Crown Court worked was not great, and I relied on the senior caseworker to make most of the running in these meetings. There were generally no issues of any great moment which arose, however, and the group met only four times a year.

The only real 'high-level' meeting I had to attend regularly was definitely the most pointless and unproductive, in my view. Once every five or six weeks there was a meeting, at police headquarters in Penrith, of the Chief Constable, the Director of Social Services, the Chief Probation Officer, one of the Magistrates' Clerks and myself. Ken Hay had dubbed the meeting "the knitting circle". This was an apt title, since what we did was to sit round and discuss various highbrow and academic topics which had no bearing at all on the operation of the criminal justice system in Cumbria. As far as I can recall there was no agenda; no actions came out of the meetings and no-one brought anything to the meetings. I never understood what purpose the meeting served other than to operate as a vehicle for the non-operational members of the group to air their uninteresting views on one airy-fairy subject or another. Fortunately, after the then Chief Constable retired and the then Director of Social Services 'resigned' her post following a massive budget overspend in her department, the meetings withered on the vine and died an unlamented death; unlamented by me, anyway!

There was at this time a seemingly unending series of initiatives being generated by criminal justice groups at national level, often spearheaded by the CPS. These were passed down to local level, and we in the Cumbria criminal justice system were expected to implement them. Naturally this required more meetings!

One such initiative was for the police and the CPS to monitor each other's performance and meetings were, of course, required in order to give each other feedback. It also required us to keep reams of statistics on timeliness of file submission by the police to CPS, so that we could confront them with their shortcomings and they would faithfully promise to shake up their systems so that they would improve their performance. This was known as "Joint Performance Management" or JPM (we became inundated with acronyms!). I cannot remember now what aspects of CPS performance in particular were under the microscope but, if there were expected to be improvements in timeliness of file submission by the police, it was a vain hope. To this day, or certainly when I left the CPS, the single enduring failing by police in Cumbria, and almost certainly everywhere else, was their inability to deliver files of evidence to the CPS within acceptable time limits in many, many cases.

Then we were asked to devise and implement an agreement between local agencies in the criminal justice system to provide a service to witnesses and victims - a Witness Care Agreement, no less. Yours truly was volunteered by Area Management to chair the Cumbrian group and to drive forward the initiative towards a formal agreement. Lots more meetings, of course!! These would involve a chief inspector, the Clerk of the Crown Court, a magistrates' clerk, Victim Support and others. It proved almost impossible to get all the parties together at regular intervals and, in the end, I found the easiest way was to draft the agreement myself and circulate it for comment. Comments were thin on the ground, so either the document was perfect or not everyone actually read it in any detail! I suspect the latter! Anyway, we had the agreement signed at a ceremony at police headquarters, and many bound copies were sent out or made readily available for inspection. I gave an interview to Radio Cumbria.

In theory, an agreement signed by all the agencies, committing themselves to minimum standards of conduct and service in their dealings with victims and witnesses, was an excellent thing. Or it would have been if we had all honoured the terms of the agreement. This was never going to happen, however. Courts, and the Crown Court in particular, may join such inter-agency groups and sign up to agreements which emerge from discussions but, in my experience, do not regard themselves as bound by the agreement in practice. The courts have other needs, such as making the best use of the time of judges and magistrates, which will always take priority over the interests of witnesses, victims, defendants or anybody else. Thus, although courts might agree on paper to, say, the attendance of witnesses at court being staggered so that they are not waiting around too long to give their evidence, they don't like it if the judiciary is kept waiting because the next witness has not yet arrived at court! The courts will pay lip service to "witness care", but that is as far as it goes.

There were many other meetings locally, regular and irregular, *ad hoc* and otherwise, which apparently required my attendance. Looking back, it is difficult to see how anything much was achieved by many of them. If they hadn't taken place I am quite sure the criminal justice system would have been no worse off, and all they did was to take people away from doing what they should have been doing, or certainly in my case.

Then there were the national meetings, and these ate even more deeply into one's time. For example, suddenly in about 1997, national management decided they needed the input of Branch Crown Prosecutors around the country into various focus groups that were convened. Month after month for about a year, I found myself summoned down to London to meet with others in groups to discuss such topics as domestic violence, child abuse, etc. For me and, no doubt, many others, this involved the best part of two days away from the office and an overnight stay in London. To this day I do not understand what was achieved by this exercise, which must have cost the Service an enormous amount of taxpayers' money.

Then there was a "conference" of all Branch Crown Prosecutors at a *Ramada* hotel near Heathrow. Six of us flew down from

Newcastle Airport for two days, stopping in a hotel which I think cost about £140 a night just for bed and breakfast, let alone the full board which we received. The overall cost must have been astronomical. Very interesting to meet colleagues from elsewhere and swap tales, but surely totally unjustifiable expense!

⋆ ⋆ ⋆

Despite the oppressive demands of the 'meetings culture' I was determined to make a full contribution to the core business of the Branch, and not to waste what skills I had as a lawyer and an advocate. I therefore made a point of going to court at least once, if not twice a week, and of carrying a personal caseload of serious casework.

Although I went as frequently as I could to Barrow and Kendal courts, most of my advocacy was done in Carlisle, Workington and Whitehaven courts, as this was where our resources were most stretched.

There was an interesting collection of defence advocates which practised in these courts at these times. In the west, our Workington advocates had been jousting for years with Joe Kelly and Kevin Commons, and they were still dominating the scene in 1995/6.

Joe Kelly was a paradox. Out of court he was charming and generous to a fault. In court he could be aggressive and downright rude. He treated the court with something close to disdain. He was often pointedly disrespectful to the magistrates and the clerk, and thought nothing of openly criticising their decisions if he did not agree with them. He seemed to get away with this sort of approach, no doubt because he had been appearing in these courts for so long and was given a good deal of latitude as a result. Outrageous statements were the norm, and unorthodox tactics and scant regard for the laws of evidence and procedure an almost daily occurrence. As a prosecutor one had to be forever vigilant when Joe was one's opponent, and one never quite knew what was coming next. There was never a dull moment, but it could be quite stressful at times trying to anticipate his next move or trying to counter his more outlandish tactics and assertions! Very sadly, Joe became afflicted, probably only in his early fifties, with what may have been Parkinson's disease. He carried on beyond what he should have done and, before he finally gave up his advocacy, he had become rambling and incoherent, and a sad shadow of his former self.

Kevin Commons was a much more conventional advocate but an eloquent and formidable opponent. He had been a court clerk in Workington Magistrates' Court in earlier times and had then left to set up his own practice. By 1995 he had a large and expanding business and, in due course, it became the largest criminal practice in Cumbria. As his business expanded, so Kevin himself began to take more of a back seat as far as advocacy was concerned, and he had a host of assistant solicitors who gradually took over that role in the magistrates' courts. Eventually the firm, Kevin J Commons and Co, had offices in Workington, Whitehaven and Carlisle and was doing a significant amount of criminal defence advocacy in all three courts. Reputedly, Kevin and his partner, Marcus Nixon, were not easy people to work for and there was always a steady turnover of assistant solicitors in the firm, at least three of them in due course joining the CPS.

Kevin himself was one of the first solicitors in Cumbria to qualify as a Higher Courts Advocate. To my knowledge, he never made use of the qualification but it adorned his headed notepaper and, no doubt, was calculated to impress would-be clients. I imagine this was the real object of the exercise in obtaining the qualification! What Kevin did do, however, was assume sole responsibility for the firm's Crown Court work and, for ten to twelve years, I had many 'interesting' telephone conversations with him about pending Crown Court cases. His approach was what you might call "direct", his language colourful, blunt and earthy, but he was always ready to 'do business' in appropriate cases, and I have no doubt that his clients always took his advice! There were never any introductory pleasantries when he rang up - it was straight to the point: "Case of …. You'll never get a conviction for a fucking section 18. But the twat would plead to a 20!" We "settled" many cases in short, unsophisticated telephone conversations!

Sadly, Kevin was another who did not live to enjoy his retirement. In his case, however, it was not the demon drink that did for him - he was more or less abstinent in this regard. He was the victim of one of his own clients. On 2nd June 2010 he was gunned down on his own driveway, the second victim of the notorious Derrick Bird, who had already killed his own brother that morning and went on to murder another ten people that day before turning his firearm on himself. Although we will never know the precise reasons, it seemed that Bird was aggrieved about the content of his mother's will. Kevin was the solicitor acting for the family in the matter. Most of the killings were clearly random, but Kevin and the brother were more obviously targeted by Bird.

There was one victim of the "lawyers' curse" in West Cumbria in this period. Rowland Earl was a sole practitioner with offices in, I think three different locations in the area. It was never clear, in fact, how he circumvented the Law Society's rules, which required the permanent presence of a solicitor in each office maintained by a firm. The Law Society was, apparently, just about to pay him a visit when, shortly before they were due, he was found in his car one morning on a remote fell road, having ended his life courtesy of a length of hose connected to the exhaust. When the Law Society subsequently took over his practice it was discovered that a good deal of clients' money was missing.

There were a number of very good advocates in West Cumbria at this time but, in my view, the best was John Dugan. He, too, was one of the first solicitors in Cumbria to qualify as a Higher Courts Advocate but, in his case he actually began to appear regularly in the Crown Court in Carlisle as an advocate. In my first-hand experience he was at least as able and as competent as any of the barristers who featured regularly in that court at this time, and more so than most. Had he carried on, I am sure that he would have made a considerable success of Crown Court advocacy. Unfortunately, his Crown Court career was cut short by health problems which greatly affected his mobility, and he was obliged to give up this part of his work. A great loss!

* * *

In Carlisle, too, there were a number of solicitors who became Higher Courts Advocates, giving them the same rights of audience in the higher criminal courts as barristers.

Malcolm Dodds was another early "qualifier" and certainly, in the early part of the 21st century, he was a regular advocate in Carlisle Crown Court, and then more sporadically thereafter. He may, or may not, have been discouraged by one early experience he had in front of the then senior judge in Carlisle Crown Court, His Honour Judge Robert Brown. Malcolm was defending a man charged with Dangerous Driving and the case was proceeding as a trial before judge and jury. At the end of the prosecution evidence, Malcolm asked the judge to send the jury out so that he could make a submission that there was no case to answer and that the case should therefore proceed no further. The submission would have been misconceived, as there was clearly a case to go to the jury, but Judge Brown would not even allow Malcolm to make his application, dismissing him in front of the jury with a curt "Don't be so foolish, Mr Dodds," or words to that effect. This must have been a humiliating experience for Malcolm, and his Crown Court appearances were less frequent after that.

Malcolm Dodds, in fact, did not often have trials for his clients, even in the magistrates' court. His clients invariably pleaded 'guilty' to something, even if it was not the original charge. The one trial I was involved in with him, however, led to the same sort of abortive application that he had made in the Crown Court in the case referred to above. This was a case in Barrow Magistrates' Court. A policewoman was alleged to have caused an accident by going through a red traffic-light. There were at least two independent witnesses to this contravention and, although the defendant was later found 'not guilty', there was manifestly a case to answer. This, however, did not stop Malcolm making a submission at the end of the prosecution case that there was not a case to answer. The submission was as misconceived as the one in the Crown Court, although the magistrates did at least listen to it before rejecting it! I am not sure what induced Malcolm to make such hopeless applications - perhaps if he had conducted more trials he might have appreciated that they were a waste of time?!

There were quite a few sole practitioners like Malcolm Dodds carrying out criminal work in Carlisle. One of the unusual features, however, was that several of them had banded together in a sort of "chambers" so that, although they were separate practices, they shared a building and, apparently, secretarial resources, etc. Most of these also became Higher Courts Advocates in due course and appeared in the Crown Court to a greater or lesser extent - solicitors like Patrick Shimmin, John Smith, Margaret Payne and Mike Reay.

Another sole practitioner who appeared at this time was one David Allen, who then disappeared as abruptly as he had first appeared and apparently leaving no indication of his whereabouts. I don't know if there was a police investigation or whether the Law Society found any evidence of dishonesty, but it was certainly a mysterious occurrence!

One instance where the "lawyers' curse" had struck, however, was in relation to another sole practitioner, Geoff Clapp, who was probably the busiest criminal advocate on the defence side in the city, at least in the magistrates' court, where he appeared on a daily basis. Geoff had been in partnership with one Bill McKenna.

When the latter died it was apparently discovered that the firm had massive debts as a result of his activities. Even if he wanted to retire, Geoff probably had to keep working and, to my knowledge, was doing so into his seventies, despite a couple of severe health warnings. He may still be working even now.

Geoff Clapp was the "Joe Kelly" of Carlisle. Like Joe, he had an in-court and an out-of-court personality which were totally different from each other. Out of court he was affable, generous and solicitous. I had one very obvious reminder of his virtues one day, when he rang me in the office from Wigton Court. Our prosecutor there, Peter Bailey, had been taken ill. Geoff had taken it upon himself to look after Peter and also arrange to have all his outstanding cases adjourned.

In court, like Joe Kelly, Geoff often displayed a familiarity with the magistrates that bordered on disdain. He was invariably dismissive of, and aggressive to the point of rudeness towards, his opponent in court. He also had this irritating habit of 'personalising' his opponent. As an advocate, one would usually refer to one's opponent as "my friend" or "my learned friend", or just the "prosecutor" or the "prosecution". There is a way of doing things which keeps exchanges between advocates on a detached level and above the personal. Geoff's tendency, however, was to refer to the opposing advocate by name and make it appear that, as a prosecutor, you had a personal vindictiveness towards his client – e.g. "Mr Binstead wants you to lock up my client because he says that he will commit further offences..." This totally failed to take account of the fact that the prosecutor was an impartial and independent advocate and not someone with a personal grudge against the defendant! As an advocate, at least, Geoff's approach did not endear him to many of the CPS advocates!

* * *

As far as my personal caseload was concerned, the demands of the job meant that my capacity to handle casework was limited. However, I resolved early on that I would do as much as I could. From the first, therefore, I took on the responsibility of dealing with all the cases in the Branch that arose from fatal road accidents and all potential and actual prosecutions of police officers. Occasionally, there were also other individual cases that I felt warranted my involvement.

In the event, I dealt with almost all fatal road traffic cases for the next thirteen years from 1995, inevitably developing a degree of expertise in handling these very sensitive and sometimes difficult cases. I also built up a very close working relationship with the police Accident Investigation Unit at police HQ. This unit comprised the "experts" who went to the scene of road accidents, examined the scene in detail, analysed physical and witness evidence, and gave opinions on the cause of accidents. Their expertise and opinion were crucial to decision-making in such cases. In time the unit changed its name to "Collision" Investigation Unit –this, I believe, was intended to show more sensitivity to the victims of such occurrences who were blameless and might, therefore, be unfairly stigmatised by being described as being involved in an "accident".

The number of road traffic fatalities per annum in Cumbria varied over this period, ranging from almost one a week at one time to less than half that in later years. Leaving aside those incidents where there was only one vehicle involved and, therefore, no 'live' potential defendant, every case needed a decision on whether there should be a prosecution or not. The completed files of evidence came to me, and in many cases I had consultation with the investigating officers and the Collision Investigation Unit before advising. The first decision was whether there was a realistic prospect of conviction for any offence against any person. If there was, then prosecution would normally follow unless it was one of those cases where the deceased was a close relative of the defendant and the potential charge was no more than Driving without Due Care and Attention. We called these "Nearest and Dearest" cases and, in these circumstances, there was likely to be no public interest in prosecuting, say, a man who had lost his wife.

The more difficult decision was the level of charge. There were two choices - Driving without Due Care and Attention or Death by Dangerous Driving, assuming that the death was the result of the manner of driving. For the latter, the manner of driving had to be likely to cause serious injury to other road-users or serious damage to property and to fall far below the standard expected of the safe and competent driver. The decision was sometimes obvious, sometimes marginal, but the police and I always managed to reach a consensus, and we were invariably vindicated by the ultimate outcome when we chose the more serious offence. Most defendants pleaded 'guilty' to whatever we charged; where they went to trial, most were convicted of the specific charge they faced. Although I say it myself, it was a history of successful collaboration and decision-making.

Many of the prosecutions I undertook myself. Most of those for Due Care I conducted in the magistrates' court, to full trial where necessary. Once I acquired rights of audience in the Crown Court after 1999, I took the cases there also, although I never managed to take one to actual trial. In cases of Causing Death by Dangerous Driving there were detailed sentencing guidelines to be observed by the sentencing judge, and the judge would expect the prosecutor to be able to draw attention to all the aggravating features of the offence and identify into which bracket the case fell for sentencing purposes.

The other aspect of handling such cases was dealing with the next of kin and family of the deceased. Eventually there was a victim's code laid down by the CPS which necessitated early contact with the family by the prosecutor, explaining decision-making and offering a meeting with the police and prosecutor, including counsel where instructed. Long before this formal procedure was introduced, I had developed my own process for dealing with next of kin and family. As soon as a decision had been made about prosecuting or not prosecuting, I would contact the next of kin in writing, providing my details and inviting contact or a meeting, or both. I learnt early on not to ring a next of kin direct, as some did not want any contact or engagement with the prosecution and court process. I managed to upset one widower, whose wife had been killed in a collision near Ambleside, by telephoning him. He simply did not want to know what was going on and did not welcome my intrusion into his life. I did not make this mistake again. In most cases, however, I found that the family were keen to be involved in events as they unfolded, usually by my keeping them abreast with developments by phone, and most of them wanted to be at court whenever there was a hearing and to meet me there as well as the police family liaison officer who had been allocated to their case. I found that I was devoting a lot of time to this sort of contact, often well out of office hours, but it seemed to me to be proper and worthwhile and I got a lot of satisfaction out of keeping families in the loop and explaining decisions which had been taken, court procedures and likely outcomes.

Whilst it is fair to say that most next of kin or family members were reasonable people, inevitably some became quite angry when they learnt of the maximum sentencing available for Driving without Due Care and Attention or that, even for the more serious offence, imprisonment was going to be in single figures and, of course, some became quite distressed even months after the event. CPS national management expected lawyers and caseworkers to deal, and deal sensitively, with bereaved relatives, angry victims and awkward witnesses, but never did they contemplate providing any training for these purposes. You just had to do it but, if you got it wrong and there was a complaint, then you were held to account! But then this was typical of an organisation that, by the late nineties, had become over-centralised and bureaucratic, so politically correct, and so target-driven, that it was completely careless of the needs of those who worked for it or whether they were equipped for the tasks they were expected to carry out.

The other category of casework in which I was routinely involved was the prosecution of police officers. There was a reciprocal arrangement with other branches within the area of CPS North that we would deal with each other's errant police officers, except where the alleged offence was a minor road traffic matter. Over several years, whilst this arrangement lasted, I reviewed probably nine or ten files of evidence relating to officers on North Tyneside who had been interviewed for alleged offences of assault. Most of these arose from complaints by defendants who had been arrested and they, and usually their witnesses, if any, were clearly the worse for drink. In none of these did I find there was a realistic prospect of conviction. There were, however, a couple of cases where I did advise prosecution and two officers were convicted of serious offences of dishonesty and Causing Death by Dangerous Driving, respectively.

Most of the files I looked at, however, related to Cumbrian officers who had been involved in road traffic collisions. Ninety-five per cent of these were never going to see the light of day as prosecutions, usually because the officer was blameless. The practice was, however, that in the interests of complete transparency all cases of damage to police cars in road collisions, however minor, were to be referred to CPS for advice.

I did, however, prosecute about five officers in appropriate cases for Driving without Due Care. It was right that I gave the advice and did the prosecution, as the local CPS lawyers would probably be more likely to know the officers in question, or would be more likely to have had dealings with them at some point. In two of these cases, both involving women police officers, I did encounter hostility from the defendants.

The first was a West Cumbrian officer, who managed to turn a police Volvo Estate over on a notorious stretch of dual carriageway on the A66 between Keswick and Cockermouth one winter's night, whilst carrying a prisoner to Workington Police Station. She maintained in evidence that there "must have been extraordinary slipperiness" on the road at the point where she lost control of the car. We had, however, an expert constable from the Collision Investigation Unit who had been to the scene at the time of the accident and had found no such defect in the road. It was simply a case of driver error. The officer was convicted, and afterwards pointedly 'cut' both me and the expert officer when we tried to speak with her. She appealed to the Crown Court against her conviction, where she was represented by Graham Duff, lately the joint "deputy" to the DPP. Her appeal failed, as it was bound to do. Her attitude was unattractive and would be rarely found in a civilian defendant in the same circumstances.

The other such case was the one I have alluded to previously, in which I was against Malcolm Dodds in Barrow Magistrates' Court. The defendant was found 'not guilty', despite some good, independent evidence, a decision which both the magistrates' legal adviser and I found difficult to understand. One lesson I learnt, however, was this - if the defence are going to use "expert" evidence, as they did in this case, then so must the prosecution, however strong the case may otherwise appear.

Following her acquittal, however, the officer made a complaint against me. Not for the way in which I had conducted the case, not for advising proceedings in the first place, but because her daughter found out that she had been prosecuted!! Her daughter was at the Sixth Form College in Barrow and a contemporary there of my daughter. My daughter was aware of the nature of the case I was prosecuting and had mentioned this to her colleague - the latter, however, was apparently unaware of the case because her mother had not told her about it! The officer wrote to Mike Graham in Newcastle complaining about my shameless conduct. Mike asked me to respond to her complaint.

I did respond, but it should have been totally unnecessary. As a police officer, the complainant should have known that the proceedings were in a court to which the public and the press had access and, indeed, the latter could have published the details of the case had they chosen to do so! I was not giving any secrets away and neither was my daughter - the case was in the public domain. I couldn't understand why, even if the officer was ignorant of that, Mike couldn't have written to her and reminded her of the realities!

This, however, was how the CPS operated! Complaints, however misconceived, had to have a response, and the response had, in the first instance, to be prepared by the target of the complaint. Thereafter, who sent out the definitive reply depended on the status of the target and the status of the complainant. Complaints by MPs, for example, had to be responded to by the Chief Crown Prosecutor, although it was likely to be someone at my level who would actually draft the response for the CCP to sign. A definitive reply had to be sent to all complaints within ten working days, and woe betide anyone who failed to meet this deadline - explanations would be demanded and possibly even disciplinary proceedings may follow! The pressure generated by the need to respond to the many complaints we received contributed very much to the climate of fear which pervaded the CPS in this period! I probably spent at least five or six hours a week investigating complaints and drafting replies. To make matters worse, letters had to be drafted in a particular way - there was a format laid down and specific terminology to be used. The DPP even required the date to be set out in a particular way!

We used to get a lot of complaints, some justified, some not, but all necessitated a response. MPs were the worst complainers - if a constituent raised a matter of complaint with them then the MP fired off a letter to us, without, apparently, considering whether the complaint might have any substance or justification!

On occasions, our local MP in Carlisle at this time, Eric Martlew, would ring me up about a particular case brought to his attention by a constituent. He would seem to expect me to have detailed knowledge of the specific case and be able to give an instantaneous reply to his query. He couldn't understand why I didn't have an intimate knowledge of every case we dealt with, notwithstanding that there were thousands of live cases across the county at any one time!

I had first encountered Eric Martlew back in the eighties, when he was a mere local councillor and had come to talk to members on a management course I was attending. He didn't endear himself to many of us then, and came across as something of a "champagne socialist". He came to visit us in the office at Carlisle once in the late nineties. His main concern then, it seemed, was that a case of criminal deception against a councillor on Eden District Council had "collapsed", as he put it, and he seemed to regard this as evidence of inefficiency and poor preparation on our part. I explained to him that the case hadn't "collapsed", but had gone to the jury, who had found the defendant 'not guilty'. Mr Martlew, however, didn't seem to recognise the distinction!

* * *

As well as the particular categories of cases that I dealt with personally, I also occasionally involved myself in the high-profile cases that arose from time to time. Undoubtedly the most significant case in Cumbria between 1995 and 1999 was the infamous one of the "Lady in the Lake", and I was intimately involved in this matter from charge to its end - or at least its 'end' at this time.

The "lady" in question, Carol Ann Park, had 'disappeared' from her home in Leece, near Barrow, in the summer of 1976. Her husband, Gordon, didn't report her as missing for some weeks as, he later told police, she had done this before when she had had extra-marital affairs, and it was only when she didn't return in September to take up her duties as a local schoolteacher that he realised something more sinister might have occurred. The police commenced a "missing person" enquiry, took lots of witness statements and eventually treated her disappearance as "suspicious", leading to them digging up the garden and questioning Mr Park under caution at Barrow Police Station. No trace of Mrs Park was found, however, at this time, alive or dead, and there was no evidence to charge Park or anyone else with any criminal offence. By coincidence, in 1969 Mrs Park's sister had been murdered by her partner and the latter, serving a life sentence, was apparently on home leave at the time of Carol's disappearance. There, for the moment and, indeed, for the next twenty-one years, the case rested.

Then, in August 1997, a team of amateur divers found a suspicious package on the bed of Coniston Water and, believing the package to contain human remains, they contacted the police. The police recovered the package and confirmed that it did contain a badly decomposed body - the body was later identified from dental records as being that of Carol Ann Park. The body had been bound in the foetal position by ropes, the knots used being typical of those deployed by the boating and also the climbing fraternity - Gordon Park was, or had been, both a boating enthusiast and a climber. The body was dressed in a short nightie and was retained within several layers of materials, two bin-liners and a nylon rucksack, the whole within a man-made sack which turned out to be a pinafore dress. A lead weight, identified as a cistern pipe, had been attached to the package. Post mortem examination showed that death had been caused by several blows to the head with a blunt instrument.

There was now, of course, a full-scale murder investigation, which was hampered to some extent by the fact that the original "missing person" file, containing the evidence that had been gathered in 1976, had mysteriously disappeared. So the police were virtually starting from scratch, interviewing witnesses who may have been seen in 1976 and who were being asked to recall events that had occurred twenty-one years before. Many of the officers involved in the original investigation had died or retired, and many of the survivors were unable to assist much as to what had taken place in 1976.

The investigation, however, proceeded apace and a considerable volume of evidence was gathered. I became involved within a week of its commencement, at a conference with the senior investigating officer, Detective Superintendent Ian Douglas and other investigating officers (one of them, Detective Superintendent "Ned" Kelly, had been involved in a previous successful investigation into the recovery of a body from another Cumbrian lake). It was clear to me at this point that all the officers were firmly convinced that Gordon Park was the killer, and it also seemed to me that this was a perfectly justifiable conclusion to draw now from all the evidence, including the circumstances surrounding recovery of the body. At this time, of course, the police did not need the consent of the CPS to charge defendants (unless the offence was one which by law required the consent of the DPP or the Attorney General) and they informed me that it would be the intention to arrest and charge Park. I did not disagree with this proposal.

Park at this time was on holiday in France with his third wife (he had divorced Carol five years after her 'disappearance' and a subsequent marriage to one Cath Sillars had not lasted and had also ended in divorce). He was arrested on his return and questioned again by the police. He was apparently aware that the 1976 file was missing and, in his confident and arrogant responses in interview, would often preface his remarks with "...as I said in 1976...". He denied responsibility for the murder, but was charged and kept in custody pending a first court appearance.

There was still much work for the police to do. I actually attended a briefing at Barrow Police Station shortly after Park was charged, and heard Ian Douglas urging the troops with these words: "We've charged the bugger, now let's go out and get the fucking evidence!"

Park was originally remanded in custody by the court. I conducted the first hearing. His solicitor, Mike Graham, told me that Park knew me. I didn't know him but realised that I had heard of him in the past. His third wife was "Jenny Marshall" before the marriage. She had previously been married to Mike Marshall, who was a solicitor in Barrow and well-known to me and the local CPS lawyers. Jenny had also been in the same baby-sitting circle as my first wife and I in the 1980s and I recalled then that there had been rumours abroad that she was having a liaison with a music teacher at the school at which she taught. This would have been Park. In Barrow, it was not unusual for locally-based prosecutors to find that they knew defendants or witnesses other than in connection with criminal proceedings. It was that sort of place. This didn't, however, stop us from dealing with the case. Phil Bates, the local team leader, was, in fact, a close personal friend of Jenny's ex-husband. Park's legal representatives were also closely involved with him inasmuch as Gordon had been a friend of the brother and ex-partner of Barbara Forrester, who was at this time a partner in the practice.

Within a day or two of Park being charged I was summoned to Area HQ to brief Mike Graham and David Farmer. I was made aware that the DPP knew about the case and needed to be briefed by them. As soon as I had outlined the case to them I detected a distinct lack of enthusiasm for the prosecution, and I was instructed to arrange a conference with suitable counsel so that advice could be sought on whether there was likely to be a realistic prospect of conviction. I was also advised that it would be appropriate to withdraw our objections to bail, providing that stringent conditions were secured.

Before the conference with counsel, we had a "brains trust" in Cumbria to dissect the evidence and consider its sufficiency. This consisted of Ken Hay, the Special Casework Lawyer, Phil Bates and me. We all agreed that we felt there was, on the evidence, a realistic prospect of conviction.

It is fair to say that the evidence was entirely circumstantial. But in my view, it was compelling circumstantial evidence. I always thought the correct way to look at the case was, as it were, through the 'other end of the telescope'. It was clear that the killer did not want Carol to be found, and went to extraordinary lengths to achieve this. To my mind this had to rule out a "stranger" killing. From this point, who else could it be other than Park?! The killer needed access to a boat, knowledge of Coniston Water, the means to get there, and specialist and very esoteric knowledge of how to tie some unusual knots. Park had all these requirements. He also had a motive - there was some evidence that Carol was embarking on yet another affair and that Park himself was nurturing a liaison with another woman. The only other obvious candidate in the frame was the man Rapson, the murderer of the sister, but he appeared to have none of the above attributes and no obvious motive for killing Carol. To me, Park's guilt stood out like a sore thumb!

Unfortunately we had difficulty in securing the services of a QC of calibre sufficient to deal with a case of this sort. I had cherished notions of hiring Brian Leveson, who had prosecuted Rosemary West, but he was not available at this time. We ended up with, and I do not mean this in any disparaging way, an elderly QC in Manchester called Jack Price. I sent him the brief, which also contained my views on the sufficiency of evidence.

The conference with Jack Price took place just into the New Year, 1998. Counsel felt there was insufficient evidence to provide a realistic prospect of conviction, although he did not think the defence would be able to successfully claim that the absence of the 1976 police file would amount to an "abuse of process", something our managers were anxious about. Four of us at the conference - Phil Bates, the two officers, and I - were disappointed, but knew what the outcome was going to be. David Farmer was also there. I found out from another source afterwards that he had spoken to Jack Price on the phone before the conference and conveyed to him that the DPP and Area Management felt the evidence was not good enough and didn't want there to be prosecution if it was felt the evidence did not meet the CPS criteria. This would no doubt have amounted to strong pressure on Jack Price to "make the right decision"!

So that was that, at that time anyway, and I shortly after issued a notice of discontinuance, putting an end to the prosecution. As a postscript, and I don't know whether there was any truth in this, but I later heard through the grapevine that Jack Price had discussed the evidence with Brian Leveson before the conference and that the latter's view was that the case ought to proceed! Six years later, when the case was resurrected, I took much comfort from the views of the then QC instructed, Alistair Webster, that he would have been inclined to prosecute the case on the evidence that was available in 1997. More on this later but, as it turned out, Park was eventually convicted on evidence that wasn't substantially greater than that in 1997!

* * *

The magistrates' courts' landscape in these years between 1995 and 1999 was much changed from that in my first period in Cumbria. A lot of the smaller, rural courts had gone - Millom, Ulverston, Hawkshead, Shap, Kirkby Lonsdale, Sedbergh, Alston. The days of Wigton, Windermere and Keswick were numbered. Eventually Penrith and Whitehaven were to go as well, despite the fact that both were relatively new courts or relatively recently refurbished! At the time of writing there are magistrates' courts only at each main point of the compass - Carlisle, Workington, Barrow and Kendal. Greater expense and inconvenience for defendants and witnesses, and I seriously doubt whether court users received a better service as a result. All about money, of course! It is interesting, however, to compare the situation of the magistrates' courts in Cumbria with that of the Crown Courts in the county. Despite the fact that Barrow Crown Court has not sat for more than four days a month for as long as I can remember and, as a result, has a very limited capacity as to the type of cases it could deal with, it has stubbornly resisted all attempts to close it down! Perhaps political considerations outweighing cost considerations in this instance?!

There were, by 1995, just three magistrates' clerks in the county, as I said at the beginning of this chapter. Two of the three, Chris Armstrong in the west and Trevor Dearnley at Carlisle, were 'graduates' of the Nottingham City magistrates' court 'school' of clerks; Simon Evans, who covered the south and east, had come from Portsmouth in about 1987. Just prior to my return to Cumbria, the powers that be had decided to appoint a non-operational, overall "chief executive" for the magistrates' courts in Cumbria. In their wisdom, they had appointed someone with no knowledge of the criminal justice system whatsoever. He had, in fact, previously been employed by one of the utilities and he came to be referred to as the "gas man", a term of abuse rather than of endearment! I never found out what his role was, and the only times I came across him were at meetings of the "knitting circle" where, as far as I can remember, his sole contribution was to remonstrate with the meeting secretary for spelling his surname incorrectly! His tenure was relatively short-lived, needless to say, and in a few years he was replaced in the post by Simon Evans. By this time Trevor Dearnley had retired and, in another bout of "rationalisation", Chris Armstrong became the sole Magistrates' Clerk for the county.

In a generation, the magistrates' court infrastructure in Cumbria had been completely decimated. Much the same had happened across the country.

Apart from those in the Collision Investigation Unit and those I met in court, most of the police officers I had contact with in these years were of superintendent rank and above. The Chief Constable for most of this period was one Alan Elliot, not a man towards whom I instinctively warmed. His senior officers did not appear to be much enamoured either, and I discovered that he was affectionately known to them as "shit for brains". However, he did appear to be popular with the lower ranks. One or two of them appeared to have a 'hot line' to him and, on a couple of occasions, he rang me up to ask me to investigate some occurrence in court which had been brought to his attention by an officer of sergeant rank. On both of these occasions the "occurrence" had taken place just that day and neither were of great moment!

We in the local CPS were engaged in a long-running battle with Alan Elliot at this time on one particular issue. There were two offences of basic "assault" by this time - Common Assault, and Assault Occasioning Actual Bodily Harm. In the magistrates' court, both carried a maximum of six months' imprisonment, but the latter was more serious because it could also be tried in the Crown Court, where it carried a greater penalty. Otherwise, the only difference between them was that the latter required proof of "actual bodily harm", as the name suggests. We had guidelines we followed when deciding which offence was more appropriate and, in most cases where the injury suffered was comparatively minor, we would opt for the lesser offence. Alan Elliot, however, for reasons I never quite fathomed, had instructed his officers to charge only Assault Occasioning Actual Bodily Harm, whatever the degree of "harm" suffered by the victim. This meant that we were constantly having to "downgrade" charges in order to reflect the criminality of the case. Alan Elliot, however, could not be persuaded of the absurdity of the situation and remained convinced that his course was the right course "in law", despite the fact that, as far as I am aware, no other police force in the country followed the same course. I began to appreciate the perceptiveness of his senior officers!!

Some of the divisional and sub-divisional police commanders I had known when they were more junior officers in the 1980s. Most of them, at one time or another, invited me to join them in their local public meetings, where members of the public had the chance to ask questions about local policing, etc. On a number of occasions I addressed these meetings on the role of the CPS and answered questions thereafter. I found these meetings quite useful and enlightening, because it was apparent that most people did not understand what the CPS was about and had no idea that we took over the conduct of criminal proceedings from the police, despite the fact that we had been in being for at least ten years by then! Just an illustration of how effective our publicity machine was - the police have always been much better at self-publicity than the CPS! The police service does, of course, get bad publicity, but it is a much 'sexier' organisation than the CPS, which rarely if ever gets a good press - the CPS seems to be forever either damned for prosecuting when it shouldn't be prosecuting, or damned for not prosecuting when the media thinks it should be prosecuting!

At one of these local meetings I met a police officer I had not seen since my time in Barrow. He was now at Police HQ at Penrith but close to retirement, which may explain why he was keen to get something off his chest. He reminded me of a trial I had conducted in Barrow Magistrates' Court in 1982, where he and two other officers had been the witnesses for the prosecution. He was a police constable then, and the other two officers involved were a sergeant and an inspector respectively. The defendant had been charged with a public order offence outside a nightclub in the town one Saturday night. I remembered the case, because it was possibly the first trial I had conducted in that court, and I recall the defendant being very vehement in his assertion that the officers were inventing the evidence against him. Be that as it may, I had no reason, then or since, to suspect that the officers were lying. Now, however, this officer told me that this indeed had been the case and that the inspector had coached the other two officers and 'instructed' them on what evidence to give! For reasons known only to himself, the senior officer was anxious to see the man convicted.

I would like to have said that I was shocked and disillusioned by this revelation. Sadly, I was not. Police officers are just as capable as civilians of telling lies in the witness box and, although it has been rare for me to have suspected perjury by officers in cases going back more than forty years, I am sure there have been more than a handful of occasions where this has happened, for whatever reason.

Sometimes, although very rarely, it has been obvious that a police officer has been less than truthful in the witness box. On these occasions, however, justice has been done and defendants acquitted. I recall one case in the late 1990s in Whitehaven Court, where an officer, a police constable with a good deal of service, gave evidence on oath in a trial about a relatively minor traffic offence. He wasn't telling outright lies, but he was certainly 'gilding the lily', and obviously so. As a result, he laid himself wide open to being completely discredited in cross-examination and the defence advocate, John Dugan, did not miss the opportunity. As his evidence was challenged and ridiculed, the officer became more and more angry and strident and, eventually, totally lost his composure. At the end of cross-examination he stormed out of court, loudly slamming the court door behind him. I was given no chance of re-examining him, and nor were the magistrates given the opportunity to ask him questions. The result of the case was, of course, a foregone conclusion. His behaviour, however, was disgraceful and I had no hesitation in reporting him to his senior officers.

Most police officers do not lie in the witness box, and the best of them learn that the way to give their evidence is low-key and without exaggeration, agreeing with the defence advocate where appropriate, and remaining unflustered and composed. They do not take challenges to their evidence personally, knowing that the defence advocate is only doing a job, and they are philosophical about defendants being found 'not guilty', realising that the burden of proof on the prosecution is heavy and that some cases are going to be "lost".

During my tenure as Branch Crown Prosecutor in Cumbria there were significant changes in the criminal law, and there were, inevitably, further big changes in the structure and organisation of the CPS looming on the horizon.

The Criminal Procedure and Investigations Act 1996 created a statutory framework for the now very important matter of disclosure of unused material to the defence – i.e. material that was not relied upon as evidence by the Crown. In essence, the test to be applied by prosecutors in deciding whether to disclose such material was: did it "undermine" the prosecution case or did it "assist the defence case", as this was known to the prosecution? If the material satisfied one or other of these tests then it should be disclosed, unless it was material that was not "in the public interest to disclose". Previously, we had been required to disclose all material that was "relevant", irrespective of whether it helped the defence or not, so the category of material to disclose was now more restricted.

To my mind, neither the police nor the CPS has ever entirely got to grips with the issue of "disclosure". The police have got better at telling the CPS about material they hold and listing it on schedules, but they haven't necessarily always succeeded in identifying the material which ought to be disclosed and flagging it up, or in adequately describing material so that the prosecutor can assess whether it is disclosable or not. CPS lawyers have been too superficial in the way they have approached the question of disclosure, relying too much on what the police have identified as disclosable and failing to carry out a proper investigation of other material. Probably the only really satisfactory way of dealing with the matter is for the prosecutor to examine all the material held by the police and make up his own mind whether it is disclosable or not. As CPS resources diminish, this is less and less likely to happen, however. In later years, when I became a regular Crown Court advocate, I repeatedly came across examples of material that should have been disclosed and hadn't been, and even recently there are instances of cases that have failed because of lack of proper disclosure. I cannot see that matters will ever get much better than they are now!

The Crime and Disorder Act 1998 introduced the concept of the ASBO (Anti Social Behaviour Order), as part of the New Labour Government's pledge to be "tough on crime, and tough on the causes of crime". The ASBO is still with us today, although its days are apparently now numbered. I don't know whether ASBOs succeeded in curbing anti-social behaviour in local communities, but the worst aspect for me was that it led to courts drawing up orders with very stringent and restrictive provisions that almost guaranteed that the subject was "set up to fail". Breach of the order was an offence which created the anomaly of an offender being liable for imprisonment, for up to five years, for, say, being found drunk in the street, although as an individual offence this did not carry imprisonment and only a fairly trivial penalty!

The Act also signalled the eventual end of "committal proceedings" by requiring "indictable-only" charges to be sent immediately to the Crown Court by the magistrates' court. This meant that, although we still prepared a set of "committal papers", it was served on the Crown Court rather than the magistrates' court. The reality, however, was that this didn't necessarily reduce the time that elapsed between the first appearance of a defendant in the magistrates' court and his or her first appearance in the Crown Court.

More significant were the changes that were now beckoning for advocacy rights in both the lower court and the Crown Court. From

1999 the DPP was able to "designate" unqualified persons to be able to prosecute certain categories of cases in the magistrates' court. These were to be known as "lay presenters" (and later as "associate prosecutors"). And the CPS began to train some of its lawyers to exercise rights of audience in the Crown Court, rights that had been made available to suitably qualified persons a few years previously, but had not been taken up by the CPS. These were historic and profound changes that would literally revolutionise the way we operated - but more of this in the next chapter!

* * *

By 1998 the CPS had reached a low point. Under the "Dame", morale in the Service had reached rock bottom and it was being publicly criticised from all directions. There were TV programmes which highlighted its shortcomings and unpopularity. In one of these programmes, lawyers in the CPS were actually interviewed airing their discontent with what was termed "a climate of fear" created by the national management and the burdens of subscribing to the gathering of performance indicators, and the target-related culture which detracted from their carrying out the core business of the CPS, i.e. prosecuting! One of the lawyers who put his head over the parapet in one TV programme in this respect is now a Chief Crown Prosecutor in a large area, so it didn't do his career any harm!!

At one point national management seemed to acknowledge that there was "something rotten in the state of Denmark". Gathering of certain statistics and performance indicators was abolished at a stroke. And two Headquarters people were sent round the country to deliver a message about what the core business of the CPS actually was - believe it or not, it was the preparation and prosecution of criminal cases!! As if we didn't know, but it really said something about how the Service had lost its way if we actually needed to be reminded what our core business was!!

There was a strong rumour in 1996 or 1997 that the government was about to abolish CPS. This didn't happen of course but instead, Lord Justice Glidewell was appointed to carry out a full enquiry into the CPS and all its workings. The Glidewell Report was published in 1998 and was very critical of CPS management. No surprise there! It recommended a number of radical changes to the Service and the way it operated. More of this in the next chapter, but the main proposal was that the organisation should be broken up into smaller areas which coincided with chief constable jurisdictions. Each area would be headed up by a "Crown Prosecutor for…", who would work more closely with the police and concentrate far more closely on "prosecuting". Indeed, this lead person should spend at least 40% of his or her time in court or preparing cases for prosecution. Music to my ears!!

Implementation of the headline proposal of the Report required, of course, yet another structural upheaval in the CPS. Having gone from small to medium-size in 1986, and from medium-size to large in 1993, we were now going back to small! There were to be forty-two Areas - the counties in effect - each with its own designated "Crown Prosecutor", who was to be a robust, high-profile person, on a par with the chief constable, with whom he or she would work closely as "crime-fighters".

As a temporary measure in 1998, I was designated as the "Crown Prosecutor for Cumbria", but it was only a temporary measure. All those so designated were to be interviewed by the DPP and her "deputies", to ascertain if we were suitable to fill this new post. In 1998 we all went through this lengthy and, no doubt, expensive process. I mentioned earlier the interview I had with Barbara Mills and the panel, in which she never once looked directly at me and showed signs of utter boredom throughout! It was a waste of time and money anyway, because the Attorney General apparently wasn't satisfied with the results of the process and decreed that the whole appointment procedure would be open to the wider public, no doubt so that persons of proper stature could be obtained! So back to the drawing-board, and we all had to complete formal applications in order to be considered.

I had a fairly good idea by now that my application to be a Chief Crown Prosecutor in the new regime would not be successful. I was quite satisfied with the achievements of my four years as a Branch Crown Prosecutor. Our case results were very good in terms of conviction rates and timeliness. We had lived within our budget. We had excellent working relationships with all our criminal justice partners. This was not going to be enough, however, as far as I was concerned. I was quite confident that I was not regarded at the centre as a "company man", and this is what they wanted. I had made no great progress in implementing their precious "team-working" initiative, although this was by now largely dead in the water. I was too fond of being hands-on, going to court and carrying a caseload, instead of being a "manager". They didn't really approve of this approach, never mind that it was how Glidewell saw things!

Furthermore, by this time I had local difficulties on my hands which undoubtedly came to the notice of the centre and didn't work to my advantage. In 1998 a number of complaints were made to me that one of the Divisional Crown Prosecutors had been touching female members of staff inappropriately and, indeed, a female member of a visiting team from HQ. I passed these complaints on to Area Management and the person in question was transferred to another branch pending a disciplinary investigation. The problem was then compounded by his opposite number on another team, with whom he formed an 'item', approaching one of the witnesses in a not-too-subtle attempt to make her withdraw her complaint. This person, too, was transferred to another branch pending investigation of this latest complaint.

In late 1998 the "Dame" finally departed and was replaced by David Calvert-Smith, Treasury Counsel, whom I had instructed once or twice whilst in London. He wrote to me in early 1999, giving the results of my application. It was, in fact, on my fiftieth birthday that I received this polite letter from the DPP, thanking me for my previous contribution but informing me I was not to be the CCP for Cumbria. What next for me? Theoretically I was redundant…

CHAPTER TWELVE

1999 to 2002: Onwards and Upwards…

The redundancy notice never came. Nor did I receive any communication from CPS headquarters about my position. From 1st April 1999, the job I had been doing for the last three and a half years had ceased to exist. No-one told me my services were no longer required, but no-one told me what I would be doing from that date. I was left in professional limbo. The silence was deafening!

This was, in fact, typical conduct by the CPS. For an organisation which claimed to be so politically correct, so committed to diversity and transparency, which demanded high standards of formality in record-keeping and decision-making endorsements, in its dealings with its own employees the CPS again and again displayed an amazing degree of naivety, incompetence and insensitivity, and an astonishing lack of formality.

There is any number of examples of this over the life of the organisation. At least two lawyers in London had been dismissed from the Service or effectively downgraded, and failure to observe proper procedures or to have sufficient grounds for the action led to adverse findings in industrial tribunals. A lawyer in Cumbria was "retired" on medical grounds, but then he had to be allowed to return because the procedure was not followed correctly. My wife was also "retired" on medical grounds in 1994, as a result of a physical condition sustained in years of carrying heavy bags of files through the streets to the Crown Court. The failure of the CPS to have in place any system to prevent employees being used as 'donkeys' cost them dear in compensation.

Then there was the remarkable story of Shirley Grisedale. Shirley was partially-sighted and was appointed in the early 1990s as a typist to work in the CPS Carlisle office. The appointment was made by the Chief Admin Officer at Preston at a time when Cumbria and Lancashire formed one Area. This may have been considered an excellent decision and a triumph for "diversity" at the time, but the reality was that it lacked foresight and ultimately proved disastrous. Even in the early days, a good deal of money had to be spent on adapting equipment so that Shirley could do her job, and a good deal of time was invested in specialist training. What the organisation failed to realise, however, was that as time went on and IT came in and developed, the kit was to become more and more sophisticated and less and less user-friendly for Shirley. Everything was tried but, in the end, Shirley simply couldn't do the job. I suppose there were grounds to get rid of her at this point but this apparently, and not surprisingly, was not an option for management. She was offered a voluntary redundancy package, but didn't want to take it. And so we ended up in the ridiculous situation where she was retained on permanent "special leave", on full pay, for several years! She finally took voluntary redundancy, I think in 2012. By that time, most of the staff in the Carlisle office had never met her!

In my case in 1999, as I understood the position, having in effect been rendered redundant, I should have actually been made redundant and paid off, or at least been placed in a central redeployment pool until a suitable post in the Civil Service came up to which I could be appointed. In the meantime, I could continue to be employed in the CPS in another job in an "overbearing" role - this meant I would retain my existing salary for twelve months and then my pay would drop to that applicable to the job I was doing. None of this actually happened!

On 1st April 1999 David Farmer came to Cumbria as the Chief Crown Prosecutor for the Cumbria Area. He had been my line manager for the last four years and was now to continue as my line manager for the next six years. Having known him well for some time, I had no difficulty in meeting up with him on his first day, and awaited news of my future with keen anticipation and curiosity! In the event, he had no more idea than I did as to what I should be doing henceforward. As it was, there was only one avenue open to me if I was to remain "on Cumbria's books". There was no management vacancy, so we agreed that I would move to an empty office on the first floor of the Workington office and become the Area "special casework lawyer". (The CPS North Special Casework Unit had ceased to exist, having 'died' with the CPS North Area itself).

This was perfectly acceptable to me, particularly as there was no mention by anybody about the role being "overbearing". Whether my new job merited the same level of salary as I had been on before I seriously doubt, but I was happy to benefit from the inertia of CPS management and continue drawing the same pay as I had been as Branch Crown Prosecutor. In fact, whatever job I was allocated to over the next fourteen years, there was never any suggestion that I should have been on a lower pay scale!

★ ★ ★

The restructuring of the CPS in 1999 and the switch from a few large Areas to 42 smaller ones brought a lot of new faces into the ranks of Chief Crown Prosecutors and saw the departure of some old ones. It also provided an opportunity for the CPS national management to indulge its passion for political correctness and diversity. The standing joke amongst the rank and file at this time was that the best qualification for a CCP job was to be female, ethnic, and preferably disabled and lesbian. This was probably a gross exaggeration, but there were certainly a significant number of female appointees at this time; some I had never heard of, and some, if not exactly plucked from obscurity, were at least propelled through the ranks. Many of these were no doubt worthy of their promotion, but there were some who almost certainly were not!

One example known to me of this phenomenon was the case of a woman who had lived close to us in Essex when I was at Stratford. She was black and of Zimbabwean extraction, I believe, and had been a team leader, a Principal Crown Prosecutor, with Essex CPS. It was said that she was perfectly adequate at her job, but no one ever thought of her rising higher in the ranks of the organisation. All of a sudden, in 1999, we learnt that she had been appointed an Assistant Chief Crown Prosecutor for the new CPS London Area, the biggest Area in the country. This was at least two grades above her previous post and was a very senior, high-profile job. Although I cannot say that it was a misconceived appointment, or that she was to be out of her depth, suffice it to say that within twelve months she had ceased to be in that job and had quietly 'disappeared'!

The appointment of David Farmer as the CCP in Cumbria was no great surprise, although no doubt he had hoped for a bigger Area than ours. He was very much a company man and had been involved in national projects, so he ticked at least some of the right boxes for the purposes of advancement. He had also been a Chief Crown

Prosecutor before, for the Northumbria/Durham Area before 1993, but had been somewhat eclipsed by Mike Graham thereafter, Mike beating him to the CCP post in CPS North when Dickie Dickinson went to Yorkshire.

David was a very affable individual and very capable in many ways. He had, however, little interest in being involved in advocacy or having a caseload, and the "Glidewell" notion that he should spend 40% of his time in these activities would be anathema to him. It was perhaps indicative that his most recent involvement nationally in the CPS at this time was to chair a group looking at the forms used in the organisation! David was very much drawn to the 'form' of things. He had an orderly and organised mind and all his files (not casework files!) were beautifully colour-coded and set out in neat and ordered fashion in his bookcases, which themselves matched his other office furniture. I think he had little stomach for being a strong manager, and the disciplinary situation involving two senior lawyers that he inherited from me, I know caused him a lot of heartache (in the event they were allowed to return to the Area in due course, albeit not as managers, or not for some years, anyway).

* * *

In this, my second incarnation as a "special casework" lawyer, I pretty well wrote my own script. David Farmer more or less left it to me as to what cases I took on and very shortly I found that the police would contact me direct if they thought I should be handling a particular case. I continued to deal with all the road traffic fatal accident cases, and soon I was also immersed in cases of Conspiracy to supply Class A drugs, armed robbery, fraud and Attempted Murder. I also found that neighbouring Areas were keen to make use of me if they had no special casework lawyer or limited resources in this regard, and I soon had the odd case from Lancashire and Merseyside.

If I had any residual disappointment about not getting the CCP job in Cumbria, it did not last long. I was back closely involved in real crime and, furthermore, there was soon another exciting dimension to my role…

Whilst I was still Branch Crown Prosecutor I had managed to persuade the Area Management that I should be one of those selected to be in the first wave of prosecutors to be trained and to qualify as

"Higher Courts Advocates" – i.e. to be able to exercise rights of audience in the Crown Court (and, indeed, all of the higher courts in the country). The first stage of training was the theoretical side of things - basically acquainting ourselves with the content of *Archbold's Criminal Pleading Evidence and Practice* - a vast work which was the 'bible' of the Crown Court practitioner. We then had to sit an examination on criminal law and Crown Court procedure. This was an 'open book' exam, which meant we could consult *Archbold* during the exam, although I did not find this any great advantage! It was the first exam I had sat for more than twenty years, and I was utterly convinced that I had failed. To my surprise, I passed!

The practical side of the training that followed involved learning how to present cases in the Crown Court and deal with the various scenarios - Committals for Sentence, 'guilty' pleas, 'not guilty' pleas, etc. Then we had to perform in front of assessors from Nottingham University Law School. This meant, amongst other things, preparing opening and closing speeches to a jury and delivering them in front of the assessors and one's fellow candidates. This also had to be done in full regalia - gown, wing collar and "tabs" (and wigs for the barristers amongst us). A thoroughly nerve-wracking experience but certainly, I found, one that stood me in good stead for the real thing in due course.

I came through all this and became a fully-fledged Higher Court Advocate in 1998. Two other lawyers on my Branch, Ken Hay and Pat Dwyer, also qualified at this time. After spending some time in the Crown Court at Carlisle to observe proceedings in real time, we tentatively embarked on Crown Court advocacy.

At first we did little more than cases that had been sent from the magistrates' courts for sentence and appeals against sentence from those courts. My first appearance was before a senior Crown Court judge who was "visiting" Carlisle Crown Court. Two of the three committals for sentence I presented were straightforward, but the third involved a series of dwelling-house burglaries and I basically made a hash of it, managing to confuse both myself and the judge in the process. Eventually I managed to tidy things up, but it was not an auspicious start! I'm pleased to say that matters only got better from that point, as I conquered my nerves and confidence increased!

Because of our other responsibilities, there was a limited amount of advocacy we could do in the Crown Court in these early days, and it was not really until the turn of the century that we were able to expand our repertoire to include doing a few Plea and Direction Hearings. These were cases that were having their first hearing in the Crown Court and, basically, involved the parties, where a 'not guilty' plea was entered, completing a form identifying the issues in the case, witnesses required, etc., and the judge then setting a trial date. If the defendant, when arraigned, pleaded 'guilty' then usually the case would be adjourned for a Pre-Sentence Report to be prepared on the defendant by the Probation Service although, as advocates, we always had to be prepared for the case to proceed immediately to sentence, so we had in effect to prepare each case we were dealing with in the Plea and Directions List as if it were a sentencing case. This meant a good deal of preparation before the hearing.

In the next two or three years, other lawyers in CPS Cumbria qualified as Higher Courts Advocates (HCAs) and eventually we had, at one point, as many as ten who could do Crown Court advocacy. This high point was reached in 2008 or 2009. There were also two lawyers who had qualified but needed to do the CPS practical advocacy course to be able to actually go into court. This gave rise to some resentment amongst the other HCAs and, indeed, other lawyers. The reason for this was that as HCAs we were given an allowance on top of our salary by the CPS of £1500 per annum. This included the two prosecutors I have just referred to, even though they actually did not do any advocacy in the Crown Court. Both of them, in fact, steadfastly refused to apply to go on the course, which would have then allowed them to practise in the Crown Court - one, Peter Bailey, was by now having difficulties with his hearing and was never going to do the advocacy anyway, and the other one, apparently, because he didn't see why he should do the course when he was getting the allowance without having, in effect, to do the job. I constantly brought this up with the Chief Crown Prosecutor because, I said, they were "not available" to practice in the Crown Court because they had not done the CPS course and, therefore, should not be entitled to the allowance - they should be compelled to apply for the course or lose the extra money. Needless to say, nothing happened and the two continued to draw the allowance, much to the annoyance of others. Another piece of ineptitude by the CPS national management!!

By 2005 or 2006 we were doing a lot of business in the Crown Court. We were able to do most of the cases in the Plea and Directions Hearing list, which was every Monday, and were routinely doing most of the Committals for Sentence, and Appeals against Sentence. We also kept most of the PDH cases which were adjourned for sentence. The result was that we had prosecutors in the Crown Court at least two, if not three, days a week. The downside was that, with so many HCAs, it reduced the number of occasions an individual HCA could go to court to two or three a month, which was frustrating for those of us who wanted to do much more.

One type of case we were not doing much of was the "contentious" sort - appeals against conviction from magistrates' court decisions, and jury trials. We did cover some of the former, but no-one in Cumbria prosecuted a trial before a jury until I did the first one in 2006. Several times before this I had prepared a case which was listed for trial, only to find on arrival at court that the defendant was to change his plea on the morning of the trial or the case couldn't proceed for some reason.

There is a lot more to say about "the Crown Court experience", but I will save that for Chapter 14.

Another restriction on my ability to go as often as I would have liked to the Crown Court was the sudden onset of my career as a trainer.

Prior to 1999 the only delivery of training I had done was to lawyers and caseworkers in the Area. Notably, whilst in Newcastle I had been part of a small team tasked with delivering training on the subject of Disclosure of Unused Material. Now I suddenly discovered that I was in demand to be a "national" trainer and, from 1999 to 2003, I spent a lot of time travelling round the country to deliver training, firstly in the matter of the Human Rights Act 1998, and then as a trainer of other prosecutors seeking to qualify as an HCA.

The Human Rights Act brought the European Convention on Human Rights into English law. It was heralded as bringing "sweeping change" into the criminal law, as well as other branches of the law. We trainers were put through a rigorous training course ourselves, inundated with reams of European Court case decisions, training material and acetates, and then sent out into the shires to train the troops. In pairs, we travelled to locations all over the country to spread the word. The cost of delivering this training must have been astronomical. I think I must have done about fifteen training sessions, involving about three hundred lawyers or caseworkers, most of them and us two trainers having to be accommodated in hotels for three nights at a time.

As it happened the Human Rights Act, when it came into force, was, at least as far as the criminal law was concerned, a complete non-event! We were told, and we told others, that the European Convention would be quoted by the defence and would be cropping up in court and in our review work every day. I cannot, however, remember anyone ever referring to it in court and it had no noticeable impact in the office - save that we now included a line in our endorsement of review decisions in files to the effect that there were "no ECHR issues"!

I hesitate to say that the whole training exercise was a total waste of time and money, but…

The HCA training was more relevant and appropriate. The CPS was rapidly increasing its establishment of HCAs in this period, and there were many lawyers to prepare for the CPS practical advocacy tests (it seems there was no longer any requirement by this time to sit the written exam!). I regarded myself as barely qualified or experienced enough to deliver training in this field, particularly as I had done no trial advocacy in the Crown Court at this point but, over a period of time, I found that I was just a step or two ahead of the trainees and that they could benefit from the experience of myself and my co-trainers. Most, if not all of them, went on to qualify as HCAs. It would be interesting to know, however, how many of them are still exercising their rights in the Crown Court!

Most of the casework I handled between 1999 and 2002 consisted of continuing to review and prosecute all the fatal road traffic cases in the county, and a series of Conspiracies to Supply Class A drugs.

As far as the former were concerned, the number of such accidents continued to run at more than one a fortnight during this period. Of the ones that proceeded to prosecution, either for Driving without due care and attention, or for Causing Death by Dangerous Driving, very few failed to result in conviction, although there were a couple of cases where the more serious offence was charged where the jury returned a verdict for the lesser offence. I took most of the Due Cares to the magistrates' court myself and prosecuted several to trial, some before District Judges who were brought in especially to hear the cases. I also started to take the odd case personally into the Crown Court and prosecute them to sentence where 'guilty' pleas were entered. There were detailed sentencing guidelines laid down for Causing Death by Dangerous Driving (and indeed, for the no less serious offences of Causing Death whilst driving without due care, being over the alcohol limit, or being unfit through drink or drugs). The sentencing judge required the prosecutor to be able to identify appropriate "aggravating" features in the manner of driving, and to indicate in which category the case fell for sentencing purposes. Prosecutions had, therefore, to be prepared to a high standard and I would spend a good deal of time preparing for a single hearing in this type of case.

There was also the matter of keeping the deceased's family 'on board' and up to date through the life of the case, ensuring they had the opportunity of making a "victim impact" statement, and speaking with them after sentence when they may not always be happy with the outcome. The "victim impact" or "victim personal" statement was a statement made by family members setting out how the death had impacted on their lives, and the prosecutor would read them out or summarise them to the sentencing judge. As far as level of sentence was concerned, I had always prepared the family for what the likely sentence would be and, although I was not always right, I was more often than not, and this would take some of the sting out of the occasional adverse responses I got from families.

Regarding drug trafficking, there were drug squads in Carlisle and in West Cumbria, both of whom were active in running surveillance operations directed against known drug dealers, mostly in heroin or cocaine. Later, more sophisticated methods of surveillance would be developed and used but, at this time, the surveillance consisted of observations carried out by numbers of plain-clothes officers over a period of time or by deploying an undercover officer who would be infiltrated into the drug user's fraternity and ultimately would lure the dealers into supplying him or her. Both methods were notably successful and a number of conspiracies were cracked and gangs of dealers convicted and sentenced to imprisonment. The sentences for Class A dealers were severe and, even for previously unconvicted traffickers, ranged from three years to eight years or more. The higher sentences were reserved for those further up in the hierarchy of dealers, those closer to the source of the imported supply of the drugs.

These cases tended to involve significant numbers of defendants and would generate vast amounts of evidence, so I did not as a rule take them to the Crown Court myself at this time. There was one case I did, however, where most of the conspirators pleaded guilty, and I saw the guilty offenders through to sentence.

The one case which dominated the scene during this period, however, and in which I was to be involved from the start, was that of Michelle Dickinson. This was identified as a case involving *Munchausen's Syndrome by Proxy* - seeking attention by doing harm, not to oneself, but to others. The "others", in this instance, were the defendant's children. She had three children and, over a period of time, she was systematically poisoning them by overdosing them with prescribed medication, anti-epilepsy drugs, and steadfastly avoiding contact with the medical authorities. Ultimately the eldest child, Michael, died in hospital, although the other two, both very ill, were saved from the same fate and taken into care. Dickinson was eventually charged with Murder and Child Cruelty, and was tried at Liverpool Crown Court in 2002. We realised during the trial that the Murder charge was not going to succeed, as there were difficulties linking Michael's actual death with the actions of the defendant, but the judge allowed the Crown to add another charge of Attempted Murder to the Indictment. She was convicted of this and the Child Cruelty counts, and was sentenced to sixteen years' imprisonment. The Attempted Murder count was quashed on appeal, because of a misdirection to the jury by the judge – ironically, had the judge adopted the direction proposed by Prosecution Counsel as opposed to that suggested by the defence, then this would have been acceptable to the Court of Appeal. Be that as it may, the sentence of sixteen years' imprisonment for the other charges was upheld.

This was a very difficult case to get to grips with, in every sense. The evidence gathered was voluminous, there were more than a hundred witnesses and the trial took many weeks. More than this, however, it was difficult to comprehend the sheer wickedness of the defendant and the absolute tragedy of the case. All of the investigating officers were deeply affected, and the defence team also had severe problems in keeping their professional detachment.

My casework also took me into Lancashire and Merseyside. These were both cases of the "lawyers' curse" once again. One involved a solicitors' clerk and the other the inevitable sole practitioner solicitor, both of whom had been misappropriating clients' money. Both were convicted. There seemed to be an unending supply of dishonest lawyers, and these would not be the last!

* * *

While I was engrossed in serious casework, training, and Crown Court advocacy, the CPS as a whole was seeking to implement the recommendations of the Glidewell Report, and also those proposed by Martin Narey. Martin Narey was a senior Home Office civil servant who had also been looking at the criminal justice system at this time and, in particular, how to speed up the transit of criminal cases through the courts. He had suggested the immediate sending of indictable-only cases to the Crown Court, with an early first hearing in that court - this we had already put in place by 2002; and also an early first hearing in the magistrates' court for other cases, with abridged files and immediate disclosure of the prosecution evidence, in an attempt to encourage early 'guilty' pleas. This, too, was implemented at this time.

So far so good, but implementing "Glidewell" was another matter. The CPS had moved from thirteen to forty-two Areas, as already mentioned. But the other main plank of the report was for police and CPS to cease to duplicate each others' work by CPS and police civilian staff merging in a single "Criminal Justice Unit" with just one file. This unit would be collocated and would include lawyers, CPS admin staff and police civilian staff. Other CPS lawyers would then be released to deal just with the casework going to the Crown Court - to be called "Trials Units".

Good idea; and it probably did come into existence in some places, but it was never going to last in my view and indeed, in Cumbria it basically never got off the ground. A committee, consisting of the CPS Area Management Team and a police team led by the Assistant Chief Constable, met many times over three or four years to find a way to create Criminal Justice Units in the four corners of the county. Only 25% success was achieved in even finding accommodation! The exercise involved, in effect, a reversal of what had happened in many places in 1986. Then, in the interests of creating an 'independent' CPS, we had moved out of police stations, where many had originally been accommodated, and into separate buildings. Now we were looking to move back into police stations! Before many more years had passed, we were all moving out once more, if, of course, we had ever moved back!

No suitable premises could be found in Carlisle or Barrow to house such a unit. In Workington there were grandiose plans to build another storey on top of the new police station which would accommodate not just the Criminal Justice Unit but also the Probation Service! The plans never came to fruition.

In Kendal, room was found for a unit in the police station and CPS staff actually moved onto the same floor as the police civilian staff who had made up the police CJU. But I think that was as far as it got and there never was, as far as I know, any "joint working" between the two sets of staff.

The problem, as I saw it, was that the police never had any real enthusiasm for joint Criminal Justice Units. Who was going to manage the units? Would it be police-led or CPS-led? It was all too political - the police were never going to permit a situation to develop where police civilian staff were being managed and directed by CPS people, and it would have had to be this way round. And so, in Cumbria at least, and I suspect in many other places, it just never happened.

In Cumbria the whole process eventually just withered on the vine and, within a few years, no-one ever mentioned "Glidewell"! Another abortive enterprise!

As for the proposal that all prosecutors should be devoting at least 40% of their time to "prosecuting" - why, fond hope!! David Farmer did go to the magistrates' court a couple of times, but his heart was never in it and the experiment soon lapsed. Nor did he suddenly take on a caseload. The team leaders, of whom by now there were only two, were hands-on prosecutors to a greater or lesser extent, but this was as far as it got.

Lord Justice Glidewell was later reported as being very "disappointed" with how the CPS and the police had dealt with his recommendations. Well might he have been!!

* * *

From 1998 to 2003 the Director of Public Prosecutions was David Calvert-Smith. He came in as a breath of fresh air after the stultifying and oppressive regime of the "Dame" and certainly, for a good while, he enjoyed a great deal of popularity within the CPS and much acclaim outside it. He was never as bad as his predecessor at any stage of his five-year tenure, although both his popularity and his patience were wearing a bit thin well before the end. He did break the mould on one or two occasions by prosecuting a list in a London magistrates' court, something which I don't think any other DPP has done during their period of office!

In Cumbria we went through a mini-reorganisation which was partially designed, I think, to meet with "Glidewell". It was decided that two Trial Units for the Area was the right number and so two such units were created, one in the north headed up by Pat Dwyer and one in the south headed by Charles Leyberg. The change was, however, largely superficial. All it meant was that the team leader now had to manage two offices rather than one, thus at a stroke doubling his management span and responsibility, but not his salary, which remained the same as before!

Unfortunately for me, but much more so for Pat, after a couple of years at the helm he discovered that he had a brain tumour and, although surgery was happily successful, Pat decided that early retirement was appropriate. No-one doubted that this was the right decision.

What I anticipated correctly came to pass! I was, in theory at least, supernumerary in CPS Cumbria and it was inevitable that I would be asked by David Farmer to fill the vacant "Unit Head" post. He actually presented it to me as though I had a choice in the matter. But he was simply being nice. There was no choice and, reluctantly, I took the job on. This job was most certainly graded at a level below my existing grade, and the CPS should have told me that I was "overbearing" in the post, that I would keep my existing salary only for so long, then would revert to the salary that applied to that job.

They, however, did nothing of the sort. Nothing was said by anyone and I kept my existing pay throughout the time I did the job. Another ineptitude by the management, but why should I complain?!! Charles Leyberg, of course, was doing the same job as me but paid significantly less than me! I don't know if he ever realised this, probably not but, if he did, he had every right to be very aggrieved…

CHAPTER THIRTEEN

2002 to 2005: ...And Down Again

And so it was back to the trials and tribulations of management once more. This time, however, the experience was to be much less congenial than my previous ones. Managing one team in one place is reasonably achievable. Managing a branch with four sub-offices was also comfortable enough, because the running of the individual offices and teams could be left to the four local team-leaders and one simply had the overview. But this now was neither fish nor fowl. I was having to manage two teams in two different locations, and without any intervening layer of management between me and the rest of the lawyers. It was a constant battle to keep a decent balance of resources between the two teams. I also had the additional task of managing our attendance of HCAs in the Crown Court. My choice I know, but I also continued to handle all the fatal road traffic accident cases in the Area and also retained a small caseload of other cases. I was determined to carry on with my hands-on involvement in casework, not to mention advocacy, and so I still appeared in the magistrates' court as well as the Crown Court as often as I could. There is no doubt that I over-stretched myself in this period, and it all ended in near oblivion for me! The pressures of work, however, were not in fact the cause of the life-threatening illness I contracted in 2005 - this was pure coincidence. It did, nevertheless, put an end to one of the less satisfactory periods of my career!

On paper we had adequate resources in Carlisle and West Cumbria; certainly, when I look back to the dark days in London, we had a wealth of resources! But there always seemed to be not enough lawyers at any one time, particularly in Workington. The demands of training, illness and holidays deprived us of lawyers constantly and, as time went on, the changing nature of our work also added to these demands.

We often had to resort to using barristers from the Manchester and Liverpool Bar, or solicitors from private practice to prosecute in the magistrates' court. As well as being an additional expense, this was not a practice I had ever particularly liked. One or two of these agents were very competent - and these tended to be the solicitors rather than the barristers. Many of them, however, were a liability. We tried to get the court files to them in advance of the hearing, but this was not always possible. Very often barristers would turn up at court half an hour before the start, knowing full well they had a pile of files to read and having no chance at all of being properly prepared. The feedback I used to get from the courts on their performance invariably reflected their lack of preparation, and often their lack of competence as well! I tried as much as possible to avoid using agents, but it was simply not possible for much of the time.

* * *

The latest CPS enterprise which impacted on our time and manpower in this period was the advent of what quickly became known as "Charging". This was, as far as I was concerned, one of the better ideas that came out of CPS headquarters, and is still with us, albeit in a qualified way, to this day. Basically, I believe it was designed to meet the growing level of cases that were being discontinued by the CPS lawyers, which, in some parts of the country, was getting to quite astronomical proportions.

The scheme was to transfer the decision to charge defendants from the police to the CPS, in all but minor traffic cases and some offences that didn't carry imprisonment. This would involve a lawyer being stationed in an office in the police station all day and officers turning up with their cases, discussing the evidence with the lawyer, and the latter making a decision whether to charge and, if so, with what, and also setting out, in either situation, what further evidence could or should be obtained. For out-of-hours situations, a new department, known as CPS Direct, was created - this meant lawyers being set up at home with computers, faxes and phones and dealing with police forces all over the country, making decisions and giving advice. These were volunteers who were, of course, then entirely removed from daytime prosecuting and were paid an allowance for anti-social hours working. Surprisingly enough, there were quite a few volunteers from the outset - some preferred the nocturnal shift to daytime prosecuting!

We set up offices in both Carlisle and Workington Police Stations, and lawyers attended there on a rota basis. I took my full share in this. Soon we found we were dealing with up to twelve or fifteen cases a day on occasions. By now we were entering into the digital age and using computers to type out our decisions and advice so, after every discussion with the police, we had to get everything down in writing before the next "conference" - no mean feat for those lawyers who were not accustomed to typing! It was definitely hard graft, particularly as one was dealing with cases from cold, with little or no paperwork being provided by the police, and having to make decisions largely on what one was being told. By the end of the day, after a shift of this work I found that I was physically exhausted, and my colleagues had the same experience.

I found the "Charging" experience rewarding. Not just because we were getting involved in the decision-making process but because we were dealing with officers face to face - officers who might just have been names on a file before. Also, certainly in the early days, officers might just turn up for "a bit of advice", not connected with the need for a decision. This took me back to the days of running a 'surgery' in Lincolnshire and I learnt that the police liked this very much and, in many cases, the CPS went up in their estimation. The whole exercise was, in my view, very beneficial for police/CPS working relations.

Some of my colleagues felt that Charging was an unnecessary extension of CPS powers. Not me. I had never been able to understand why we hadn't been given the power to make the decision in 1986 when the CPS was created. It always seemed absurd to me that the police retained the power to make the charging decision but, as soon as it was made, the CPS could change or reverse it! A political decision at the time, no doubt; a sop to the police for depriving them of the control of the prosecuting process? As far as I was concerned, Charging rationalised the situation. Unfortunately things didn't altogether stay this way. After a year or two it was apparent that in some areas of the country, and in London in particular, backlogs and delays were occurring, largely because CPS was putting off charging decisions for too long when the police were being asked to obtain further evidence before the lawyer would make a decision. Nothing wrong, in principle, with that as far as I was concerned, but it seems decisions were being delayed for weeks, or even months in some cases, and this was not acceptable to the government, who insisted that the system be altered to reduce or remove delay. The upshot was that the decision to charge was, in due course, returned to the police in a significant category of cases.

The system was eventually changed again, firstly by introducing an appointment process, so that officers could no longer just turn up for advice or a charging decision, but had to make an "appointment". Whilst this made the system less frenetic, it removed the element of officers dropping in for a bit of quick advice, which to me had been one of the benefits of the original scheme and, to my mind, very much enhanced CPS/police relations.

Then, later still, for whatever reason, the CPS seemed to give up altogether on face-to-face consultations, and everything was done by telephone, thus making daytime charging decision-making no different from the out-of-hours process. Again, in my view, this was a detrimental step. The result was that lawyers were making decisions on cases largely from other parts of the country, speaking to officers they had never met and never would meet, and dealing with cases they would never handle. In my experience, dealing face to face with officers from one's own 'patch' meant that there was a significant incentive to get it right - after all, one may be handling the case oneself ultimately or, at least, one of one's colleagues would be!! The detached, 'disembodied' system that was now being followed by night and by day, however, removed this imperative. If you got it wrong, there would be no comeback - it would be someone else's problem! I am not suggesting that there was an irresponsible, unprofessional approach by "Charging" lawyers, but there must have been a great temptation to make a quick decision and gloss over the evidential shortcomings - to make a decision, in short, which was likely to satisfy the officers seeking that decision! Certainly, I was to come across many decisions made by "Charging lawyers" that left much to be desired and seemed to have been made in haste and without much consideration. Needless to say, many of these decisions were later overturned by the local CPS which had to prosecute the case, rather destroying the point of the whole exercise!

Charging, to me was a good idea which the CPS centre, in its usual inept way, first implemented and then undermined. I believe that the only effective way to carry out the process was for face-to-face consultation, whatever the time of day or night. If this meant paying lawyers more to be on call at police stations during the night, then so be it! I have been in police stations making decisions in individual cases as late as 11.00 pm. I would hate to think what decisions would have been made in some of those cases by a lawyer on the other end of a telephone! It was never going to happen, of course, and in the end we got a system which was less than satisfactory!

* * *

Another good 'wheeze' by the CPS national management at this time was to devise for all lawyers a "proactive prosecuting" course. All lawyers were despatched on this course. What it was designed to do was to educate lawyers, not just in the need to make decisions on whether or not a defendant should be charged and if so with what, but to go further and actually consider if there were other lines of enquiry the police could pursue, and other evidence they could seek to reinforce and strengthen the case, or, indeed, to make the case one that could be pursued rather than not pursued! To me this was an exercise in stating the obvious! For years I had always written long minutes to the police when giving advice on cases - either there was insufficient evidence at present, but has this been considered and could such and such evidence be obtained? Or there is sufficient evidence to proceed, but the case could be better if this or that evidence could be acquired… To me, this approach was an absolutely fundamental complement to the basic advice one was giving or the decision one was making.

It seemed, however, that the centre was not satisfied that many lawyers were doing this! They were simply looking at the evidence the police had gathered and making a decision on that, or giving advice on that, and saying no more. In other words, the police investigate, we prosecute, and never the twain shall meet! I suspect many prosecutors believed that the police would not take kindly to CPS lawyers trespassing on their territory and suggesting other lines of enquiry. I had never found this to be the case with the police, however. They tended to welcome the dialogue - sometimes they would agree that another line could be followed, sometimes they would tell me that they had already done that without success. Either way, I would consider it an appropriate approach by the prosecutor - whilst the police have the investigative skills, it is the prosecutor who knows from his experience what he has to prove in court, what is going to pass muster and what isn't, and what additional evidence might turn the case in the prosecution's favour. It should be a two-way approach to case preparation, a dialogue, not a compartmentalised situation!

The course was well-conceived for these reasons, even if it should not have been necessary!

* * *

These years mark the start of the government's obsession with putting the victim of crime "at the heart of the criminal justice system". It was felt that the pendulum had swung too far in favour of the defendant and that the balance needed redressing. There was a raft of measures and initiatives designed to safeguard the interests of victims and witnesses and to put them on something of a pedestal.

Applications could now be made in appropriate cases for witnesses to give their evidence behind screens or by live-TV link, and for children in sex and other cases to have their evidence in chief recorded on video by the police so that their only 'live' evidence was in cross-examination, which would also be over TV link.

We were encouraged to consult with victims before dropping or downgrading charges, and we were now required to write to victims with a detailed explanation if charges were materially changed, discontinued or dropped. In certain circumstances victims could demand a meeting with the CPS lawyer - this was introduced for cases in which a fatality was involved, giving next of kin the opportunity of meeting with lawyer and police at several stages of the case. This was, in fact, just an extension of what I had been doing in such cases for years.

Then, in an initiative called "No witness, no justice", the CPS and police had to plan and set up a new body called the "Witness Care Unit", which would take over the responsibility of warning witnesses for court and also generally looking after witnesses throughout the life of a case. This complemented the service which was provided at court by the volunteers and salaried head of the Witness Service. The latter would meet witnesses at court, both defence and prosecution (keeping them apart where necessary) and provide refreshment, information about court processes and a visit to the courtroom itself if required.

In many ways much of this was to be welcomed, and it really only firmed-up earlier schemes such as the moribund Witness Care agreement and the "Victims Charter". Attending court and giving evidence was always, at best, going to be an ordeal for civilian witnesses (and, indeed, many police officers as well!), and any measures which mitigated the ordeal and encouraged and facilitated the attendance of witnesses at court had to be a positive development. Getting witnesses to court, let alone persuading them to go into the witness box, had always been fraught with difficulties.

There was also a danger, however, in my view. Cosseting witnesses and victims throughout the life of the case, consulting with victims, offering them meetings and giving them written explanations for decisions, was putting them on a pedestal. It was tending to give many of them an impression that they had more influence on the course and outcome of a case than they in fact did or could have. It also tended to convey to some the impression that attending court and giving evidence was an option and not a requirement! Indeed, it tended to create the false impression that the prosecutor was 'their' lawyer in much the same way as a solicitor or barrister in civil proceedings, there to be instructed!

To my mind a balance had to be struck. I had always made it very clear to victims and next of kin that, although I was talking to them and listening to them, at the end of the day any decisions about the direction of the case were mine, and I was acting for the Crown, for the State, and not for them! It was important to make it clear to witnesses that attending court and giving evidence was both a duty and a legal requirement, and that there were sanctions for refusal or failure, that they might be arrested if they failed to come to court when required, and that they could be sent to prison if they refused to testify. It was also incumbent on the CPS prosecutor to remain detached from witnesses and victims, and to safeguard his or her independence because, in the last analysis, decisions may have to be made by the lawyers which might not be palatable to the victim. The CPS, after all, was an independent prosecuting authority and not a body 'in bed' with victims and witnesses.

I rather felt that this portfolio of measures tended to work against the independence of the prosecutor. In particular the dreaded "DCV" letter. This refers to "Direct Communication with Victims" and to the letter we had to write to "victims" where we changed or dropped charges. There were many such letters which had to be written and there was, I believe, a deal of resentment on the part of many of us that we had to account to victims for the exercise of our statutory and independent discretion.

Putting a high priority on the interests of victims in the criminal justice system and diminishing the importance of the defendant was, no doubt, a 'sexy' message for the government to be putting out and attractive to much of the electorate, so it was bound to be given to us as a package that had to be delivered.

The same sort of thinking no doubt coloured the message we were being given by the centre at this time in relation to the 'victims' of rape. The government felt that the conviction rate for Rape was far too low. It was certainly right that not many such cases resulted in conviction, even where we felt they should be prosecuted and, in all probability, we were prosecuting some cases which didn't pass the "sufficiency of evidence" test. But it really should have been no great surprise that few were convicted. It is the nature of the beast that there are rarely any witnesses to the alleged act, and not very often that there is any other physical evidence. Very often the act of intercourse is not in issue anyway - it is simply a question of whether the 'victim' consented to it or not or, more likely, whether the defendant believed the victim was consenting. The case will invariably boil down then to the word of the complainant against that of the defendant. Given the heavy burden of proof on the Crown, is it surprising that juries acquit so often in such cases?!

It also strikes me as offensive that we are told that "not enough defendants are being convicted" of rape. Might not some of them be innocent!!? Who is to say that the figures aren't right? It is not uncommon, as we know, for some women to falsely claim rape, for whatever reason, and there are a good few recorded instances of women being convicted of exactly that!

Nonetheless, we in the local CPS Areas were tasked with improving the stats! Special "Rape prosecutors" were created to deal with such cases and to do whatever was necessary to improve the conviction rate. I do not know whether this objective was, in fact, ever achieved - I doubt it! The 2014 examples of celebrities being acquitted of such charges after jury trial serve as a continued reminder of the infrequency of conviction!

⋆ ⋆ ⋆

By 2005 the Magistrates' Court landscape in Cumbria had been transformed in two significant ways.

First of all, by that date we had three "Designated Case Workers" (later to be renamed "Associate Prosecutors"). Within a year or two of this we had a further two. The DCWs were able to prosecute most 'guilty plea' cases in the adult court and later also conduct remand hearings. Some, I believe, would also go on in due course to be able to do simple trials. They were not, however, able to exercise the power of Crown Prosecutors to drop charges at court and had to consult with a CP before doing so or to accept pleas proffered by defence advocates. This meant that, in practice, they could operate only in a court building where two courts were going at the same time.

The proposal to create DCWs led to strenuous objections and institution of litigation by the First Division Association, the trade union that represented Crown Prosecutors. It required a radical amendment to the law to allow unqualified persons to prosecute, and the CPS lawyers argued that it was contrary to the Prosecution of Offences Act 1985. Their real objection, however, was that they had undergone years of training and exams to reach their status as Crown Prosecutors and now people without qualifications were being let loose in court as prosecutors after, in effect, no more than a couple of weeks' training provided by CPS trainers.

As a Crown Prosecutor myself, I sympathised with and understood the fury of the lawyers. By allowing unqualified prosecutors, the status of the Crown Prosecutor was seriously diminished. If caseworkers with two weeks' training could do the job, why did we need qualified lawyers prosecuting in the magistrates' court? And think of the money that could be saved, as the DCWs were paid a lot less than the CPs!

Many saw this development as part of a general 'dumbing down' in the criminal justice system, designed to cut escalating costs. They would point to the arrival of the HCAs in the Crown Court as also part of this process. It seemed to me, however, that there was little similarity between the position of the DCWs and that of the HCAs. There is a world of difference between the situation of unqualified persons becoming prosecutors after two weeks' training and qualified lawyers with years of experience taking their advocacy skills into the Crown Court, where life is different, but not that much different!

Objection and litigation proved futile, however, and the DCWs came to stay. They came to cover up to 30% of the magistrates' court advocacy and, these days, one is just as likely to find an "Associate Prosecutor" doing a full court list as a Crown Prosecutor. I can't say that I have seen much of them prosecuting in court, but the feedback I have had over the last ten years or so is that most of them are perfectly adequate and as good as many of the qualified agents the CPS use to prosecute in the magistrates' court. One cannot expect many APs to aspire to or attain the advocacy skills of the excellent prosecutors and defence solicitors I have known over the years but, if they are 'cutting the mustard' as far as the bench is concerned and comparing favourably with "qualified" advocates in court, then this is surely good enough, whether or not standards of advocacy and expectations are lower than in the past!

The world of the Crown Prosecutor has changed. There is no longer the routine daily experience of magistrates' court advocacy and, these days, he or she is just as likely to be sitting in the office dealing with case preparation as prosecuting in the narrow sense of courtroom advocacy. But they should change with it if advocacy is their choice! Certainly, in 2005 there was every opportunity and encouragement for Crown Prosecutors to become HCAs and take their advocacy skills to new heights and to the ultimate experience of jury trials. Many did take the chance, and many of those who did not then take it may now regret that they didn't, as the opportunities of becoming an HCA have somewhat reduced in recent times.

★ ★ ★

The other big change in Cumbria was the arrival in 2004 of a full-time District Judge. Gerald Chalk had been a criminal lawyer all his career, having begun as a prosecuting solicitor in the County Prosecuting Solicitor's office in Newcastle (where he was, apparently, mentored by my friend, Paul Grieveson!) and then spending twenty years as a defence practitioner in Nottingham. Most of our prosecutors were at first somewhat daunted by the prospect of appearing before a professional judge. I was less so, perhaps because I had had this experience for a while in London and had also prosecuted fatal accident "Due Care" trials before DJs and deputy District Judges in Cumbria. They needn't have worried, as it didn't turn out to be a daunting experience, and soon everyone was quite comfortable with appearing in the DJ court! He had an easygoing style, although he could express anger when it was required. He had the common touch with defendants and could speak to them in language which they could understand. One story, which may or may not be apocryphal, was of an occasion when, granting bail to a defendant in Kendal Court, he told him "not to get pissed" on Saturday night or he would be back in court!

I believe that, at first at least, many of the lay magistrates were less than happy with the advent of the DJ. He could, of course, take a much bigger share of the business, as he would get through cases in half the time. As far as I am aware, however, any such lingering resentment has long gone.

After the conviction and sentence of Michelle Dickinson, the other stand-out case in Cumbria at this time was the resurrection of the prosecution against Gordon Park for the murder of his first wife, Carol, in 1976 - the infamous "Lady in the Lake" case. The reader will recall that the first prosecution had been discontinued in 1998 for "lack of evidence" - although that was not the view of all those involved, including myself. Now, in 2004, a new investigating team, on the case in Barrow, announced that they believed they had uncovered fresh material evidence which would justify the proceedings being revived. I attended a conference with the officers, along with Phil Bates, the senior lawyer in the Barrow office, and David Farmer, who had, of course, been instrumental in the decision to discontinue the case in 1998.

At first glance the 'new' evidence was strong. We had statements from two fellow inmates of Park when he was remanded in custody in 1997 at Preston prison; they had 'come forward' with stories that Park had confessed to the murder to them. Also, we now had a new "knot expert" - a man with experience of making comparisons of sailing knots and giving evidence to that effect, who now maintained that he had examined the knots on Carol's body and compared them with examples of knots in rope-work found in Park's house in Leece and, in his opinion, they were tied by the same person! There was also now a piece of stone which had been recovered from the bed of Coniston Water, near where the body had been found, and this appeared to be very similar, if not identical, to the stonework in the walls of Park's bungalow. Finally, there was a statement from a woman who had come forward on reading of the previous case in the newspapers and recalled that, on a date in July 1976, she had been sitting by Coniston Water and seen a tall man in glasses standing in a boat, appearing to push something into the water - she had remarked to her husband that "perhaps he was getting rid of his wife"!

It was decided to arrange a further conference with a new prosecuting counsel and to invite the knot expert to attend. Alistair Webster QC, who had prosecuted Michelle Dickinson, was now instructed. At that conference we all agreed that the new evidence justified the reinstitution of the proceedings against Park, and that he would be rearrested and recharged with the murder of his first wife. Alistair Webster went so far as to say that he "would have had a go in 1998"!

The knot expert turned out to be an affable but elderly gentleman, who gave us an interesting exposition on his theory that the knots had been tied by the same person. As it happened, however, Alistair Webster found him a rather 'flaky' witness and his evidence was, in the event, not used at the trial.

As to the other 'new' evidence, that of the two cell-mates of Park, who had allegedly heard him confess to the murder, it would not have been difficult to dismiss their accounts as fictional and attention-seeking. Wainwright and Banks were hardly men of good reputation and Banks was a person with significant learning difficulties. Neither account was consistent with the known facts or, indeed, with each other. The evidence was led at the trial but can hardly have carried much weight with the jury. The evidence of the lady on the edge of the lake in July 1976 was also led at the trial but was really too nebulous to be of much value. Indeed, the type of boat she was describing didn't match the type of craft that Park was known to have had in 1976. And finally, the recovery of the piece of "bluestone" near the body was hardly conclusive, as the type of stone was to be found in places other than the house in Leece.

The reality is that the evidence upon which the jury convicted Park was not really different from that which was available in 1998. The case was presented on the same basis as we had thought it should have been then - that this was not a stranger killing, it could only have been Park, and the strong circumstantial evidence pointed emphatically to Park.

Park's legal team made strong attempts to persuade the Court of Appeal that there was significant new evidence that showed the conviction was unsafe. This was rejected by the Court of Appeal judges, who found that there was "strong circumstantial evidence of Park's guilt".

Gordon Park hanged himself in his prison cell in 2010, on his sixty-sixth birthday.

* * *

By the autumn of 2004 I was finding life in Cumbria increasingly difficult. The demands of Charging, advocacy in both Magistrates' and Crown Courts, carrying a caseload, organising the rota for attendance of some nine or ten HCAs at court, training, and dashing between two offices to manage some twelve lawyers and about twenty other staff, were running me ragged, and my work/life balance was severely out of kilter. Of course it was at least partially my fault, as I could have cut out the advocacy and the caseload, as many managers undoubtedly would have done, but this was not my way and the job would have been even more unpalatable than it was becoming had I taken this course!

David Farmer was a pure manager and no longer made any pretence of fitting the "Glidewell" profile of devoting 40% of his time to "prosecuting" in any shape or form! Even he by this time, however, the much-vaunted Glidewell reforms being a dead duck, was starting to realise that structural change in Cumbria was a necessity, even more so than it had been when I had devised the blueprint for change back in the 1990s. There were no economies of scale in our structure and the management span of the unit heads was too great. There were also no separate arrangements for the handling of complex casework, these having 'gone west' when I became a unit head in 2002.

With the blessing of national HQ, David secured the services of an independent expert in management systems and various other things; he became a regular visitor to the Area and regularly attended our Area Management meetings. I seem to recall that his name was John Sprachan, or suchlike, although I have no great cause to remember him. He was forever demanding interviews with me and other staff, forever creating elaborate graphics on his computer, but never actually coming up with any practical scheme for reorganising CPS Cumbria. He made no secret of the fact that he thought I was wasting my time being involved in casework and advocacy.

I came close to never witnessing the 'brave new world' that was eventually conceived. In May 2005, whilst on a walking holiday in Scotland, I contracted severe leg pains and had to come home on the train, leaving Charles Leyberg, who was also on that trip, to bring my car back. The next few days were somewhat of a blur, although I visited A & E and the GP without ever getting any medical diagnosis of my condition. One of the last things I remember before coming round in a hospital bed was driving down to the office in Workington to look at my emails. Then nothing! Apparently a friend was sent to fetch me when I didn't return home, and tells tales of finding me reading the phone directory, shouting about the lack of evidence, and declaiming in Latin! My wife called *Cuedoc* out and I was shipped off to hospital. Still no diagnosis, and my wife was told to "prepare for the worst". Fortunately, there was an Australian registrar who had seen encephalitis before, for this is what it was, and the appropriate treatment was started...

It was more than three months later that I returned to work to find that the world had moved on in my absence, or, in some respects, had moved back in time!!

David Farmer had gone. He had been "persuaded" to take a year doing "other work" for the CPS with a commitment that he would then be allowed to leave with a "package". I don't really know whether he wanted to go or whether he didn't - I would be speculating. But gone he was. Charles Leyberg was acting Chief Crown Prosecutor.

Not for the first time, or indeed the last, my job had also "gone". The momentous and 'earth-shattering' outcome of the months of John Sprachan's planning was that we had gone back to where we were in 1999! There were still to be four offices in Cumbria and, once again, each was to be headed by a Divisional Crown Prosecutor. I find it difficult to believe that this was the best they could come up with in my absence, or perhaps they just gave up in tedium and frustration. The only positive result to come out of all this was that there was to be a Complex Casework Lawyer for Cumbria. I was given the "option" of taking this post or… If there was an option it was, as far as I was concerned, a 'no-brainer'. And guess what? Nothing again was said about me "overbearing" in the post or that it was anything less than worthy of the grade I was still on! I grasped the job with both hands and said goodbye to management for the last time.

CHAPTER FOURTEEN
2005 to 2011: ...Out of the Trees and into the Sunlit Uplands

The temporary stewardship of Charles Leyberg came to an end in November 2005, when Clare Lindley was appointed Chief Crown Prosecutor for Cumbria. Charles had applied for the job and was interviewed; I also applied, but was not interviewed. I was not surprised at all at the way things turned out in this regard. HQ were, no doubt, looking for a 'new broom', someone untainted by association with the previous regime, which had been mauled somewhat in reports by the CPS Inspectorate and had exceeded its annual budget, apparently, on more than one occasion. As for me, I had clearly passed the sell-by date as far as the CPS were concerned, although this had probably already taken place in 1999! No matter - I was doing what I wanted to be doing!

Clare Lindley was a feisty lady in her mid-forties. She had been acting Chief Crown Prosecutor in Cheshire recently and came with a reputation for getting things done, and getting them done with a high degree of efficiency. This reputation was quickly vindicated. She mended one or two 'broken bridges' and got us working within budget and, although she did no more advocacy or casework than her predecessor, she did show a keen interest in what casework was being done and what was going on at court. She was especially keen that we stepped up our attendance at the Crown Court, and I was tasked to continue managing this process and to meet targets for saving Counsel fees that were to be set.

I was impressed by her industry and achievements, and I remained impressed throughout the four years she was with us. I found out, however, that there was a 'darker' side, and this ultimately worked to my disadvantage. By the end of her reign I had lost any trust or sense of loyalty I may have had initially. I don't think I was alone in this regard.

★ ★ ★

As far as my own work was concerned, this six-year period was the most productive and, I felt, the most successful of my career. Certainly for the first three years, as in my previous spell as a Complex Casework Lawyer, I more or less chose the cases I handled. I continued to deal with most of the fatal road accident work, but most of my business came from a close association with the Serious Organised Crime Unit. This was a squad which worked from Police Headquarters at Penrith, mainly carrying out undercover operations against "target" criminals involved in Class A drug trafficking.

I became involved in a series of multi-defendant cases in which large numbers of accused were charged with Conspiracy to supply heroin or cocaine. Almost all these persons were convicted, and long sentences of imprisonment were imposed on many of them. We then followed up this success with equally successful applications to confiscate their assets. I worked closely with the Serious Organised Crime Unit throughout the life of these cases, being consulted well before charge, making the charging decisions, and then conducting the first remand applications at court and often the first hearings in the Crown Court. At the arrest stage of the operation the police would have a planned timetable for the sequence of arrests and I would make myself available, often by mobile phone outside normal working hours, to make charging decisions. I can recall coming out of a pub on a Friday night to take a call following the arrest and interview of a number of persons, and of agreeing over the phone that they should be charged and the nature of the charges. Strictly speaking, this should have been put in writing there and then and not done verbally and, indeed, done by the out-of-hours team, CPS Direct, but this would have been quite impractical. I soon found, however, that custody officers were prepared to charge defendants on my verbal say-so and for the necessary paperwork to be sent on afterwards! I was, of course, making decisions without any written evidence and relying on the word of the officers as to what had happened in the interviews, but I was dealing with skilled and competent officers I came to trust and, of course, I already knew what evidence had been gathered before arrest. It would have been quite impossible for a CPS Direct lawyer to have made any sort of positive decision in the circumstances he or she would have found themselves in and without my knowledge of the case, and it was important that a decision was made as it would have been detrimental to the case for many of the defendants to have been released without charge at this stage.

The first of these cases arose out of a police surveillance operation called "Operation Acquiline". This was targeted against a well-known Carlisle criminal called "Bimbo" O'Neil, who had recently been released from an eight-year sentence of imprisonment for supplying heroin. He was a member of a notorious local family of ne'er-do-wells, others of whom I was to encounter further in the years to come. The O'Neils were probably descendants of the Border Reivers, and criminality was deeply ingrained in their genes! I had been involved in the previous prosecution of "Bimbo", and he had been out of prison barely a couple of months before he was once more at the centre of a large-scale heroin-supply enterprise.

The surveillance device used by the police in this operation was a probe inserted in "Bimbo's" car. They had managed to enter his vehicle whilst it was in a garage for repair and to conceal a listening device, which they would monitor from their office at Police HQ. By this means they picked up and transcribed dozens of conversations O'Neil had with 'customers' he met by appointment and, although many of these discussions were conducted in the coded language used by the drug-trafficking fraternity, most of the officers were sufficiently experienced in this field to be able to interpret the conversations as being about drug supply. The evidence gathered by the probe was complemented by visual surveillance by officers who observed O'Neil meeting with known persons in his car. Much of the evidence, therefore, had been gathered before the arrests and interviews, and there was enough to be able to charge even if defendants made no admissions in these interviews.

What the evidence from the listening device revealed was that the persons O'Neil was meeting were themselves 'street-level' heroin dealers and not merely heroin users. We were thus able to charge each of these individuals with Conspiracy with O'Neil to supply "others" with heroin, and to depict O'Neil himself as at the top of the local hierarchy of dealers. It was instructive, indeed, that when O'Neil and many of the other defendants were remanded in custody following charge, the number of burglaries and the incidence of shoplifting in Carlisle dropped, at least for a while. There was, temporarily at least, an absence of available heroin for the users, and the need to commit crime to fund its purchase was removed. Needless to say, the vacuum was soon filled by others and crime returned to its normal levels!

As a result of this operation, some sixteen or seventeen defendants were convicted of Conspiracy to Supply heroin - all of them in fact, albeit one or two after trial (most pleaded guilty). There were substantial prison sentences all round, and O'Neil himself received a sentence in double figures.

We built upon this success by making use of the provisions of the Proceeds of Crime Act 2002. It had been possible prior to this legislation to seize and confiscate the assets of drug dealers and others, but now it was easier and became a routine part of the prosecution process. Many of the "Operation Acquiline" defendants were 'men of straw' and had no assets worth confiscating, but O'Neil and his wife (also convicted in the case) had a house and other assets. I had already been to court during the life of the case to obtain from a judge a "Restraint Order" which, in effect, 'froze' these defendants' assets and prevented them disposing of them, and now we went on to apply successfully for the frozen assets to be confiscated and sold to meet what was determined to be the defendants' benefits from their criminal activities.

The Proceeds of Crime Act is a splendidly draconian piece of legislation. Not only does it allow the prosecution to secure the confiscation of a convicted defendant's assets to pay for the benefits that have accrued to him or her as the immediate result of his crime, but also there is, in many cases, an ability for the court to make assumptions that any property that has come into the possession of, or been transferred by, a defendant over the six years before criminal proceedings were commenced, is the proceeds of crime and liable to be confiscated. The provisions of this legislation have been used to claw back successfully enormous sums of money as "ill-gotten" gains in the ten or so years of its existence. In the past, many serious criminals have gone to prison secure in the knowledge that, on their release, there were still substantial assets awaiting them - no longer the case in many instances!

In the "Acquiline" case, a later connected investigation against various relatives of the O'Neils uncovered large sums of money concealed in houses and bank accounts that represented the laundered proceeds of the O'Neils' dealing. Not only were the various relatives convicted of money-laundering offences (created by the Proceeds of Crime Act 2002), but the money was confiscated as benefits of the O'Neils' criminal activity.

Surveillance operations using a probe were used sparingly, but with considerable success. One was that directed against "Tarka" Robinson in about 2002 (see before - Chapter Seven). Then, following Operation Acquiline, the Serious Organised Crime Unit launched another such operation against a notorious West Cumbrian drug trafficker, John Roe. This resulted in about twelve persons, from West Yorkshire, the north east and London, as well as Cumbria, being convicted of Conspiracy to supply cocaine, followed by another raft of heavy custodial sentences with, of course, the now routine sequel of confiscation of assets. One of the interesting features of this case was that one of the defendants had a previous conviction for drug trafficking in either Thailand or Laos, and had actually been sentenced to death in that country. The sentence had eventually been commuted to life imprisonment to be served in the UK, and the defendant had not long been released from the sentence when he became embroiled in this new conspiracy and was now facing another lengthy period of custody.

* * *

My caseload at this time, however, was not all about Class A drug dealing. There were four other stand-out cases in which I was involved and which were not under the auspices of SOCU, although they would have had input into one of the investigations and one of their officers was the investigating officer in another.

"Operation Cadillac" was a unique case at this time because it was the first occasion that we had made use of the provisions of section 73 of the Serious Organised Crime and Police Act 2005 in order to secure convictions. Basically, this allows the prosecutor to enter into an agreement with certain defendants whereby they agree to plead 'guilty' to what they are charged with, make full disclosure about the criminal involvement of other, more important defendants and, if necessary, testify against them; in return their "assistance" is brought to the attention of the sentencing judge, who may then reflect that in their sentence. They may be sentenced before the need to give evidence arises but, if they welsh on the deal, they can be brought back before the sentencing judge and their sentence reviewed.

Defendants may from time to time have benefited in the past from giving evidence against co-defendants, but this was giving statutory recognition to such arrangements.

In this case the principal defendants were the three directors of a Northern Ireland haulage firm, Boyles Transport. In an operation conducted by the Cumbria Constabulary Road Policing Unit, about fourteen of their employed drivers were found to have regularly interfered with their digital tachograph equipment, enabling them to drive for significantly longer hours and carry out more trips than they would have been able to do if they had complied with the Drivers Hours Regulations. The road safety implications of exceeding hours in this way are obvious, but then so are the likely consequences for the profitability of the firm. It was easy enough to prosecute the drivers in this case, but the real test for the prosecution was whether we could demonstrate that the directors had aided and abetted, indeed solicited, the actions of the drivers. In police interviews, the directors insisted they had not and were unaware of what the drivers were up to!

We felt we had enough evidence to secure convictions against the directors on the circumstantial evidence that had been gathered, but success was by no means guaranteed. Before the matter came to trial, however, there was an unexpected turn of events. I was approached by two of the defence solicitors, who represented half a dozen of the defendants, indicating that their clients would be prepared to "assist" the Crown. Initially they were looking for us to discontinue the proceedings against these defendants, but my response was that this was not an option! In due course, however, I was able to draw up and get them to sign agreements whereby they would agree to enter 'guilty' pleas to the charges they faced of Using False Instruments, agree to be re-interviewed by the police and make full disclosure of their employers' criminality, and give evidence against them if necessary. They duly made statements implicating the three Boyles in having, in effect, coerced them into falsifying tachograph records, on pain of dismissal from their employment if they failed to comply. When we served these statements on the Boyles, it had the desired effect and they changed their pleas to guilty. They were sentenced to imprisonment, the drivers were not.

"Operation Tandem" generated the most paper I have ever seen in a case in my career. Ironically, it was a case about the disposal, recycling and management of 'waste'!

The defendants were the proprietor and the management team of a waste disposal company based in Barrow-in-Furness. The company had a contract with Cumbria County Council to manage waste recycling sites in the south of the county and dispose of harmful waste such as refrigerators, TVs and computers. Essentially the allegation was that the firm was, in its returns to the Council, grossly and falsely inflating the volume of waste it was "managing" and thus substantially increasing its income, at the expense of the council-tax payer. It was a million-pound fraud.

One of the difficulties that confronted the police and me throughout the life of the case was that this was a joint investigation by police and the Cumbria County Council Trading Standards Department. It was, to say the least, an uneasy relationship between the two investigative bodies. The police lead was Detective Constable Barry Cowin, a very experienced detective, and he really should have been allowed to direct the investigation. The Trading Standards officers did not have the experience to run an investigation of this sort, but they had 'hired' as a 'consultant' a retired detective superintendent from West Yorkshire. The result was that Trading Standards were frequently on a 'frolic' of their own, their 'consultant', Brian Steele, encouraging them to take witness statements and gather material left, right and centre, long after this was necessary, against the advice of Barry Cowin and, subsequently, of prosecuting counsel.

This unrestrained approach by Trading Standards created difficulties and embarrassment for the prosecution. I had authorised charges against six defendants, I had served the prosecution case on the defence, and we were well past the Case Management hearing in the Crown Court, and yet Trading Standards were still showering me with statements and material they had gathered. All this had to be sifted. Some did have some evidential value, but added little to the case we had already built; most was just "unused material". The defence complained to the trial judge about the apparently endless process of evidence and unused material being served upon them, and the judge set deadlines for the process to halt, deadlines we failed to meet more than once. Counsel seemed powerless to stop the Trading

Standards officers collecting more and more material as the trial date drew nearer.

Ultimately we had served something like three thousand pages of evidence and had about three times that in unused material. Counsel decided the volume of evidence was too unwieldy and we then spent a lot of time chopping out a good deal of the evidence, repaginating the statement and exhibit bundles, and re-serving them on the defence. More complaints from the defence and more exasperation from the judge! Then, to cap it all, about two weeks before the scheduled start of the trial, Trading Standards let slip that they had seized a computer months ago from one of the County Council's offices and that this contained reams of material which would have at least some bearing on the case. This resulted in days of intensive work, identifying this material, downloading it, sifting it, sorting out what was disclosable and then arranging service on the defence in an acceptable format. The defence were getting this new material only a few days before the trial and, not surprisingly, they were very fractious about it!

As the trial got ever nearer, the defence put us on notice that they would be raising preliminary issues with the judge about the admissibility of some of the evidence. As with "Operation Cadillac", there were persons who were involved in the criminality in a smaller way than the principal defendants and who were prepared to testify against the latter. These were employed drivers of the defendant company's vehicles and employed operatives at waste recycling sites. Like the "Cadillac" drivers, they had assisted the Conspiracy by complying with instructions from their employers. Unlike "Cadillac", statements had been taken from these persons in the course of the investigation after Brian Steele had decided to inform them that they would not be prosecuted and we had served their statements as part of the evidence. As far as I was concerned there was nothing wrong with this - it is perfectly legitimate for the prosecuting authority to decide that some offenders are small fry and need not be prosecuted whilst going after the bigger fish, and to use them as witnesses. I had endorsed what Brian Steele had done here and, certainly, prosecution counsel had never made any adverse observations on what had happened. Nonetheless, the defence meant to challenge the admissibility of this evidence and were threatening to demand that Brian Steele and I give sworn evidence as to what had gone on.

In the event this was a damp squib. On the first day of the trial, and before it started, there were a lot of negotiations between the parties. The upshot was that we agreed to let three of the defendants go if the other three pleaded 'guilty' to an amended indictment that alleged a lesser amount of money obtained by deception. This was perfectly acceptable to us, since the three acquitted defendants were really only one step up from the drivers and other operatives in the hierarchy, and we were securing convictions against the proprietor of the company and his two senior managers. The cash figure in the indictment was not unduly important either. The three convicted defendants were each sentenced to imprisonment for terms of between eight and eighteen months. All in all, the prosecution team was very happy with this result.

⋆ ⋆ ⋆

The other two significant cases I dealt with in this period were both homicide cases. Both attracted attention from the national media. They were both unusual cases, if not entirely unique.

The "Woolpack Baby" case ran from 2005 to 2006. It began when a dead foetus was discovered in a pedal bin in the ladies' toilets of the *Woolpack Inn*, a pub in the far reaches of Eskdale in the western lakes. The 'mother' was quickly identified as a young, quite inadequate lady from East Anglia, who admitted giving birth in the toilets and abandoning the baby, but maintained that the child had been stillborn. The post mortem was carried out by the eminent Home Office Forensic Pathologist Dr Alison Armour, a feisty individual who was noted for her tendency for uncompromising and forthright views, never afraid to stick her neck out! She was quite certain that the child had been alive when it emerged from the birth canal and that death had been caused subsequently by asphyxiation, probably by using the umbilical cord. On the basis of her evidence, I authorised a murder charge.

Unfortunately, or perhaps otherwise, this was the highpoint of the case as far as the prosecution was concerned. Although they had no chance to conduct a second post mortem, a number of other forensic pathologists were recruited by the defence to look at the PM photographs. They were equally as adamant as Dr Armour that the child had been strangled by the cord in the journey up the birth canal. Given the range of expert evidence against the Armour view, we felt that likelihood of conviction had disappeared and the murder charge was dropped, leaving just a conviction for Concealing a Birth.

There was no wailing and gnashing of teeth by any of the prosecution team as a result of this outcome. Rather, a feeling that perhaps it was, at the end of the day, the right result!

The "Tractor" case was a very bizarre case, the stuff of crime novels and TV homicide serials. It also had the special added ingredient of Dr Alison Armour.

The death of Jane Wilson came to light when, in December 2007 her husband, Cumbrian farmer Robert Wilson, made a hysterical 999 call to the police to announce that he had killed her in a tragic accident by running over her with his tractor as he was manoeuvring the vehicle in a barn. Police officers from Carlisle attended the scene and, indeed, found the lifeless body of Mrs Wilson in circumstances which tallied with the husband's story. With the benefit of hindsight it is easy to be critical, but now it seems remarkable how the police and, indeed, the pathologist at Carlisle Infirmary who carried out the autopsy on the body, readily accepted the husband's account that he had run over her body after she had been knocked over by cattle. Foul play was not suspected.

The matter would, in all probability, have rested there had it not been for a chance visit to the farm by Mrs Wilson's son and daughter in early 2008 whilst Mr Wilson was away from the area. By this time the funeral had taken place and the body had been cremated. Whilst looking amongst their mother's possessions the children made an important and, for them, devastating find in the marital bedroom - greetings cards, clearly addressed to Robert Wilson, from "Kathy". The messages in the cards left little doubt that there existed a deeply amorous relationship between Wilson and "Kathy", and that it was not one of recent origin.

The children initially brought their discovery to the attention of a retired police officer who, in turn, took the evidence to the police. Inevitably, a full-scale police investigation was then mounted into Mrs Wilson's death.

There was, of course, no body to be examined, but Dr Armour was called in to look at the photographs that had been taken of the post mortem and of the scene of the "accident". Her opinion as to the cause of death completely confounded that of the original pathologist.

Basically, she asserted that the total absence of blood at the scene and on the body made it highly improbable that Mrs Wilson had been crushed by the tractor while she was still alive. In other words, Robert Wilson was running over a dead body.

Then the investigation started to uncover details about Wilson's lifestyle and his finances. It turned out that he had been in serious debt prior to his wife's death, and had taken out several policies of insurance on her life not long before the incident. The proceeds from these policies would have paid off all his debts. It was also discovered that he had been making regular trips to Spain, running up more debts, but had also purchased an expensive sports car that was nowhere to be found.

The mysterious "Kathy" was tracked down and identified as one Kathy McNeill, an attractive, blonde lady in her late forties who at this time was living in Spain. Her story 'squared the circle'. Wilson had been living a double life for some two years before his wife's death. He had met Kathy in a bar in southern Spain and a full physical relationship had developed between them. He had lavished her with gifts, including the sports car. He told her that his wife had died previously from cancer. It was quite apparent that Kathy was completely oblivious to the fact that Mrs Wilson was, at this time, still very much alive. The pair contemplated a more permanent relationship back in the UK, to where Kathy was intending to return.

Wilson's two 'worlds' in late 2007 were about to 'collide'. Arrangements had been made for Kathy to visit Wilson at the Cumbrian farm. By coincidence, this would have been the very weekend that Mrs Wilson met her unfortunate end in the "accident"!! Not surprisingly, Wilson had asked Kathy to delay her visit to the farm by a few days, and he invented a pretext for this purpose. When Kathy finally arrived at the farm the deed was done, although Wilson had to be careful to ensure that she got no wind of the fact that Jane Wilson had died only a short time before. Wilson was 'walking a tightrope' but by March 2008 he must have thought he had got away with it.

I had been put in the picture as to the progress of the investigation and in April 2008 Wilson was arrested, the investigating officers being confident that they had enough evidence to charge him, whatever he might say in interview. I had at this time primed the Chief Crown

Prosecutor, Clare Lindley, and told her what I knew about the evidence that had been gathered. She was sceptical about its strength and counselled me against authorising any charges at this stage unless there were admissions made in police interviews.

Matters, however, took an unexpected turn and I was put in a position where I had to make a very quick decision. The police had conducted several interviews with Wilson, and he had denied that he had murdered his wife, although he admitted his illicit relationship with Kathy McNeill. The investigators intended to interview him further and had made an application to the magistrates' court to extend the detention period beyond the normal length. Unfortunately the application was, apparently, flawed and the District Judge refused it! This meant that when I was summoned to Carlisle Police Station late on a spring evening, the PACE clock had almost run its course and the defendant, within about half an hour of my arrival, would have to be charged or released. There was no doubt as to which course the police were wanting. It was clear they were quite anxious as to the prospect of Wilson being released and being able to communicate with witnesses, particularly Kathy McNeill.

Despite the views expressed to me by my boss, I decided to put my head on the block and I authorised a charge of murder. It was a pressure situation, but I had always felt that the circumstantial evidence on which the case would be based was strong and that a jury would have no trouble in concluding that Wilson had done away with his wife in order to further his relationship with Kathy, not to mention cashing in on the insurance policies! Clare was good enough to respect my decision when I told her what I had done but, had I been proved wrong, no doubt I would have come in for some criticism!

Happily, my decision was vindicated in the outcome of the case. Wilson was convicted by a unanimous decision of the jury after a trial in late 2008, and was sentenced to life imprisonment with a minimum term of twenty-two years. His later appeal against conviction was rejected by the Court of Appeal. Wilson turned out to be a less than convincing witness, in stark contrast to the elegant Kathy McNeill, who gave a strong performance as the woman betrayed and scorned.

The case was presented on the simple basis that Wilson's two worlds were about to collide and he had to remove his wife. To me this was always an utterly convincing and irresistible argument. It was an altogether unacceptable coincidence that the "accident" occurred on exactly the same weekend that Kathy would have made her first appearance at Wilson's home. There was an obvious parallel with the case of Gordon Park where, again, coincidence could not explain how anyone else could have murdered the wife in the circumstances in which it took place. In both cases the jury clearly had no difficulty in reaching the common-sense conclusion!

* * *

Before the "Tractor" case had reached its trial, I had been knocked off course, once again, by yet another upheaval in the structure of the CPS. Having gone from small Areas to large and then back to small ones again only nine years before, we started to 'go big' again in 2008. There had already been moves in 2004 to merge Lancashire and Cumbria Constabulary, the moves only failing because of irreconcilable differences over Council Tax arrangements. There were no police force mergers at this time in fact but, nonetheless, the CPS decided that it would head in this direction, mirroring similar developments in the Court Service. Thus, in 2008 CPS Cumbria became part of the "Lancashire/Cumbria group", and the Chief Crown Prosecutor in Lancashire, Bob Marshall, became the "lead CCP" for the two counties. The Complex Casework Unit for Cumbria was abolished and a new unit for Lancs/Cumbria, based at Preston, was created. Thus, at a stroke, my job had once again disappeared!

To be fair, I was actually offered the post of Head of the new unit by Bob Marshall. It was, however, a no-brainer! I would have had to relocate to Preston at my own expense - this was something I was simply not prepared to do at this late stage in my career, having finally settled in West Cumbria after a lifetime of moving around! I declined the offer and Bob went ahead and advertised that job, and also lower-graded posts for Special Casework lawyers to cover both Cumbria and Lancashire. It looked as though my third 'incarnation' as a Complex Casework Lawyer was at an end and, indeed, in April 2008 Clare Lindley asked me to take on a new role in Cumbria once I had wound up my existing complex casework. This would entail managing the Higher Court Advocate unit in Cumbria whilst retaining my "fatal accident" casework and, of course, putting in a lot of time personally as an advocate in the Crown Court. Whilst the head of the HCA unit at Preston, a much bigger unit than the Cumbrian one, was on a salary grade one below the one I was on, there was, again, no suggestion that I would be "overbearing" or that my salary would drop after a period of time!

As far as I was concerned this was a very acceptable arrangement and I gladly agreed to the new role. I also decided at this time that I could take advantage of a new pension 'wheeze' that had been introduced, known as "Partial Retirement". This involved reducing one's working hours and drawing part of one's pension entitlement and, in my case, this was particularly favourable as I could work 3.5 days a week and still retain the same level of income, without compromising very much the amount of my eventual full pension. Another no-brainer, and I seized the opportunity to become "partially retired"!

There was also further structural upheaval taking place in Cumbria. Clare Lindley, to her credit in my opinion, thought the "Sprachan" arrangements were absurd and finally, twelve or thirteen years after I had submitted my blueprint for Cumbria to the management of the old CPS North, we began to move towards just two prosecution units in Cumbria. The Kendal office was closed - only a few years after it had become the sole manifestation of the "Glidewell" experiment in Cumbria - and the Kendal office staff moved into a new building in Barrow. The offices in Emlyn Hughes House were big enough to accommodate both the Barrow and the Kendal staff. Four of the Kendal lawyers, including the Divisional Crown Prosecutor, Charles Leyberg, decided, however, that the move was not for them and resigned - three of them were some way off pensionable age. They were not all replaced, as the move meant that some economies of scale could be achieved.

For me, however, my settled state did not last long. There were dark forces at work. I came back from holiday in mid-May 2008 and, in a chance conversation with one of the caseworkers at Workington, she asked "what was happening" to me. When I asked her what she meant, she went on to tell me about a recent meeting the Workington staff had had with Clare Lindley. The meeting was principally for Clare to explain the proposals for merging the Workington and Carlisle offices, although not until spring 2010. When numbers and levels of managers in the new set-up were being spoken about, the caseworker had picked up that it was intended that there would be only two lawyer managers, one to manage the team and one the HCA unit, and these posts would be filled by the two existing managers. It was clearly the case that I did not fit into these arrangements, despite the promises that had been held out to me by the CCP in April. To use the vernacular, I was being 'shafted'!!

I did nothing immediately, but decided to await developments. I did not have long to wait. In June Clare called me in and told me that, although the post of Head of the Complex Casework Unit for Lancashire/Cumbria (the one I had previously been offered by Bob Marshall) had been filled, no "suitable candidate" had been found to fill the post of Complex Casework Lawyer to cover Cumbria. As a result, according to Clare, Bob had said to her:"Never mind, you have an excellent candidate in Cumbria anyway." (i.e. me!). I was led to believe that this conversation had just taken place. Clare than asked me if I would "be prepared" to do this job. This was, however, not presented to me as mandatory and I came away from this meeting still believing I had an option to take the HCA manager role instead. In view of what I had been told in May by the caseworker, this was naïve of me!

In truth, I would have been by no means unhappy to carry on with Complex Casework. However, I had built up in my mind the notion of finishing my career in the Crown Court, and I informed Clare I would rather take the HCA manager role. The reality, of course, was that there was no option. Within a few days I was summoned to Preston to see Bob Marshall. Although he made a point of stating that "coercion" was not his style, I was left in no doubt that if I wanted to stay in the CPS I had to take the Complex Casework role.

I was quite bitter about what had happened. Not just about the deceit and pretence, but also that others knew I wasn't going to get the promised job before I knew. The point was made once again that, although the CPS was forthright in demanding high standards of integrity and transparency in dealing with the public, victims and witnesses, defendants and other agencies in the criminal justice system, it could resort to arbitrary and underhand methods in the way it treated its own staff.

I was angry enough to contact my trade union representative in Manchester about the situation. I needn't have bothered, as he was clearly uninterested and it seemed clear to me that his sympathies were more with management than with me. This was not my first, or last, contact with the union, but it was certainly the most unsatisfactory.

Thus I swallowed my indignation and became the Cumbrian arm of the Lancs/Cumbria Complex Casework Unit, and resumed the Special Casework role I had, in fact, never actually left since 2005...

* * *

Fortunately, after I had adjusted to having work allocated to me at a distance and working with a new set of caseworkers, I found my 'new' role very fulfilling. Over the last three years I had been dealing mainly with Cumbrian cases and mainly with drug-trafficking crime. Now I found myself working with police squads, not just in Cumbria, but also in Merseyside, Lancashire and Manchester, and handling cases not just of Class A drug-dealing, but also of Corruption and serious Robbery, armed or otherwise.

The members of the Complex Casework Unit, based at Preston, were, to a man or woman, highly motivated and extremely committed and efficient. Once I had become used to their ways they were a pleasure to work with. The unit head was John Dilworth, who was a very experienced lawyer and, indeed, a very able one. He was affable and easy to get on with, as were the caseworkers on the team.

I retained the existing Cumbrian casework I was involved in, although I now dropped the "fatal road accident" cases after thirteen years of handling these. Over the next three years I picked up other casework from the Serious Organised Crime Unit in Cumbria, but the standout cases in this period were from elsewhere in the north-west. Two of these related to attacks on security vans carrying large amounts of cash from or to banks.

As it happened, one of these cases first gave rise to arrests as a result of a robbery in Cumbria. A 'cash-in-transit' van was attacked by a gang in the Harraby area of Carlisle one morning, the security guards overpowered and a large amount of cash seized. Fortunately the local police were quickly on the scene, and four gang members were rapidly tracked down and apprehended in the locality, or within ten miles of it. Most of the cash was recovered in the process.

It turned out that the four defendants were part of a much bigger gang that was targeting such vehicles throughout the north-west. Shortly after the Carlisle arrests, I attended a case conference with officers from a cross-border squad based in Liverpool, known as "Titan", who were investigating a series of robberies and attempted robberies of such vans across the north-west. Large amounts of cash had been stolen and, whilst leaving the scene of one such crime, a car driven by a gang member had run over a police officer who had sustained very serious injuries and had, indeed, been lucky to survive. The officers had gathered a good deal of evidence of a criminal conspiracy to commit these robberies, much of it from mobile telephone records and "cell-siting" of these phones, which showed links between the suspects and their proximity to scenes of offences. There were a number of suspects and, after much discussion, we agreed that we would focus our efforts on four or five of these, one of them being one of the arrested defendants from the Carlisle offence.

The principal defendant was one Christopher Jones, who was believed to be in Holland at the time of our conference. He was captured, however, when he nearly killed himself by trying to abseil off the Harwich ferry in an attempt to evade arrest when he returned to the UK. Eventually he was convicted, after trial, of Conspiracy to commit a number of robberies and also complicity in causing PC Marshall grievous bodily harm with intent. He was sentenced to nineteen years' imprisonment. Seven other defendants were also sentenced to long periods of imprisonment as part of the gang, either for Conspiracy to rob, or for involvement in the Carlisle robbery or another separate robbery near Preston.

In another case involving an attack on a security van, this time with a gun being used, two notorious Lancashire villains were convicted and sentenced to substantial prison terms. Again, much use was made of mobile phone evidence in this case.

I was also involved in several cases of conspiracy to steal from petrol stations or isolated rural guesthouses, caravan sites and dwellings. These were all different gangs, roaming the country, often visiting targeted premises earlier and disabling CCTV cameras by spraying cameras with silicon or suchlike. Almost all those charged were convicted.

One case that was very different involved civilian employees of Merseyside Police Authority and various company directors. The main defendant, a man called Kell, was responsible for awarding contracts on behalf of the Police Authority to companies for doing building work at police stations throughout Merseyside. We were able to show that over a period of time he was enjoying a lavish lifestyle at the hands of these companies, receiving regular hospitality at race meetings, football matches and golf tournaments, as well as holidays and Christmas hampers. After a long trial at Liverpool Crown Court, eight defendants were convicted of offences under the Prevention of Corruption Act although, somewhat surprisingly, none received an immediate prison sentence.

The period from 2005 to 2011 was, almost certainly, the most successful of my career in terms of outcomes. I claim little of the credit for this. I may have made the right decisions about charging but, by and large, these decisions were not difficult. Thereafter, I was involved in vast amounts of work to prepare the cases for trial, but the evidence was all present, having been expertly gathered by elite and diligent police squads. Whilst I often found that the process of evidence-gathering by police left a lot to be desired, when it came to routine, 'volume' crime, I had only the greatest admiration for the work of detectives in the various squads who investigated the most serious crime. I had the distinct advantage of being able to spend a good deal of my career in the CPS working with such officers.

One case that I handled in this period, however, which did not have the benefit of skilled investigators, was that of Pauline Butler. This was another in the long line of what I have termed "lawyers' curse" cases. Pauline Butler was a solicitor in Carlisle and, almost inevitably, a sole practitioner. I went one day in 2009 to Carlisle Police Station, where I met with an investigator from the Solicitors' Regulation Authority; also the investigating officer who, I discovered to my surprise, was a "temporary detective constable" and very inexperienced, and also his detective inspector, who was to play no part in the case thereafter. I was told that evidence had been gathered that showed that Pauline Butler had stolen more than two hundred thousand pounds of clients' money over a period of time. Astonishingly, complaints had been made by various clients of hers and the police had commenced an investigation but, having gathered evidence, had done nothing more, for whatever reason. We were only having this conference now because a local reporter had buttonholed the Chief Constable at some function and had demanded to know what was happening about the investigation. Equally astonishingly, I was now being asked by the police at this conference if it was "in the public interest" to pursue the matter to prosecution. The solicitor had ceased to practise and would certainly be struck off the roll of solicitors by the Law Society; the clients' losses would be met by the Solicitors' Compensation Fund.

Was it "in the public interest" to prosecute the poor woman!? Not only was it a six-figure fraud, but it was also a very serious breach of trust by a professional person. Why would it not be in the public interest?!! The man from the SRA looked relieved. Basically, I believe, the police had no interest in pursuing the case. It was in the "too hard to do" pile. And they did not think the ultimate sentence would justify the work that needed to be put into the investigation. They were somewhat surprised when I told them that, on conviction, a prison sentence would be inevitable and it would be measured in years, not months. The allocation of the case to an inexperienced officer was no doubt an indication of the police's lack of interest!

In any event, the police now had little option but to conclude the investigation. They did not, however, add to their investigative resources, and I found that I was constantly having to push the officer into gathering appropriate witness statements and securing the right exhibits before I was in a position to authorise charging and to select the correct charges. Eventually we got there, and the evidence was strong enough to ensure that the defendant pleaded 'guilty' in the Crown Court. Even with her 'guilty' plea and some strong mitigation, she was sentenced to two years' imprisonment.

This was a case I handled, in effect, 'from cradle to grave': authorised the charges, input into the investigation, drafted the indictment and put the case together, attended all the hearings, drafted a case summary for the sentencing judge, and presented the case at both the plea hearing and the sentencing hearing. The defendant was represented in the Crown Court by the youngest-looking Queen's Counsel I had ever seen. Had he not been in QC garb, one could have easily mistaken him for a first-year law student. Not that he was incompetent, I hasten to add - far from it. But there again, nor was he anything out of the ordinary, and his speech in mitigation was no better than I have heard from decent solicitor advocates in the magistrates' court!

* * *

Throughout this six-year period , I was spending a good deal of time as an advocate in Carlisle Crown Court as well as on my casework. At first, we still had as many as nine or ten HCAs in Cumbria and it was difficult to do more than a couple of sessions a month. As time went on, however, some of these fell by the wayside or left the CPS and, within a year or two, there were only about four of us available to carry out regular Crown Court advocacy. By 2007 I was in the Crown Court at least one day a week and often more, particularly when I was engaged in an effective trial. Nor did the reduction of my working week with partial retirement in 2008 serve to decrease my Crown Court time. What it did mean, however, was that I was probably putting in nearly as many working hours as I had been before this stage. So much for "winding down"!

How did prosecuting in the Crown Court differ from prosecuting in the magistrates' court? Well, although the basic principles are the same, there are two important distinctions - firstly, there is a judge and, secondly, there is also sometimes a jury!

Dealing with bail applications in the Crown Court was very different from opposing bail before magistrates. As I have said before it was sometimes, indeed, a non-event. Whilst in the lower court it was an occasion for using one's skills in the "technique of persuasion", these were often not required in the Crown Court. The judge would be in possession of at least a summary of the case and also the defendant's previous convictions and would, very often, have decided the matter before the application was made. Sometimes he wouldn't even want to hear from the prosecutor, and at best he wouldn't want to hear very much. Sometimes he would tell the defence advocate before he started that he had "an uphill task". Very often it was a case of the prosecutor simply shortly outlining the case and re-stating the objections to bail without actually trying to justify them! That's not to say that defendants didn't sometimes get bail, but one learnt to identify the sort of case where this was going to happen and one withdrew one's objections at the outset.

Presenting the facts of the case following a 'guilty' plea is broadly the same format as in the magistrates' court, except that the prosecutor needs to know the case inside out, as the judge is always likely to ask questions which wouldn't get asked in the court below, and one needs to anticipate what these are likely to be and be prepared to answer them. The prosecutor in the Crown Court also needs to be familiar with the judge's sentencing powers in individual cases and, moreover, the content of sentencing guidelines for the offence and even, sometimes, the case authorities on sentencing for that offence. This is the sort of thing you never get asked by magistrates, who will rely on their legal adviser for this sort of information. The prosecutor in the Crown Court will also be expected to correct the judge if he is passing a sentence he is not empowered to pass, so a familiarity with the wider general sentencing powers is required.

What also happens much more often and routinely in the Crown Court is that the defence will offer to plead 'guilty' on a particular 'basis', which may not always accord with the prosecution evidence. If the prosecutor accepts the basis, then he or she has to be careful, in presenting the facts of the case, that what one is telling the judge does not conflict with that basis. This may mean, in effect, diluting or toning down the content of a witness' evidence or omitting some of that content. This can be difficult where a victim, for example, alleges that he was set upon and assaulted without justification, when one has accepted a basis of plea that the defendant had been acting in self-defence but had used unreasonable force in so doing. It is axiomatic that the prosecutor has to exercise care and judgment in deciding whether to accept a basis, even though the temptation may be to accept it to avoid a long trial where the outcome may be uncertain!

The most obvious difference from prosecuting in the magistrates' court is in the "trial" situation – i.e. the presence of a jury rather than a single District Judge or a bench of magistrates!

In the magistrates' court, the District Judge or the lay bench is required to determine issues of both law and fact. In the Crown Court, however, only the judge can deal with points of law that arise, and the jury are the sole arbiters of the facts. This means that, if any issues of law arise in a trial, they will be heard by and determined by the judge, either before the trial starts or in the course of the trial but, in either case, in the absence of the jury.

When the trial proper starts, the prosecutor will make an opening address to the jury - as in the court below - setting out the Crown's case by reference to what the witnesses will say. But the prosecutor will have to take a somewhat different approach in the Crown Court. Most, if not all, the members of the jury will have had no experience of being in a courtroom, let alone sitting as a tribunal required to hear evidence and decide on guilt or innocence of a prisoner. The whole situation will be strange and alien to them. They will, moreover, have only just taken their seats and are likely to be unsettled and wondering what is going to happen next! The prosecutor, therefore, will to some extent have to lead them by the hand - he or she will have to explain to them in simple terms the nature and content of the indictment; also the burden of proof, that the prosecution bring the case, the prosecution must prove it, and that they cannot find the defendant guilty unless they are "sure" of his guilt. These are the basics, but there may be more issues to be dealt with in many cases.

Whilst the rest of the opening address may be similar in content to one in the magistrates' court, it will probably be necessary to give a little more detail of what witnesses will say in evidence, so that the jury has a clear picture of the prosecution's case. At the same time of course, as in the lower court, the prosecutor will want to be careful about not making himself or herself a hostage to fortune by making assertions that he or she is uncertain will come out in evidence. There is a balance to be struck.

Examination, cross-examination and re-examination of witnesses will take the same path and be conducted in the same way as in the magistrates' court. But, at the end of all the evidence, the prosecutor has a right to address the jury again, something which, until fairly recently, was not an automatic right in the lower court.

If it has been a short trial, the prosecutor may come under some pressure from the judge not to make a final address to the jury. I have always felt that this pressure should be resisted, and a final speech made, even if it is short and succinct! Otherwise, one is leaving the stage entirely to the defence, who already have the advantage of having the last word to the jury (apart from the 'neutral' input of the judge), and they are free to exploit any weaknesses in the Crown's case which have emerged and to milk for all they are worth the mantra that members of the jury must be "sure" before they can find the defendant guilty!

I have always believed that the prosecutor's final address to the jury should be short and 'punchy'. The approach I always tried to adopt was to identify three main points of strength in the prosecution case and to hit them with these..."The first point, members of the jury, is this...," and so on. I could never see the point of laboriously going through the evidence given - they have heard it and they are likely to quickly lose interest. Moreover, the defence are probably going to do this at length and then the judge will also sum up the evidence. They don't need to hear it three times! I always felt the prosecutor's final address should be a bold and emphatic highlighting of the strengths of the evidence and avoiding any mention of any weaknesses that have emerged. Something forceful and memorable, something that will resound with the jury members and stay with them whilst they listen, at greater length almost certainly, to the pleadings of the defence!

* * *

After 2005 we had annual financial targets to meet in terms of "counsel fees saved", and so we had to keep up regular and constant presence in the Crown Court in order to get near these targets, which increased incrementally from year to year. We got into the habit of presenting as many as 90% of the cases at first hearing - these are known as Plea and Direction Hearings. This meant we often went down to court mob-handed on a Monday morning, when these hearings took place. If a defendant pleaded 'guilty' at these hearings, sometimes the case would proceed to sentence there and then, so we had always to be prepared to outline the case, make ancillary applications, know details of previous convictions, and be aware of sentencing guidelines, etc. So preparing four or five cases each for a PDH court would often involve several hours of preparation.

More often than not, however, the defendant who pleaded 'guilty' would have his case adjourned for the preparation of a pre-sentence report by the Probation Service. Unless it proved to be impossible for some reason, we always covered the eventual sentencing hearing as well. The only cases we did not cover at PDH courts, in normal circumstances, would be serious sexual cases or child abuse, homicide cases, or multi-handed Conspiracies.

Finally, we also started to do jury trials. I was the first HCA in Cumbria to prosecute before a judge and jury - in 2006, I believe it was. Before this I had, on a number of occasions, identified suitable cases for me to do but, as I have already said, none of these actually proceeded to trial, usually because the defendant on the morning of the hearing decided to plead guilty, either to the indictment or to acceptable lesser or alternative charges. Then, inevitably, one did not "crack". This was a trial on a charge against a young lady of twenty-two years of age of Malicious Wounding on another woman of the same age in the ladies' toilet in a nightclub. I had spent many hours preparing, and had written and re-written my opening address to the jury. When I stood up to make that address I was certainly more nervous than I had ever been in my life in a courtroom, and certainly more so than on my first appearance in a magistrates' court. To my surprise, however, my bowels did not turn to water and I did not become incoherent! In fact, as I got into my stride I found that I became more and more confident, and could look away from my notes to make eye contact with the jury.

The rest of the trial went smoothly enough. The witnesses came up to proof, more or less, without being entirely convincing; I managed cross-examination well enough, I thought; and I had time overnight to prepare my final address to the jury. One thing I had been dreading was the scenario where the defence case finished mid-afternoon and the judge asked me to make my final address at that point; before, in other words, I had had time to consider the entirety of the evidence. I had never had to make a "final speech" in the magistrates' court, so my experience of being in this sort of situation was nil. In time, however, I got used to writing most of it well before the defence case was over, making any quick adjustments necessary really in the course of delivering that address. Ideally, however, and certainly in a case of any length, it is far better if one can prepare one's final address at one's leisure!

My opponent in this trial was our old friend Greg Hoare, once of CPS and my fellow candidate in the interview for the Barrow job in 1982. He had left CPS in 1986, at the time of the transition to the new "CPS" and, after a period in private practice apparently doing probate cases, he had decided to change direction completely and applied to join the Bar. By 2006 he had been practising as a barrister, almost exclusively in Carlisle, for probably ten years. He very rarely prosecuted, but had carved out something of a reputation for himself as a reasonably successful defence advocate. He attributed his success in jury trials to not patronising the jury and keeping it simple. Rumour had it that he had but three basic formats for his final address to the jury, and every time was just a variation on one of these themes. His favourite one was what he called the "charge of the light brigade". I don't know which theme he used this time, but it was quietly impressive and was good enough to persuade the jury to acquit after not much more than an hour's deliberation.

So I 'lost' my first jury trial and would lose others over the next seven years. There were also successes, however, and probably by the end I had 'won' more than I had 'lost'. I don't necessarily attribute this success ratio to brilliant advocacy, because I tended to pick my trials to prosecute and only go for those which, on paper at least, seemed to present an even chance, or better, of success. It was always my experience, however, that juries were much less predictable than magistrates, and there were one or two cases where I expected a 'guilty' verdict and got the opposite. It never happened the other way round.

As I have already said, this was not altogether surprising, or not in my view. Juries consist of twelve people selected at random, most of whom will have had no experience of being involved in a criminal trial or, indeed, any sort of court procedure. The last advocate they will hear from will be the defence counsel, who will be stressing for all he or she is worth that they must be "sure" before they can convict, and this will then be echoed by the judge in his summing up to the jury. We will never know whether some juries do not interpret "reasonable doubt" as "any sort of doubt".

There is, of course, no intelligence test for juries. You get what you are given! There have been occasions when I have looked at the selected jury with dismay. One shouldn't stereotype, of course, but it doesn't fill one with confidence that a sensible verdict will be reached when most of the men are in jeans and T-shirts, and shaven-headed and tattooed, and most of the women are not much different. This is what we used to term a "Cleator Moor" jury - a reference to one of West Cumbria's notorious crime-ridden areas. On other occasions, however, one can be heartened by a jury of sensible-looking people who look interested and listen attentively!

Advocates often say that they can tell what the verdict will be when they see the jury members returning to court after their deliberations. It is said that a jury as a body will not look at the defendant in the dock at this point if it is going to convict; otherwise if it is to be a 'not guilty' verdict! Usually, in my experience, if the jury has been out less than twenty minutes it will convict unless, of course, the case has fallen apart from the prosecution point of view. One could say that the longer the jury is out the more likely it is to acquit, but this doesn't always follow.

The summing up by the judge to the jury is supposed to be an unbiased and accurate summary of the evidence, as well as directions on the law. There have been occasions, however, when I have detected non-too-subtle attempts, in my view, to influence the jury one way or another. Sometimes the judge will tell the jury that he agrees with their verdict. Less often, perhaps, he might demonstrate his disapproval in some way: it is not unknown for a judge to keep jury members in their seats where they have acquitted, so that they can hear about another indictment to which the defendant has pleaded 'guilty' and a long history of previous convictions. This can be quite embarrassing for such a jury and it may well show on their faces and in their body language!

More often than not the judge will thank the jury for their services before letting them disperse. I can remember one occasion, however, where the judge, clearly dissatisfied with their verdict, dismissed the jury without a word of thanks or appreciation. They would have been left in no doubt that they had 'got it wrong'!!

In the first trials that I was involved in, I felt at a disadvantage because I was dressed differently from the defence counsel. In those days, as solicitor advocates, we were not entitled to wear wigs - although the HCAs who were barristers could! I was always conscious of the likelihood of the jury looking upon me as a lesser advocate, not properly qualified, and taking more heed of the "fully-dressed" defence barrister. It was not, I felt, a level playing field. The rules changed within a few years to permit solicitor advocates to wear wigs, and I needed no encouragement to acquire one. Not cheap, I hasten to add - about £300, and another £100 for the box to keep it in!! Nonetheless, I felt much more comfortable in front of a jury from then on.

* * *

Inevitably, when I first started appearing as an advocate in the Crown Court, I was very apprehensive as to how I would be received by the judges and the Bar. My colleagues who started at the same time felt much the same. The Bar is the biggest 'closed shop' there is and most of the judges, certainly then, were drawn from its ranks. We were interlopers, trespassers on their private territory where they had enjoyed exclusive 'rights to roam' for generations. Moreover, we were the junior branch of the legal profession and had had no specific training as advocates. Worse still for those of us in the CPS, we were salaried employees and, apart from the stigma that might convey, we couldn't be expected to be able to exercise an 'independent judgment'. Worst of all, we were decimating the income of the Bar - by covering the majority of first hearings and sentence hearings we were preventing new counsel from getting the prosecution work they would have picked up previously; and by doing jury trials we were eating into the work of other junior counsel.

It is true we represented an obvious threat to the living standards and well-being of the Bar. Even a small HCA unit like ours at Carlisle was undermining the attempts of newly-qualified barristers to get a foothold in the Crown Court, and was making more established barristers question whether there was an economic future for them as independent counsel. In places like Preston, Manchester, Liverpool and Newcastle, where there were much larger HCA units and those units were, pro rata, doing much more Crown Court work than us, the threat to the Bar and its livelihood was even greater. In those places I believe the ranks of the junior Bar were quite voluble in their opposition to the development of HCA units in the CPS and, in time, there was a small but noticeable exodus from the local Bar, either into retirement or even to joining the CPS itself, where there were the obvious benefits of a stable income, paid holidays and a pension!! It also became increasingly difficult for would-be barristers to get a pupillage or a place in a set of chambers.

As time went on, although not in large numbers in our area, solicitor advocates started to appear for defendants. These were solicitors in private practice who had acquired the "higher rights" of advocacy. And, more recently still, firms of solicitors started to employ barristers to conduct their Crown Court advocacy. Kevin J Commons and Co in West Cumbria had as many as three on their books. The Bar was being assailed from all sides!

Was I, or indeed were my colleagues, upset at the anguish and concerns of the Bar? Not a bit of it!! The reality was that there would always be work for the better junior counsel, prosecuting as well as defending, and we would never be depriving QCs of much of their highly-paid work, even though there were by 2010 a number of barristers in the CPS who could and did prosecute murders! For too long we had been paying too much for mediocrity. We didn't owe the Bar a living. If they were not now good enough to make a living, then they shouldn't be there!

The Bar, in my view, was always too big. In Scotland, I believe, it is much smaller and solicitor advocates routinely conduct much of the advocacy in the higher criminal courts. There was not now enough work to support the overgrown monster, and it needed to shrink and become leaner and more competitive.

The plans of the government in more recent times to cut the criminal legal aid rates also, of course, gave rise to further howls of anguish from the Bar. But why shouldn't they suffer cuts in their living standards like the rest of us?! I laughed out loud when watching coverage on the TV news of a recent 'protest' by the Bar at the government's plans: one very junior barrister was complaining to the camera that he got only £50 for doing a Crown Court bail application, and how was he supposed to live on that? What he failed to mention was that, on average, Crown Court bail applications last about fifteen minutes and involve about the same amount of preparation time. £100 an hour - not bad remuneration for doing not very much! And if this was all the work he could get, maybe he should rethink his choice of career!

So how did we get treated by the Bar at Carlisle Crown Court? On the whole, and by those barristers who regularly appeared there, quite well, maybe because we were not the same threat to their livelihood as our colleagues in other places. But I certainly encountered counsel who came to Carlisle from outside, from Newcastle for example, who could barely disguise their disdain, and even hostility. And even if nothing was said to our faces, what was being said behind our backs? This point was well illustrated by an incident I came upon one day in the advocates' room at Carlisle. I chanced to walk in when a quite senior junior counsel, and one we had instructed often in substantial cases, was regaling other members of the Bar in the room about the CPS instructing an in-house advocate to prosecute a Class A drug trafficking case in an impending trial. He clearly thought that he should have been prosecuting counsel. "Well," he was saying, "If they think an HCA can do a better job than me..." I exited the room before he realised I was present. I always thought he was an arrogant, self-opinionated little twat... What he failed to appreciate, in any event, was that the HCA in question had recently joined the CPS as a senior Crown Court Advocate, and was a very experienced counsel who had prosecuted such cases many times before!

* * *

And what of the judiciary? Well, even after twelve or thirteen years of appearing in Carlisle Crown Court, I still often felt that I was barely tolerated and there on sufferance only. It wasn't so much what was said by judges as their demeanour and, sometimes, what was not said! I speak for myself, but I suspect my colleagues had similar feelings. These were feelings of discomfort, of never quite being accepted.

Many of the judges I appeared in front of were Recorders, i.e. part-time judges, and most of these I found easier-going, courteous, and appreciative of any help they would receive. A lot of them had not been in the job long and were still, perhaps, uncertain of their powers or were feeling their way and, consequently, were not into giving the CPS advocates a hard time or making them feel uncomfortable. Much of their work, too, consisted of appeals and committals for sentence from the magistrates' court and they often appreciated that solicitor advocates might have a greater knowledge of what went on in those courts than ordinary barristers, and welcomed assistance as to sentencing and procedure in the lower court.

At the other extreme, I appeared quite a few times in front of visiting High Court judges. Ironically, I found them to be, on the whole, unfailingly courteous and even-tempered. I suppose that judges who have reached that level have nothing to prove, do not need to be constantly exerting their authority and, consequently, have no interest in scoring points against counsel or making life difficult for them!

Probably the most trying judges to appear before, I found to be circuit judges from other court centres, who had been drafted in to cover absences at Carlisle. There was one in particular, from Preston,

Judge Edward Slinger, whose court I used to hate being in. He seemed to be always irascible and exuding barely-concealed hostility. He had a knack of making one feel very small and inadequate. I speak for myself here, of course - others may not have had the same experience, and I suspect it was because he had little time or respect for solicitor advocates, certainly those from the CPS! On one occasion, he interrupted my opening in a sentence hearing and demanded I read out chunks from the statement of a particular witness. I had deliberately not done so up to that point, because the evidence in question was not something the prosecution were accepting as truthful. I regret to say I did as I was told and read out the offending material. On another occasion, having unexpectedly asked me the maximum penalty for an offence which could be tried only in the magistrates' court, he then rather pointedly remarked that he wouldn't be asking me for maximum sentences on the more serious offences, the implication being that I wouldn't know them!

I was highly amused, a few months after my last appearance in front of Judge Slinger, to come across a reference to him in the autobiography of the former England and Lancashire cricketer, David Lloyd. Lloyd had organised a cricket tour to an army camp in Germany and "Eddie" Slinger, a regular member of Lancashire Second Eleven, was in the party. The night before the match there had been a convivial night in the mess, and David Lloyd turned up at the ground for the game the following morning only to find that almost the entire Lancashire team hadn't arrived for the start of play. The sole exception was Mr Slinger!

Most of the time, of course, we appeared in front of one or other of the three circuit judges who were allocated to Carlisle Crown Court and, for a good part of the period between 2005 and 2013, these were respectively His Honour Judge Batty QC, who was the resident judge and latterly the Honorary Recorder of Carlisle, His Honour Judge Hughes QC and Her Honour Judge Forrester.

Judge Batty could be humorous and accommodating, but he could also be irascible and intimidating. It always seemed to me that he didn't much care for solicitor advocates and not much more for employed barristers. As a solicitor advocate who was prosecuting, I always felt that I had to be extremely well-prepared and to be ready to justify every decision that had been taken. If he didn't like what you had done, he would let you know in no uncertain terms and would often send you away to "reconsider", or even suggest that you "seek the advice of counsel" - an embarrassing suggestion, to say the least. One was always apprehensive, when prosecuting before him, about taking decisions to accept a plea to a lesser offence and, in particular, to accepting a 'guilty' plea to a charge of Malicious Wounding when the charge on the indictment was Wounding with Intent to Cause Grievous Bodily Harm. One was never sure how Judge Batty was going to react in these circumstances; he might simply nod and say "A sensible decision," or he might fly off the handle and send one away to "reconsider".

I had more than one tongue-lashing from Judge Batty, although there were times when I was aggrieved because I didn't believe I was at fault. On one occasion I was prosecuting a seventeen-year-old boy, who had hit a policeman at a road block whilst driving a stolen car. The policeman had suffered horrific injuries and his career as an active police officer was over. I had discussed the case at length with the investigating police officers and, although we would dearly have loved to have charged Attempted Murder or at least Causing Grievous Bodily Harm with Intent, the evidence simply didn't support the proposition that the car had been driven deliberately at the officer. In particular, expert evidence from an experienced officer from the Collision Investigation Unit, who had examined marks left on the road, ruled this out. It was simply a case of reckless driving, and the most serious charge we could prefer was Causing Grievous Bodily Harm (without the "Intent"), which was a much less serious offence than those we would have liked to have charged. Judge Batty was the sentencing judge and he was manifestly quite incensed by the level of charges brought, despite my best efforts to explain why we had arrived at this decision. The situation was compounded by the fact that the judge's sentencing powers were even more circumscribed because the defendant was under eighteen! This was calculated to aggravate the judicial wrath even more! When sentencing the youth, the judge publicly announced to a packed court that his hands were tied, and the implication seemed to be that it was the Prosecution, and indeed the CPS, who were responsible for this, rather than the evidence and the law-makers.

Another problem area for us prosecutors with Judge Batty was acceptance of "a basis of plea". Very often a defendant would plead 'guilty' to an offence but on a basis which was different from that alleged by the Crown. A judgment call for the prosecutor was whether to accept the basis put forward or to let the matter go to trial, or at least to a hearing for the judge to determine the facts. There were many cases where we wouldn't accept a basis, but others where we would, and we would sign a document setting out the "agreed basis of plea". This would be handed in to the judge for his perusal and he could decline to accept it if he wished. Judge Batty, if he disagreed with the basis, would let the parties know in often very strident terms. On one occasion, he laid into me for accepting a "basis" in a case of Supplying Heroin. The basis was that the defendant was just supplying to a small circle of close friends for minimal profit. I was accused of ignoring pages and pages of evidence that showed that, according to the judge, the defendant was in telephone contact with many more people who, from the evidence of text messages, were clearly involved in buying heroin from the defendant. When I was given a chance to explain my position, I pointed out to the judge that the part of the statement he was looking at related to another defendant, not the one before the court! The judge had not picked this up. There was a few moments' silence as the judge looked again at the evidence. He then looked up at me with a wry smile and nodded! No apology, but then I suppose judges don't have to apologise!?

It wasn't just the CPS advocates that fell foul of Judge Batty. I can think of two local solicitors who had rights of advocacy in the Crown Court and regularly exercised them who, if anything, seemed to incur the wrath and dislike of Judge Batty more than we did. I think probably they erred by bringing their more 'casual' advocacy ways from the magistrates' court into the Crown Court but, even so, it always seemed to me that their treatment was somewhat disproportionate.

The independent Bar seemed to get away with things in front of Judge Batty far more often than we solicitor and employed advocates did, although I did once witness him laying into a very young female barrister who was palpably under-prepared when she addressed him. I suppose the close 'brotherhood' of the Bar is always likely to mean that judges are going to be less keen to upbraid barristers, some of whom, of course, might even have been in the same chambers as the judge! I noticed this particularly with barristers from Newcastle, who occasionally appeared at Carlisle. Judge Batty, of course, had been many years in chambers in that city. What always rubbed salt into the wound was that the judge would invariably invite these counsel into his chambers for "tea" after they had finished their business.

Appearing before Judge Hughes was also often a trying experience for CPS advocates. The most difficult situations were when we were conducting Plea and Direction hearings before him, or Committals for Sentence from the Magistrates' Court. He clearly felt that many of the cases that came before him shouldn't be there and, in PDHs, he would often dissect the case in front of you, openly denigrate the quality of some of the witnesses, and demand explanations as to why the case had been brought or why the charges on the Indictment were appropriate. We learnt to be prepared for this kind of inquisition and to be even more ready than usual to weed out weak cases before they got into his court, but we would often come under severe pressure to drop cases at the PDH. Whilst sometimes he might have a point about particular cases, on other occasions I believed that he had missed the point of the case and that he was running down perfectly good prosecutions.

He also regularly found fault with cases sent for sentence from the Magistrates' Court or with sentences passed by the magistrates in cases that were the subject of appeals against sentence. Why did the prosecutor allow the court to do this, he would ask us, or why did the prosecutor allow the court to pass this sentence? He seemed to want to hold the CPS responsible for what he regarded as errors by the magistrates, even where those 'errors' were not errors in law, but what he saw as a wrong-headed sentence or course of action! He rather overlooked the fact that the magistrates had a legally qualified clerk to advise them, or that sometimes it was the District Judge who had, in his view, 'transgressed'!

Appearing before Her Honour Judge Forrester I found to be an altogether much more comfortable experience. This was, no doubt, because of the fact that she had been a solicitor rather than a barrister, and had not been steeped in the culture of the Bar. By the same token, there were one or two counsel who probably regarded her as an upstart and sometimes in addressing her would find it difficult to disguise their disdain and would come perilously close to overstepping the fine line between firm advocacy and outright disrespect. I never, however, witnessed her reacting in any way to such provocation!

The Crown Court is a world of arcane procedures and practices, and absurd and outdated etiquette and dress. There is a lot of deference and 'bowing and scraping', both physical and verbal, and a lot of traps for the unwary. It is very easy for the advocate who routinely appears before Circuit Judges to find, to his horror, that he has addressed a High Court Judge as "Your Honour" instead of "Your Lordship", and woe betide the solicitor advocate who addresses the Circuit Judge as "Your Worship" instead of "Your Honour"! The use of the address "M'lud", incidentally, is a no-no - it occurs only in films and TV series!! Then there is the convention that one never addresses the judge as "you", but always as "Your Honour" or "Your Lordship", as the case may be; this can lead to the ridiculous situation where one is constructing sentences that are overflowing with "Your Honours"... "Your Honour, I know what Your Honour is thinking and I agree with Your Honour and I urge Your Honour to take this course...." This sounds ridiculous, and is ridiculous!

Advocates' addresses to the judge will be littered with "in my respectful submission" and "with the greatest respect". The latter is a convention designed to demonstrate that you think your opponent is talking complete nonsense! Why one can't just say "I disagree...", I really don't know!

Then there is the problem area of whether to refer to your opponent as "my friend" or "my learned friend". Many barristers will assert their 'superior status' by referring to solicitor advocates simply as "my friend" or, worse still, just as "Mr" or "Ms". And how do solicitor advocates refer to each other!? I always made the point of calling all advocates "my learned friend", even though some of them were not very "learned"! This way, I thought, you can't go wrong! I have never experienced a judge intervening to 'correct' what he or she might perceive as an improper address, but a friend did once tell me his experience of appearing as a solicitor advocate in a Crown Court in 1972. This was just after the passage of the Courts Act 1971 and when solicitors, for the first time, were allowed to represent a client on a committal for sentence in the Crown Court if they had also acted for him or her in the magistrates' court in the same case. My friend found himself as the only solicitor in the Crown Court proceedings, because the prosecution and other co-defendants were all represented by barristers. Prosecuting Counsel proceeded to introduce the representation to the judge in this way: "My learned friend Mr… appears for X, my learned friend Mr… appears for Y, my learned friend Mr… appears for Z and Mr King is for A." Clearly intended to put the interloping upstart King in his place!! On this occasion, however, the judge, to his credit, pricked the balloon of posturing arrogance. "Oh," he said, "I think Mr King can be your learned friend too!"

However antediluvian all this terminology may appear to most people, I suspect members of the Bar love it as it sets them apart from the man in the street. In the same way, I am sure they like dressing-up in the ridiculous and antiquated court dress - gowns, wing collars, tabs and wigs. I believe all this is intended to impress and overawe defendants and witnesses, and to convey an impression of the 'dignity' of the court; also to prevent judges and counsel from being recognised on the street by defendants and clients, etc? It seems to me, however, that there is no real justification or need to perpetuate such outmoded dress in this day and age - it is impractical and uncomfortable and, far from impressing other court-users, it is more likely to be the subject of amusement and derision!

One thing I have observed with some judges is the development of what might be termed "judgitis". This is a 'disease' which can afflict magistrates as well, but to a much lesser extent!

I have seen this occur in judges whom one has known and has instructed as counsel before they were elevated to the bench. As barristers instructed as prosecuting counsel, they may often be down-to-earth and very 'matey', but there can then be a strange transition once they become judges (and, of course, are no longer looking to you to provide them with a living!); they seem to regard it as mandatory to be irascible, abrupt and inconsiderate. Barristers who once complained about judges who came into court late and without apology, now do exactly the same themselves. Counsel who were grateful once for being instructed by the CPS now find reasons to lambast their erstwhile paymasters again and again and to demand the attendance at court of CPS senior managers to explain decisions or shortcomings. Where, as instructed counsel, they had a very carefree and even careless approach to the issue of Disclosure of Unused Material, they now make stern orders that the prosecution must disclose material that they really have no obligation to disclose.

I'm not saying that all counsel who become judges go this way, far from it, but there are certainly some, and it is difficult to understand how they can change so much and alter from friendly, reasonable and understanding people to critical, carping and sometimes irate and hostile individuals. It is almost as if they feel they must conduct themselves in this way as part of the responsibility thrust upon them.

These days it is comparatively rare to find a judge who is out of touch. Gone, I think, are the days when the judge interrupted proceedings to ask: "Who is Gazza?" Twenty years ago, however, things were different and one could still come across some astonishing social gaffes. Judge Percy, no doubt a relative of the historic Percy family who were the hereditary Dukes of Northumberland, whilst sitting at Newcastle Crown Court decided to hand down a short lecture to a defendant who was appearing before him for sentence. The defendant was a hard-bitten old lag from the west end of the city who had been offending all his life. The judge quite rightly identified alcohol as the defendant's *bête noire* and, having passed a non-custodial sentence he spoke sternly to the man before he left court, with these immortal words: "I want you to promise me that from now on you will completely eschew alcohol - not even a small sherry before dinner…" This was the modern equivalent of prosecuting counsel in the *Lady Chatterley* obscenity trial, who memorably asked the jury if "they would allow their … servants to read this…"!

Despite all the idiosyncrasies of judges, or perhaps because of them, and despite all the irritating nuances of terminology and behaviour, I can state quite categorically that I always found the Crown Court a much greater challenge than the magistrates' court, and I much preferred appearing in the former. After many years of daily court appearances before magistrates, and although there were still some challenging situations from time to time, I became weary and complacent. The proceedings became too formulaic and predictable. The constant "retirements" of the magistrates and the countless adjournments of cases became irksome. The organisation of the business to suit the court rather than court-users was a perennial source of annoyance and irritation. I might be susceptible to being lured out of retirement to do Crown Court advocacy, but nothing would persuade me to go back to the magistrates' court!

* * *

In 2010 and 2011 the 'storm clouds' were gathering over the CPS, both locally and nationally. The Chancellor of the Exchequer announced in the House of Commons what we all were expecting: there would be a massive cut to the budget of the Crown Prosecution Service. He went as far as singling out the CPS as having "over-inflated" expenses which had to be drastically reduced. There began a process of wholesale shedding of staff, a process which continues to this day and looks set to continue apace beyond the next general election in 2015.

Before the 'axe' fell we had already, to some extent, anticipated it locally, although our restructuring in Cumbria in 2010 was also a process of rationalisation that would have taken place in any event. In 2010 the office in Workington was closed and the staff from there transferred *en masse* to the office in Carlisle, thus reducing the Cumbrian CPS operation to the two-office scenario that could and should have been implemented years before. It had previously been thought that the Carlisle office was nowhere big enough to accommodate two sets of staff, but the Civil Service had by now revised its requirement for each employee to have a specified minimum amount of space, and so the Carlisle office was now big enough! As it turned out, within four years the number of staff there had fallen to such a level that the physical size of that office could actually be substantially reduced by shedding some of the floor space.

The author of the structural changes had, by late 2009, also departed. Clare Lindley had moved on to greater and better things in another CPS Area and had been replaced by Chris Long, a lawyer from South Yorkshire, aged about thirty-two and with about five years' experience in the CPS. What he lacked in experience, however, Chris made up for in the depth of his immersion in the management culture of the organisation. I had a good deal of respect for the effortless, but seemingly compelling, way in which he could utter the 'management-speak' and churn out reams of the sort of platitudes we would expect and get from senior CPS management. I soon found, however, that I had little cause to respect his legal judgement, after I read one or two of his opinions on fatal accident cases that I took to court. Furthermore, whatever faults I may have seen in Clare Lindley, she was vibrant and had a lively sense of humour; Chris, however, was impassive, inscrutable and with no obvious sense of humour. A two-dimensional management clone!

Then, in 2011, the ever-spinning wheel of structural change in the CPS gave one more violent surge. Having gone from small Areas to larger Areas to very large Areas and then back again to small Areas, we were now to metamorphose once again from small to very large. Cumbria now became part of the North West Area, although perhaps "appendage" would have been a more appropriate word! Area HQ was to be in Manchester, all operations were to be run from there and, in order to meet the budget reduction imposed upon us, those operations were to be downsized.

Almost inevitably, there were implications for my position. The size of the new Complex Casework Unit was to be reduced *pro rata* and, in particular, there was to be no lawyer to cover the Cumbrian end of the operation, or no lawyer based in the county, anyway. My post was, yet again, to be abolished!!

As ever, management made a complete mess of the transition as far as my own situation was concerned. I was told that I would be placed in a central "redundancy pool". This meant that I could be invited to fill any job in the Civil Service which came up at my grade, providing, of course, that I had the appropriate experience and expertise to do that job. In theory, but probably not in practice, I could therefore have ended my career at HM Revenue and Customs, or running an office dealing with cattle movements in the Ministry of Agriculture! Management, however, initially at least, overlooked the fact that, as I was a "partially-retired" employee, the rules did not permit me to be moved to anywhere more than an hour and a half's travelling distance by public transport from my home. The reality, therefore, was that unless there arose a job at my grade in Cumbria, and specifically, in fact, in north or west Cumbria, I wouldn't be going anywhere! It was apparent very soon that the likelihood of such a job arising was extremely remote! So CPS North West was stuck with me - the CPS Chief Executive had apparently given an undertaking to the unions that there would be no compulsory redundancies at this time.

Another conundrum was that one could not, under the rules, be in the "redundancy pool" for more than twelve months. So, if I hadn't been placed in that period and compulsory redundancy was not an option, what happened to me then?!

There became available at this time an exit strategy. This was, in effect, an opportunity for staff to apply for voluntary redundancy, or "voluntary early severance", as it was called. The terms were not particularly favourable, as the government had succeeded in capping the amount that could be paid out under the scheme and it became less and less attractive the closer one was to retirement age. Many, however, applied for VES, far more than could actually be realistically released - there was literally a stampede to get out of the CPS! Many lawyers left the Area under the scheme, mostly from Lancashire and Manchester, and considerably more, I believe, in the north-east, and many of these were experienced people. I am quite sure that I was expected by Area Management to apply, and I have no doubt that I would have been successful. However, as a matter of principle I decided I wasn't going to do what was expected of me and make life easy for management of the new Area!!

Under the rules which applied to the "redundancy pool", management was required to find me "meaningful work" whilst I waited to be placed in a permanent job. When I enquired as to what constituted "meaningful work", I learnt that it meant any kind of work that management wanted it to be. So I could be deployed into full-time photocopying or filing!! What I was actually offered was to become a full-time Crown Advocate, working in the Crown Advocate Unit at Carlisle, with no other casework or management responsibilities.

I had mixed feelings about this. On the one hand it was, for me, a very satisfactory way of ending my career, going down to the Crown Court and prosecuting before judge and jury, especially as, once again, it was a job for which I was being very much overpaid. The other members of the Crown Advocate Unit were on salaries probably between £20000 and £25000 less than I was receiving! Once again, there was no mention of my "overbearing" at my salary grade. As I understood it, after twelve months, if I hadn't been placed in a post commensurate with my existing grade and I wasn't to be made redundant, then I should drop to the same grade as my colleagues, with corresponding decrease in salary. As ever, however, no-one said anything about this and I was still in the same job and on the same salary sixteen months later and, no doubt, would have been to this day had I remained in the CPS!

Over a period of twelve years the CPS had consistently failed to get it right as far as my grading was concerned. I have said it before and will say it again, for an organisation whose core business was applying and enforcing the law, and which demanded a high degree of transparency and accuracy in its external operations, the CPS repeatedly fell short in its dealings with its own staff. I shouldn't complain, of course, because I was the beneficiary of the organisation's incompetence! If I were being charitable I would say that the CPS was simply being a benign and compassionate employer; most, however, would say that it was simply crass ineptitude!

My conscience did provoke me into challenging this offer of "meaningful work", however. I pointed out to management that they were paying me an inflated salary to do the job in question. So why didn't they give me work to match the salary? Why couldn't I carry on doing Complex Casework as well as Crown Advocacy? It was no skin off their noses and they would be getting their money's worth out of me. Or why didn't they make me the manager of the Carlisle Crown Advocate Unit, again getting a much better return for their money? Nonetheless, however logical this would appear to me and others, it cut absolutely no ice at all with the managers. They couldn't do the first because it had been decided there was to be "no Complex Casework Lawyer in Cumbria"; they couldn't do the second because it would be creating another management post and there was "no provision for one" in the restructured Area!! They would rather pay me over the odds for doing a lesser job!! The lunatics were taking over the asylum!

The downside of the "meaningful work" was that I would be line-managed by Linda Vance, who at this point was the Divisional Crown Prosecutor for the reconstituted north Cumbria "branch". She was a grade lower than I was, and later I was to be line-managed by lawyers two grades below me who were temporarily acting up in Linda's position when she, in turn, left the CPS. How could this be, I asked? How could people on a lower grade than me write appraisal reports on me, let alone carry out disciplinary procedures should the need arise? I was to be 'managed' by people who were, in some cases, grossly less experienced than I was and who were earning at least £25000 a year less. Something wrong here? Apparently not, I was told

- it had happened elsewhere in the CPS in the past! “Lunatics” and “asylum” were the words that came to me again.

Be that as it may, in November 2011 I embarked upon the last phase of my career…

CHAPTER FIFTEEN

2011 TO 2013: The End of the Day…

From November 2011 to March 2013 I spent a good deal of satisfying time tripping down to Carlisle Crown Court, prosecuting all manner of cases, including jury trials of alleged offences ranging from Dangerous Driving to Causing Grievous Bodily Harm with Intent and Aggravated Arson. But if I and my three colleagues in the Crown Advocate Unit thought we were going to be allowed to exist in our little Crown Court bubble, unmolested by the rest of the CPS world, then we were sadly mistaken…

All around us the world seemed to be slowly disintegrating. The grip of local management seemed to be eroding and disappearing. Established systems and practices were being replaced by new, half-baked ones which had no attraction to anyone outside senior management. Members of staff who had left were not being replaced. Morale was becoming lower than even it had been under the 'reign' of the Dame in the 1990s.

National management had always, of course, had a propensity to come up with new schemes for improving working practices and 'outcomes' and, as we have observed, most of these had deservedly withered on the vine and been quietly allowed to disappear without trace. The latest idea, however, really capped them all. We had always operated what might be termed a system of "file ownership". This meant, in effect, that the lawyer who initially conducted a full review of a case and decided it was suitable for prosecution, then stayed with the case throughout its life, making any casework decisions on the file as they arose, dealing with correspondence, briefing counsel, etc. It was 'his' or 'her' case and, as such, there was a strong incentive to make sure the right decisions were made and that ultimately the case was ready for court, "trial-ready", if necessary. A specific caseworker would be allocated to the case where it was to go to the Crown Court, and he or she shared in looking after the case as it proceeded. There was inevitably, for the lawyer and caseworker, a feeling of pride and satisfaction when the case had a successful outcome and, indeed, a degree of sadness when it did not! It always seemed to me, and most of us, in fact, that this was the only logical way to handle casework, and the more serious cases in particular.

Management, however, in its enduring wisdom, felt that there was a better way of doing things! Lawyers went to court regularly, and sometimes it might be some days before they could find the time to deal with outstanding work on cases that they 'owned'. Matters could be dealt with much more expeditiously if those lawyers and caseworkers who were in the office on any given day, picked up the file and dealt with any correspondence, unused material, decision-making, etc. In other words, there would be no more "file ownership", but anybody and everybody would be required to look at files! The system, for whatever reason, became known as the "Pod". Every day there would be a number of lawyers and caseworkers sitting in the "Pod" like a hive of worker bees, waiting for files to be put in front of them, files which, in most cases, they had never seen before and, most likely, were never to see again!

To avoid accusations of negativity or of being a dinosaur, I could see some merit in the Pod system as it applied to the sort of 'volume' casework that was to be found in the magistrates' court. There was probably no need for anyone to 'own' cases of minor public order, motoring offences, shoplifting, etc. It would be easy enough for any lawyer to pick up one of these files, to assimilate fairly quickly the evidence, and deal with any correspondence or make any decisions thereon. It was a completely different matter, however, when it came to cases destined for the Crown Court, where the evidence was likely to be more voluminous or complex, there was likely to be much more unused material, there were "committal" papers to be prepared and served on the defence, indictments to prepare, briefs to do, and possibly conferences with counsel to arrange and participate in.

The scenario that could develop with a Crown Court case that went through the Pod might unfold as follows:

1. Lawyer would review the evidence in a file at an early stage and decide the case was suitable for prosecution.

2. Following a decision at court that the case should go to Crown Court, a full file is received from the police so that a set of papers can be prepared for service on defence. This full file goes to a Pod lawyer, almost certainly not the same lawyer as at 1 above. He or

she prepares papers. He or she will also conduct a "full file" review of the case - may not agree with the original decision made by 1!

3. Following service of papers, more material or unused material comes to CPS from police and goes to Pod lawyer. Unless he or she is same as 2 above, will have to read file from beginning and in its entirety if a proper decision is now to be made about new material. May not agree with previous decision or content of indictment.

4. Further material comes in, or letter from defence requiring reply. Same process as at 3 above.

5. As 4.

6. Counsel rings up with a query (or Crown Advocate if he or she is to be prosecuting). Who answers the query - lawyer at 1, 2, 3, etc?

7. Case conference with counsel or police required - who attends?

8. Judge wants explanation for decision from "the reviewing lawyer". Who is he or she?

This is really a simplified version of what might be a much more complicated and protracted sequence of events. The point, or one of them, is that no one lawyer has responsibility for the case. Further, rather than saving time, time is wasted by each lawyer or caseworker that has to deal with the file in the Pod having to go back to square one and read the file in its entirety in order to 'get a handle' on the case. The temptation is, of course, for the latter not to happen, and new material, etc., is dealt with in a vacuum and without getting to grips with the case. I suspect this happened regularly. As a Crown Advocate dealing with a case immediately before and at a Crown Court hearing, I repeatedly found evidence that material had not been dealt with, or not dealt with properly, that unanswered correspondence was lying on the file and, often, that unused material that had come in and should have been disclosed quite simply hadn't been! Indictment drafting was often sloppy or wrong and had to be redone before arraignment. The standard of case preparation, in short, was often sub-standard.

The judges at Carlisle Crown Court became aware of the Pod system, made little attempt to disguise their disdain for the procedure, and needed no invitation to expose its shortcomings. There was one notorious incident, involving a multi-handed public order case from Barrow, where Judge Hughes stopped the case in its tracks before the trial could start and demanded that CPS in Barrow appoint a lawyer "independent" of any previous involvement in the case to review the decision-making and review and case-handling processes that had taken place, and attend court to account for them at the next hearing. The ridiculous situation was that so many lawyers at Barrow had been involved as a result of the Pod system that there was, in effect, no "independent" lawyer, and the one "appointed" had had some input into the case! The upshot was that Judge Hughes stayed the case and delivered a written judgment utterly condemning the failures to disclose disclosable, unused material and other case-handling shortcomings. One point that he made very strongly was that the case suffered considerably from the lack of any one CPS lawyer having got a grip of the evidence and the case as a whole. This was a very public and thinly-disguised indictment of the Pod system and, clearly, it came to the notice of Chris Long and other senior managers in the Area. Did it change anything? Of course it didn't. They knew best! The fault, in their eyes, lay not with the system but those who should have been implementing it!!

Apart from being a totally illogical and defective system, "Pod" also had a completely adverse effect on the morale of lawyers and caseworkers. They no longer had a stake in the outcome of the case and were probably not involved in its 'birth'. They became no more than operatives on a conveyor belt. It must have been very plain to the powers-that-be that this was not designed to provide any sort of job satisfaction or incentive to perform well.

* * *

Morale, of course, was also being affected, by staff being aware that they were part of a dwindling band and by the remoteness and insensitivity of most tiers of management by 2013. Lawyers and other staff left under the VES scheme in 2011 and 2013 and, as it turned out, again in 2014. They were not, and would not be, replaced. Management locally was either largely ineffective or becoming invisible or non-existent as time went on.

I could identify four managers in the Carlisle office in mid-2012. The overall manager was Linda Vance who, by common consent, without going into detail, had negligible management skills.

However, one day in autumn 2012 she was summoned to Area HQ in Manchester and, on her return, announced that she would be leaving at the end of the month, having been "awarded" a VES package. This was occasion for universal rejoicing in the Carlisle office, although she was replaced by temporary managers - senior Crown Prosecutors with no experience or extremely little experience of managing, let alone managing a team of lawyers, highly experienced Crown Advocates, and largely equally experienced caseworkers, associate prosecutors and admin staff! As it turned out, however, it became plain that there was never any intention by Area HQ to have any further permanent management at this level in Cumbria, and I understand that after I left in 2013 the post was abolished and management was delivered, if that is the correct word, from Manchester or Preston.

In 2012 under the Divisional Crown Prosecutor there were, nominally at least, three other managers. One managed the admin staff. She went on maternity leave, however, in this period and it appeared that no-one could be persuaded to 'sub' for her. Management at this level then became, it seems, a movable feast between numbers of people!

The caseworkers were managed by a third person, who left at the same time as I did and who was not, I believe, replaced. Then another caseworker was responsible for managing the operation of the Crown Court Pod, although she too left in 2012 and, again, there appeared to be no obvious attempt to replace her!

During this period there were occasional 'visitations' by management personnel from Area HQ, notably from the Area Business Manager, Louise Rice, a charmless individual who had clearly learnt her management skills from Attila the Hun. She, and the others who came, patently had no understanding of, or sympathy with, either the day-to-day operation of prosecuting offenders or Cumbria. The latter they appeared to regard as no more than a tiresome appendage, an appendage which would have to be cut off at some stage. There were dark warnings of closing the Carlisle office and, at one time shortly before I departed, of shutting down the Crown Advocate Unit.

The Chief Crown Prosecutor apparently made one visit to the office, which I did not witness, but made no attempt to talk to any of the staff other than those he had brought with him. This was the same Nazir Afzal who had posed as a champion of the oppressed workforce during the "Dame's" regime, and whom I had seen acting as the 'life and soul' of courses when he and I were trainers of aspiring HCAs a dozen years before. Another poacher turned gamekeeper!

* * *

Another couple of edicts that were handed down by Area management at this time also served to further dent morale amongst lawyers. First of all it was decreed that if a lawyer wished to "discontinue" a case, he or she could only do so with the express consent and approval of their Divisional Crown Prosecutor or, indeed, someone higher than that! No doubt it was felt by senior management that too many cases were being discontinued, despite the existence of the Charging regime, and that a degree of control was required. Whether this was the case or not, it is a mark of very poor management to show such lack of confidence in the lawyers' ability to exercise one of their most fundamental powers, one they had been exercising for twenty-five years! Strictly speaking, the rule applied to me as much as it did to any other lawyer, but I was certainly not going to be seeking anyone's approval for any such decision I made. If my line manager or any of her superiors were aware that I was making "unapproved" decisions to discontinue cases, then they made no attempt to rebuke me for it!! As it was anyway, we Crown Advocates routinely made all manner of decisions about the future and direction of cases when we were at Court, and it would never cross our minds to seek approval from anyone else!

Then senior management, in their eternal wisdom, decided that the Crown Advocate Unit was to vet every case that was destined for the Crown Court, once such a decision had been made, to ensure all decisions up to that point were correct and appropriate. Not only was this extremely time-consuming for those in this unit, it was also another strike at the self-esteem of the other lawyers, who clearly couldn't be trusted to make any sort of important casework decision. It also added another layer to the discredited Crown Court Pod system!

* * *

In early 2013 it was announced that there would be another "exit" scheme, another opportunity, in other words, for staff to apply for Voluntary Redundancy. This time I decided to throw my hat in the ring and I made an application for VES.

I was still finding the work I was doing both challenging and fulfilling, and could quite easily have carried on with it. I was 64 by this time, but there was no longer any compulsory retirement age and, whilst I was still *compos mentis*, or at least appearing to be so, no doubt I could have gone on until I was carried out in a box. But although in the Crown Advocate Unit I was working in something of a vacuum, it was impossible to be completely unaffected by the gloom and doom that pervaded the atmosphere all around me. There was an air of *fin de siècle* about the CPS in Cumbria, and it was probably about time for me to make an exit.

The last straw was the announcement by the delightful Rice person that it was intended to shut down the Crown Advocate Unit in Cumbria because it was not "cost-effective". The argument was, apparently, that it would be cheaper to employ the Bar to prosecute the cases that we were covering. I could never understand how this conclusion was reached and, when we asked for the figures to support the conclusion, they were never forthcoming. Apart from any other consideration, we were doing more than just preparing and prosecuting individual cases in the Crown Court - it was part of our job to vet all cases going to the Crown Court, and to provide advice and mentoring to other lawyers. These additional functions were not, of course, provided by counsel. If the unit were closed down, the CPS would still be paying us to carry out other functions and they would have to pay counsel on top of this to pick up the Crown Court prosecution work. So how could it possibly be the case that we were costing more than counsel and were not cost-effective?

Nonetheless, it seemed that the writing was on the wall for the Crown Advocate Unit, and I had really had enough of being pushed around from one job to another. My application for VES was approved and, along with one or two others, I finally left the CPS on 31st March 2013.

Needless to say, our departures were barely acknowledged by the senior management. One didn't expect a gold watch, but there was a time when long-serving members of staff were given a send-off by a senior manager at a specially-arranged event. This no longer happened, and I didn't even get a letter of appreciation from anyone at that level. Two years previously the CPS had been in existence for twenty-five years, and the DPP was moved to send out a letter and a commemorative badge to those employees who had served the full twenty-five years. Even this they managed to 'cock up'. Many of us who were entitled never received this acknowledgment, and HQ had to be reminded that they had missed out a whole tranche of staff from this event. The DPP then had to send out another clutch of letters and badges weeks after, but not a word of apology.

Essentially, the CPS had become a completely soulless organisation, devoid of any warmth towards, or empathy with, its employees. The attitude had become "You've got a job, you're lucky to have one; that should be motivation enough, you don't need to be appreciated." It had long ceased to be a pleasant or congenial organisation for which to work, and it was little wonder that many established staff took the opportunity to leave in these years, and with little or no regret. It was a sad state of affairs, and the responsibility for this as far as I was concerned lay with those in the upper echelons of the CPS; many of them, including the Director, were fly-by-night, transient birds of passage, who came and went and who had little feel for what the organisation was about or should have been about, but were only concerned in furthering their own ambition and then moving on when it suited them.

Following my departure, although I kept in touch with one or two people, I made no attempt to visit the office. I always think it is rather sad to see those who have left making a return visit - although they may get an initial welcome, no-one really has time for them, they are no longer part of the set-up, part of the team, and they tend to sneak away before anyone notices they have gone. I had no intention of exposing myself to such an embarrassing experience and I kept well away. Indeed, I found that within a short space of time I had largely lost interest in the workplace and the work, until, that is, my interest was revived when I decided to write this book and, even then, most of my focus was historical rather than recent.

I did learn that there had been a few changes in the twelve months or so since my departure, some not unexpected. Management had, apparently, ultimately realised the deficiencies of the Pod system and had at least started to unravel it, and a degree of "file ownership" had been restored! Surprisingly, the Crown Advocate Unit has survived despite all the dire prognostications, although this may have something to do with the fact that two of the four lawyers, of which I was one, had gone and possibly rendered the unit more cost-effective in the eyes of management, or perhaps they hoped it would fade away of its own accord by natural wastage?!

On the debit side, Cumbria was in due course deprived of any sort of senior management, and the branch was now run remotely from Preston or Manchester. The temporary lawyer managers who had existed at Carlisle and Barrow reverted to being ordinary lawyers. At Carlisle the office was becoming a 'ghost ship'. Chris Long and the Business Manager who had been in post in 2011 had long been whisked away to Preston; more staff left in another exit strategy in 2014, both lawyers and admin staff and, like those who had departed previously in 2011 and 2013, they were not replaced. Managers' offices stood empty. Area management decided that the office now occupied too much floor space for the reduced numbers of staff, and half of the office was closed off. All the signs were that, in the not too distant future, Cumbria would essentially cease to exist as a separate entity and staff would be transferred to Lancashire or Manchester.

* * *

It is very much doom and gloom in Cumbria CPS now, and it may be that there is an 'endgame' situation in this outpost of the North West Area. Some believe that the CPS itself is an 'endgame'. Is this the case? Will it survive another twenty-five years, or even another three or four?

There are discouraging signs. Even as I write, the organisation is being vilified for poor decision-making in several cases where celebrities have been acquitted of historic sex crimes and, even more recently, of poor decision-making and outrageous waste of public money for prosecuting high-profile journalists in a celebrated phone-hacking case where most of the defendants were acquitted after a very long trial. Certainly, in my view, the CPS 'spokesman' who made public comments following this case did the organisation no favours by suggesting that the reason for bringing the prosecution was "to explore a culture of invading privacy". The unfortunate implication of this bizarre statement was that there was not considered to be a realistic prospect of conviction on the evidence, but that this didn't really matter!! Whatever happened to the Code for Crown Prosecutors? Some of the media, and notably the *Daily Mail*, have been gunning for the CPS since its inception in 1986, but there are signs now that even the more reputable newspapers are being regularly critical of the organisation.

The response to media criticism in individual cases is, of course, that established by Alan Green when he was Director of Public Prosecutions all those years ago:

"You are picking on anecdotal evidence - look at all the thousands of other cases which had successful outcomes." For every failed 'celebrity' case, of course, there are at least an equivalent number where prosecutions have resulted in conviction - thus far in 2014, for example, one can cite the cases of Max Clifford, Stuart Hall and Rolf Harris. And, every day, there are literally hundreds of criminal cases in the criminal courts where other defendants plead 'guilty' or are convicted after trial. There is hardly any sort of evidence that the system is failing!

Furthermore, it has often been the case that the CPS has been subjected to media criticism where it has not instituted criminal proceedings in various cases. It is difficult to understand how anyone can criticise a failure to prosecute without being privy to the nature and content of the evidence, but the criticism tends to stick anyway!

The reality is that the CPS is damned if it does, and damned if it doesn't. It is always in a no-win situation. Failures or omissions will be criticised; successes will go largely unremarked. In my view, also, the CPS has never had an effective publicity machine, unlike the police service. The police will always make the most out of successful cases and will always keep a low profile where there are failures. Where there is a successful outcome, there will always be a police officer on the steps of the court to take the plaudits and praise the effectiveness of the investigation which has brought justice to the victims; when there is not a successful outcome, it seems always to be the CPS spokesman who is facing the media, churning out the usual platitudes about "sufficiency of evidence" and "we respect the decision of the jury", and nary a police officer in sight! It's always another victory for the police, or the CPS "loses again"!!

The police service, of course, has had to suffer a good deal of criticism and vilification over the years, the handling of the

Hillsborough disaster being a recent example. But, at the end of the day, the ability of its publicity machine to make the most of 'good news' will always ensure that the standing of the service remains high in the eyes of most, if not all, members of the public. It is important that it does retain public esteem. The CPS, however, is never going to attract much more than indifference. Its publicity machine is poor, its role in the criminal justice system barely understood, and not at all by much of the public. It is not 'sexy'. The police service is 'sexy'. There is a continuing public fascination with the police - one only has to witness the number of TV series about police work, detection, etc. If there are, or have been, any TV programmes centring on the CPS, they are few in number, and are or were unmemorable!

We are led to believe that the CPS came close to extinction in the early 1990s but, despite everything, I suspect it will survive in some form at least because, for all its faults, the criminal justice system needs an independent prosecuting authority. Few might lament the passing of the organisation, but it is difficult to see what would replace it; it would, nevertheless, need to be replaced. Nature, of course, abhors a vacuum.

Prior to the creation of County Prosecuting Solicitors' departments by local or police authorities, the police would either make their own decisions about prosecuting or would hire private solicitors' firms to advise on decisions, unless the case was so serious that it was dealt with by the DPP's office. Going back to this, I believe, would not be considered an option. The principle that the decision to prosecute, or at least the decision to <u>continue with</u> a prosecution, should be a decision made by someone independent of the investigating authority is now too well-established and respected to be abandoned. There would not, either, be the requisite standard of independence with solicitors in private practice, who would have criminal clients and who would be governed by income-generating considerations. No doubt it was for these sorts of reasons that most police forces prior to 1986 had opted to have a separate department of salaried solicitors, who would give advice and handle the preparation and delivery of criminal prosecutions - hence the advent of local County Prosecuting Solicitor offices.

Many would regard the latter as the high-water mark of prosecuting in England and Wales and the local model as the better option to have been adopted in 1986. The national CPS model that was selected has become over-bureaucratic, over-centralised, over-prescriptive, and obsessed with political correctness. The local model might have avoided these defects, and already had a track record of success before 1986, or at least was not subject to the vilification suffered by the post-1986 organisation.

I suspect, however, that no government of any political complexion will want to unravel the national organisation. It would be a strange state of affairs, anyway, if it decided to go back in time, when there is a long-established centralised system in Scotland in the shape of the Procurator Fiscal Service. Perhaps the fact that the PFS has survived the test of time is an indication that the CPS, also in the fullness of time, will become an accepted, if not much-loved, institution? Probably the worst that will happen, as has been threatened from time to time, will be that a future Conservative government will hive off parts of the prosecuting activities to the private sector - such as the actual prosecuting in magistrates' courts, for example. But there again, why would it do that when it can secure low-cost delivery there with associate prosecutors? I may be wrong, but my guess is that not much will change, in the short-term anyway, and that the CPS will carry on in its present form...

★ ★ ★

I have seen many changes in the world of courts and prosecuting over more than forty years. There have been fundamental and profound alterations to the processes, and many of the characters who populated the scene in the 1970s and 1980s would seem very much out of place in the modern world, impossibly larger than life and quite anachronistic. I don't want this to be a final exercise in nostalgia, or a lamentation about how things "ain't what they used to be". Some of the changes that have occurred over the years have, in my view, been for the best and it certainly wasn't all 'beer and skittles' in the criminal justice system forty years ago.

I may look back wistfully at the standards of advocacy in my early days and the quaint charm of the rural magistrates' courts but, in retrospect, the idiosyncratic conduct of some of the part-time magistrates' clerks, for example, was sometimes nothing short of outrageous and there is a much greater degree of professionalism to be found in the fewer and larger local courts in these days.

The Crown Prosecution Service may have become an organisation mired in bureaucracy and obsessed with political correctness, with too many 'chiefs' as opposed to 'Indians'. It may have allowed itself to be distracted by pursuing too many half-baked, unworkable schemes to "improve" working practices. It may have become bogged down in a meetings culture and with too many performance targets. It may have become infatuated with over-focusing on fashionable topics such as "hate crime" and domestic violence, at the expense of concentrating on drug trafficking, serious violence and fraud. It may have made a virtue out of being transparent in its dealings with the public and the rest of the criminal justice system, whilst being less than transparent in its dealings with its own employees. For all that, I remain firmly of the view that the creation of an independent prosecution service was absolutely right and was the most significant and important development in the criminal justice system in the 20th century.

It surely is indisputable that the arrangements for the prosecution of criminal offences had to change. It was never right that the decision to prosecute and the conduct of criminal prosecutions should remain in the hands of those who had investigated the alleged offending in the first place. However impartial and objective they tried to be, the perception would always be that they had a stake, a vested interest, in seeing that those they had brought to book were charged and prosecuted and that, inevitably, this would militate against independent and dispassionate decision-making.

Once this principle is accepted then it makes logical sense, to my mind, that the "independent" body should not only have conduct of any prosecution but should also be making the initial decision whether or not there should be a prosecution. As I have pointed out previously in this work, in 1986 the legislators stopped short of giving this initial decision to the CPS, and the police retained the power to decide whether someone should be charged or not, whether or not they first sought advice about the decision. This was perhaps a sop to the police but, of course, it was an empty gesture because, once criminal proceedings had been instituted, the CPS had sole conduct of those proceedings and could discontinue the case if they saw fit, or amend the charges.

The introduction of the Charging scheme in the early part of this century was, I felt, the logical development and completion of the process that had been brought in during 1986. It removed the illogicality that had existed up to then, that the police retained the decision to prosecute but not any subsequent decision-making in the criminal process. The Charging scheme has, for one reason or another, been watered down, but it remains the case that, for any alleged offence of any seriousness, the CPS will make that initial decision to charge or not to charge.

Government has always wrestled with the situation thrown up by the interface between the police and the CPS and, despite opportunity, has always seemed reluctant to rationalise the arrangements. Thus we still have, effectively, two separate bodies involved in the preparation of criminal cases - a police prosecutions department or "Criminal Justice Unit", and the CPS. This has always led to duplication and delay, but attempts to reform the process have failed and, I believe, have always been resisted by the police. There is no sign of any change on the horizon!

Apart from the creation of the CPS itself, for me the other most important development in the criminal justice system, both from a prosecution and a defence perspective, was to break the near-monopoly of the Bar over advocacy in the higher courts. It was certainly a career-defining change for me and, I suspect, many others. It has been a notable achievement for many CPS lawyers, and also a significant number of solicitor advocates on the defence side, to have 'broken the mould' and to have become regular and established advocates in the Crown Court. It has not been an easy passage, with some hostility and lack of acceptance from the Bar and the judiciary to counter, but it has happened, and it is here to stay!!

⋆ ⋆ ⋆

If I had no regrets about leaving the CPS, neither did I have any regrets about devoting most of my career to the CPS, whether in its pre-1986 incarnation or in its later form. I never had any real hankering to do anything else outside the law, and I never really thought long about the occasional invitations to join the private sector. I am glad I did not become a 'fat-arsed' conveyancer, a personal injury lawyer, or someone involved in the musty world of wills and probate. Neither did I ever wish to have criminal clients and all that that entails! In short I am, and always have been, a prosecutor…